THE EVERYTHING.
KOSHER SLOW COOKER
COOKBOOK

Dear Reader,

Most recipe bloggers have fantasies about being "discovered" and magically presented with a cookbook deal. So when Lisa Laing, editor of the Everything® series, contacted me asking if I would be interested in writing this cookbook, I first had to pinch myself to make sure I wasn't dreaming. Of course I would do it! As a recipe blogger, I was thrilled at the prospect of seeing my own name on the cover of an actual book.

The thrill quickly turned into abject terror when I was given a deadline. Do I have the juice to create a masterpiece, or at least something semicoherent? Do I have the chops to be a professional writer? Can I cook up 300 slow recipes quickly, or will I have egg on my face, reduced to eating humble pie?

I had been only a few short years out of grad school, which consisted of writing one long paper after another. It was relatively easy to slip back into writing mode. Somehow I managed to squeeze in recipe testing and photographing the results along the way. I am quite happy with the 300 recipes that are in this book. I hope you enjoy using them as well.

Dena G. Price

Welcome to the EVERYTHING® Series!

These handy, accessible books give you all you need to tackle a difficult project, gain a new hobby, comprehend a fascinating topic, prepare for an exam, or even brush up on something you learned back in school but have since forgotten.

You can choose to read an Everything® book from cover to cover or just pick out the information you want from our four useful boxes: e-questions, e-facts, e-alerts, and e-ssentials.

We give you everything you need to know on the subject, but throw in a lot of fun stuff along the way, too.

We now have more than 400 Everything® books in print, spanning such wide-ranging categories as weddings, pregnancy, cooking, music instruction, foreign language, crafts, pets, New Age, and so much more. When you're done reading them all, you can finally say you know Everything®!

QUESTION

Answers to common questions

FACT

Important snippets of information

ALERT

Urgent warnings

ESSENTIAL

Quick handy tips

PUBLISHER Karen Cooper

MANAGING EDITOR, EVERYTHING® SERIES Lisa Laing

COPY CHIEF Casey Ebert

ACQUISITIONS EDITOR Lisa Laing

SENIOR DEVELOPMENT EDITOR Brett Palana-Shanahan

EVERYTHING® SERIES COVER DESIGNER Erin Alexander

Visit the entire Everything® series at *www.everything.com*

THE EVERYTHING®

KOSHER SLOW COOKER COOKBOOK

Dena G. Price

Adamsmedia
Avon, Massachusetts

An Everything® Series Book.
Everything® and everything.com® are registered trademarks of F+W Media, Inc.

Published by Adams Media, a division of F+W Media, Inc.
57 Littlefield Street, Avon, MA 02322 U.S.A.
www.adamsmedia.com

ISBN 10: 1-4405-4350-X
ISBN 13: 978-1-4405-4350-0
eISBN 10: 1-4405-4351-8
eISBN 13: 978-1-4405-4351-7

Printed in the United States of America.

10 9 8 7 6 5 4 3 2 1

Always follow safety and common-sense cooking protocol while using kitchen utensils, operating ovens and stoves, and handling uncooked food. If children are assisting in the preparation of any recipe, they should always be supervised by an adult.

Marinara Sauce photo © iStockphoto.com/Aspheric.
All other photographs by Dena G. Price.

This book is available at quantity discounts for bulk purchases.
For information, please call 1-800-289-0963.

Contents

Acknowledgments

I would like to thank my editor Lisa Laing at Adams Media for giving me the opportunity to write this book. I also appreciate the comments and suggestions provided by the Art and Production departments at Adams Media. My photography has improved a thousandfold.

Hugs to the staff at the Old Bridge Public Library, who enthusiastically ate anything I brought in for "testing," especially Pat B., who suggested the perfect herb and spice "tweaks" on several recipes.

Special thanks go to Rabbi Lisa Malik of Temple Beth Ahm in Aberdeen, NJ, who took time out of her very busy schedule to help me in explaining kashrut, the Jewish dietary laws.

Last, but most certainly not least, I would like to thank my husband. Richie, you have been incredibly supportive and encouraging, not just with the book but with everything thrown at us during our amazing journey together.

Introduction

THERE NEVER SEEMS TO be enough time for chores, family, and work. Creating delicious and wholesome meals for the family should not add to the daily stress. Luckily, a slow cooker can help. With all the demands of the day, a slow cooker is the least demanding. After assembling and preparing ingredients, it quietly does what it is supposed to do . . . all day, or all evening.

Set up the slow cooker and leave it alone to do its job while you do yours. You can literally leave it alone. Leave it on while you are off somewhere else, in a different part the house or even a different zip code. The food will safely cook in your absence. Some slow cookers have built-in timers that automatically lower the temperature to "warm mode" when cooking is done. No more overcooking or scorched food. No other cooking appliance can even come close for convenience.

Slow cookers also free up the oven and the stovetop, a huge help when company is coming and there never seem to be enough ovens or burners to get everything finished in time.

Remember when slow cookers only came in avocado green or harvest yellow? Today, those old-fashioned colors will only be found in your mother's or grandmother's kitchen, or at garage sales. The slow cooker no longer has to hide behind a cabinet door. Today's slow cookers are stainless steel or modern bright colors to match modern bright appliances. Some even come with jazzy prints! And most slow cookers have removable crock inserts, which allows you to bring them to the dining room table. The entire unit is also at home at a buffet, keeping foods at a safe serving temperature. Some models are even built for traveling! They come with special clamps or handles to make it easier to transport food to a backyard barbecue, a picnic at the park, the house of a sick friend, or a Shiva call.

Homes with kosher kitchens have their own unique requirements. While anyone can use this cookbook, the information presented is "kosher friendly." There are no recipes combining meat and dairy items. Meats are all from kosher animals. The fish are all kosher according to kashrut. There are no recipes with pork or shellfish, nor with any ready-made products containing even a smidgeon of either. And because most slow cookers are not very expensive, buying one for meat meals and another for dairy is not cost prohibitive. A more detailed explanation of the kosher laws can be found in Chapter 1.

Traditional recipes for major Jewish holidays are included in this cookbook. Recipes for Passover, which has its own set of rules, customs, and traditions, are also included. The recipes for Passover follow Ashkenazi customs. Kitniyot, such as rice, beans, and corn, as well as their derivatives, is prohibited.

Because kosher meats are salted to remove all traces of blood, some residual salt remains in the meat. As a result, less salt is required in any recipe containing meat. All ingredients referenced are either inherently kosher or can be obtained with kosher certification. Some products may not be available in all locations; Appendix B contains suggested websites where these products may be ordered online.

What is presented here is a general guideline and is in no way complete. While the kosher laws are discussed in more detail in the sources listed in Resources here as well as in other books, your rabbi is the final authority on the subject and should be contacted directly with any questions or concerns about any recipe or information provided in this book.

CHAPTER 1

The Kosher Kitchen

Imagine yourself multitasking . . . in another room in the house, outside doing chores, or at work, yet at the same time cooking dinner. Well, you no longer have to imagine it. This chapter will explain how to accomplish this miracle, give you lots of tips on using a slow cooker, plus offer suggestions on how to convert many of your favorite recipes for use in a slow cooker. Combine all this with the kosher-ready recipes in the chapters that follow and you will never bother to hide your slow cooker again!

Kashrut (Or, Why This Cookbook Is Different from the Others)

There are plenty of kosher cookbooks available. There are a myriad of slow cooker cookbooks as well. But until recently, those who follow kashrut did not have the convenience of a kosher cookbook with recipes for slow cookers.

So why is this such a big deal? Why can't those who are kosher just take any old slow cooker cookbook and make substitutions as necessary? And what the heck is kashrut, anyway?

Let's get the easy question regarding "any old slow cooker cookbook" out of the way first. Just as with cookbooks for any kind of dietary restriction, whether diabetic, no-salt, vegan, pescatarian, Seventh-Day Adventist, Muslim, or Jewish, the advantage is the convenience of having recipes that can be used "as is," rather than having to substitute or omit ingredients in order to conform to a particular diet, simultaneously hoping that the end result will be just as tasty as the original. Plus it avoids making a serious mistake by leaving in ingredients that must be absolutely avoided, be it for health, allergies, lifestyle, or religious reasons.

Now to the more important question—what is kashrut? According to most dictionaries, kosher means "fit" or "proper." Kashrut is the set of Jewish dietary laws. Since kashrut is a transliteration of a Hebrew word, there are several valid spellings in English, including kashruth and kashrus. For consistency, the spelling used throughout this book is "kashrut."

Since the Bible is not very detailed in its description of kashrut, and since present-day Judaism is not equivalent to biblical religion, many of the laws of kashrut are included in the Talmud and other rabbinic texts, codified some time during the first six centuries of the Common Era. During the 1,500 years since then, the laws of kashrut have been interpreted and reinterpreted by rabbis and other scholars as Jews dispersed around the world and encountered local customs along with new foods and methods of preparation. This book presents general guidelines of kashrut based on the interpretation and practice of kashrut within the traditional Jewish movement known as Conservative Judaism. It is in no way complete. While kashrut may be explained and discussed in greater detail elsewhere, your rabbi is the final authority on the subject, and should be contacted directly with any questions or concerns about any recipe or information provided here.

What Is and Isn't Kosher

Many people think that being kosher simply means not eating pork or pork products. It is a little more complex than that, but in a nutshell, certain foods are prohibited and certain other foods cannot be combined or eaten at the same meal. In addition to pork, the list of prohibited foods includes shellfish and certain other types of fish, meat, and poultry.

To be considered kosher, meat has to come from animals that have cloven hooves and chew their cud. Kosher meat comes from animals including (but not limited to) cows, bison, goats, and sheep. Although the Bible doesn't specify the signs by which one can recognize kosher birds, it does provide a list of kosher fowl, including chicken, pigeon, and domesticated duck, goose, and turkey. Birds of prey, such as vultures and owls, are not kosher. To be considered kosher, fish must have fins and scales. So, while tuna is a kosher fish, dolphins and sharks are not. Shellfish, such as clams, shrimp, octopus, and lobster, are also not permitted.

QUESTION

How do I know what foods are kosher?
If you are unsure if a food you want to purchase is kosher, check the label. If it has a hechsher, a special symbol or logo from one of the many kashrut-certifying agencies that inspect food products, then that food item may be brought into a kosher home.

According to the laws of kashrut, kosher meat and poultry must be killed by a kosher butcher as quickly and painlessly as possible, according to a prescribed method of ritual slaughter. The meat or poultry is then soaked and salted to remove all traces of blood before it may be cooked and eaten. Fish does not need to be killed according to any specified method of ritual slaughter, nor does it need to be soaked and salted.

To be considered kosher, milk and all dairy products made of milk (such as cheese and yogurt) must be produced by kosher animals. To be considered kosher, eggs must come from kosher birds. Although eggs are considered to be dairy products in the secular world, they are not considered to be dairy in the realm of kashrut.

Any food containing meat or poultry may not be combined, cooked, or served at the same meal with milk or with any foods containing milk or products made of milk, and vice versa. In this book (and as per kashrut), the term "dairy" refers to all products that include milk as one of their ingredients and the term "meat" refers to all products made with beef, lamb, chicken, or any other kosher animal (except fish).

Besides meat and dairy, there is an additional category: pareve. Pareve (also spelled parve because it, too, is a transliteration of a Hebrew word) means "neutral." Pareve food is neither meat nor dairy. Any food considered pareve may be used alone, or in a meat or dairy recipe. Nuts, grains, eggs, fruits, and vegetables are all considered to be pareve. Fish is also considered pareve, but some Orthodox Jews do not allow fish to be served on the same plate as meat or poultry.

Cookware and Dishes

The utensils, cookware, dishes (except for glass, which is considered neutral and may be used for either), silverware, and storage items for meat may not be used for dairy, and vice versa. The only exception to this general rule is that drinking glasses, cups, and serving dishes that are used for serving cold foods may be used for both meat and dairy drinks and cold foods. Many families have two sets of everything, one set for dairy and one for meat, usually in different styles or colors to avoid accidental mix-ups.

Passover

Passover is an eight-day holiday in early spring that celebrates the liberation of the Jewish people's ancestors from slavery in Egypt. Because they fled with no time to let their bread rise, it is traditional to only eat unleavened bread (matzoh) during this holiday. There is an additional set of kashrut rules and restrictions that apply during the eight days of Passover. Products classified as "chametz" that are permitted during the rest of the year are prohibited during this holiday. Chametz consists of any food product made of barley, oats, rye, spelt, and wheat (or their derivatives) that has leavened or fermented. Flour made of any of these grains that comes into contact with water or other moisture is considered leavened unless it is fully baked within eighteen minutes. Chametz includes bread, biscuits, cakes, cereal, coffee containing cereal derivatives, crackers, and liquids containing ingredients or flavors made from grain alcohol.

ESSENTIAL

According to kashrut, it is necessary to remove chametz from one's home, as well as from one's diet, during Passover. Jewish law also prohibits even the ownership of chametz during this period. Therefore, many Jews arrange for the temporary sale of the chametz that they are unable to remove from their homes.

The Passover home atmosphere is created each year by the practice of thoroughly cleaning the home in order to remove all traces of chametz. It is also traditional to either ritually clean the dishes, flatware, and kitchen equipment used during the rest of the year or to store away the everyday dishes, flatware, and kitchen items and bring out another two sets of these items (one set for meat and one for dairy) that have been reserved exclusively for Passover use.

While this may sound like a major hardship, there are plenty of foods that can be easily prepared during Passover. Some recipes traditionally served during this holiday are included in this book.

Choosing a Slow Cooker

A slow cooker is an appliance that, in case you haven't already figured it out, cooks food slowly. Unlike a stove, oven, pressure cooker, or microwave, it can take up to several hours to reach proper cooking temperature. Heating coils are built into the sides and bottom of the slow cooker, which heat a removable stoneware crock insert. This allows a more consistent and gentle heating transmitted to the food inside.

You don't really need a slow cooker in order to cook foods for a long time at a low temperature. Just take a lidded pot and place it over a low flame on the stove or in an oven set at low temperature. But of course there has always been the potential safety hazard of a pot of food unattended on the stove or in the oven. It was a risk most shomer shabbos (Sabbath-observing) cooks took in order to feed their families a hot meal on Saturdays. Although the slow cooker wasn't conceived and invented for this reason, Sabbath-observing cooks rejoiced at its invention!

There are several different sizes of slow cookers from which to choose. The two most popular sizes are the 3- to 4-quart and the 6- to 7-quart sizes. Generally speaking, the smaller sizes are for recipes that serve around three to four people, and the larger size is for families of five and up or to cook enough to serve dinner and again at a future time.

Less popular are the 1- or 2-quart sizes. They run at only a warm setting and cannot bring cold or room temperature foods up to safe cooking temperatures. The big advantage of these miniature cookers is using them for small batches of dips or fondues, which are great for company or buffet meals, as well as a sneaky and fun way to get kids to eat their veggies.

FACT

There are two basic shapes of slow cookers: round and oval. Do you plan to cook a whole roast beef or chicken? An oval-shaped cooker can handle a whole roast beef or chicken more easily than a round one.

Are you planning to set up the slow cooker, then leave the house? Buy one with a timer, which automatically switches to a safe warming temperature when cooking time is over, perfect for those days when you are unavoidably detained and can't get home on time. Unfortunately, some units with this option reset to "off" if power is lost, even for a few seconds. This poses a possible health risk if the food temperature drops to an unsafe level.

Speaking of temperature, most modern slow cookers have two settings: low, which reaches a maximum temperature of about 200°F, and high, which reaches up to 300°F. Older models cook at lower temperatures. According to the Crock-Pot official website, the low and high settings of its slow cookers both reach about 300°F; low just takes twice as long to get there. Many brands have a third setting: warm, which reduces the heat to a safe "holding" temperature.

There is at least one slow cooker available that comes with several sizes of crocks. By purchasing additional covers, one or more sizes could be dedicated to meat dishes and another for dairy, which saves the cost of buying multiple cookers. The disadvantage is that, unlike standard cookers, the heating element is only on the bottom, increasing the risk of burning or uneven cooking.

Other Kitchen Equipment and Tools

- **Immersion Blender:** If you don't already have one, invest in a couple of immersion blenders (one for meat and one for dairy) for purée-ing sauces and vegetables. Inexpensive ones are around $12–15; more expensive ones with bells and whistles can run up to $100. The big advantage of an immersion blender over a standard blender is that it can be quickly and safely used directly in the slow cooker without first having to cool down the food. To get the same results from a standard blender, first the sauce must cool down, then be ladled into the blender. Pulse until desired consistency is achieved, then remove and repeat with remaining sauce. With either tool, purée the entire batch, or leave a few larger pieces for a more rustic appearance. The immersion blender is easier to clean as well since, except for more expensive all-in-ones, only the immersed part needs cleaning afterward.

- **Cooking and Serving Pieces:** To avoid scratching the interior, especially if the insert has a nonstick surface, purchase scratch-resistant cooking and serving spoons, ladles, tongs, spatulas, scrubbing sponges, and anything else that might be inserted into the crock.

- **Instant-Read Thermometer:** While a little pink won't hurt most cooked meat, that rule does not apply to chicken. To ensure that poultry is fully cooked, purchase an instant-read thermometer. Follow the guidelines that come with the thermometer, and remove the food only when the proper temperature is reached.

- **Well-Fitting Lid:** Planning on transporting cooked food in the insert, or the entire unit? Make sure the lid fits tightly, or comes with a band or snap-on clips to hold the lid on securely.

Slow Cooker Tips

Slow cookers work best when they are half to three-quarters full. Smaller quantities might burn; add an extra vegetable or two (veggies with long cooking times such as onions or carrots are best) to bring the level up to at least half. Conversely, a too-filled crock might not reach a safe cooking temperature quickly enough or might not cook properly.

ALERT

Minimum cooking times in this book are based on newer slow cookers. If you own an older cooker, increase cooking time to the maximum suggested.

Cooking Temperatures

As a rule of thumb, cooking on high takes half the time of cooking on low, which is great if you are in a hurry. The main advantage of using low heat, however, is that food cooked with gentle heat tastes much better. Low heat is also more forgiving. Can't be home after six hours of cooking? Let it quietly cook on low for an extra hour or two until you get home. In fact, dinner might even be more delicious!

The warm setting is meant to be used only to "hold" food at serving temperature. This setting does not bring food up to a bacteria-killing temperature. For food safety, never cook food on the warm setting.

Always read any recipe before starting out (this is good advice for utilizing other means of cooking as well). A slow cooker doesn't necessarily equal long cooking time. Some foods, like kasha or macaroni and cheese, are ready after only one hour!

ESSENTIAL

Chilled ingredients take longer to get to a safe cooking temperature. To reduce cooking time by up to one-half, heat liquids before transferring them to the slow cooker. Remove cold food from the refrigerator about twenty minutes before cooking to reduce the chill.

Food Placement

It may surprise you to learn that many vegetables, especially tough root vegetables, take longer to cook than meat. Place vegetables and other ingredients that need a higher temperature on the bottom of the slow cooker.

Conversely, more delicate vegetables such as peas or zucchini will shrivel, fall apart, or become quite unappetizing after cooking for hours. Add these vegetables no more than thirty minutes before the end of cooking time, or cook them separately and mix in just before serving.

FACT

Because a slow cooker cooks at relatively low temperatures, the timing can be very forgiving. If an item is supposed to cook for four hours, the cooking time can usually be stretched at least another hour without overcooking.

Presoaking and Other Prep Work

Most dried beans, especially red kidney beans, need to presoak before cooking. The night before you plan to cook them, place the beans in a bowl and cover with at least an inch of water. Let the beans soak overnight. In the morning, drain and discard the soaking water. This is the preferred method, because you can then immediately continue with the remaining steps in the recipe.

Another way to pre-soak is called, ironically enough, the "quick" method. But since it involves placing the beans and water in a saucepan, waiting until it comes to a full boil, then turning off the heat and letting it soak for an hour before continuing, it actually extends the prep time.

Set the cooker on high for the first hour of cooking to more quickly reach safe-cooking temperature and to reduce total cooking time; then, if the recipe calls for it, adjust to the low setting. However, if you have to leave before the hour is up, it is safe to cook on low the entire time.

Adding Insulation

Pudding or other delicate desserts such as cheesecake benefit from an extra layer of insulation. Cook in smaller heat-safe cups or pans set in the cooker, raised up from the bottom by placing wadded-up aluminum foil balls underneath them. Because some pans, especially casserole dishes and loaf pans, have extending handles or rims, test first by placing them inside the cooker before filling with food to make sure that they actually fit. Unless the recipe says otherwise, there is no need to add water to the bottom of the cooker when using this technique.

Even if your slow cooker has a nonstick interior or you have greased it, for foods such as brownies or cake that you want to remove before slicing, first line the insert with a sheet of aluminum foil or parchment paper. Let it extend up the sides or over the edges, depending on the recipe. Use a little cooking spray on the foil or paper so that it can be easily peeled off the food after cooking. Liner bags can accomplish the same thing and are made to fit, but they are much more expensive. Unless the recipe directs otherwise, allow baked foods to cool before removing; they will shrink away from the sides as they cool, making removal that much easier.

Cooking Meats

Meat, especially tough cuts such as brisket, soften and tenderize when cooked on the low setting for an extended period of time, rather than on the high setting for a short one. Avoid using more expensive tender cuts of meat, which turn mushy or tough from long cooking.

Meats that will be shredded should be done so soon after cooking. Remove the meat from the cooker and place on a cutting board. Wait until it cools enough to handle safely, then grab a couple of forks and start shredding. For meat that will be sliced instead, let cool, then place in a covered dish and refrigerate overnight. The meat will be easier to slice and will shred less.

Boneless chicken and turkey can be cooked to perfection in a slow cooker, but they can easily be overcooked. Place boneless poultry farthest away from the coils, preferably on top of the other ingredients, or during the last few hours of cooking. Poultry is fully cooked when it is no longer pink and the juices run clear when pierced with a fork. For greater accuracy, use an instant-read thermometer.

To ensure that meat quickly reaches cooking (and bacteria-killing) temperature, cut meat into portion-sized or 1-inch cubes. Vegetables should also be cut into similar-sized chunks or dice to allow quicker, even cooking.

Remove as much skin as possible from poultry. It shrivels up, becoming quite unappetizing. It will only have to be removed before serving anyway, and contributes to the grease and scum that accumulates on top of the food.

Precooking

Many recipes call for a little sautéing prior to going into the slow cooker. There are several reasons for what seems like an unnecessary step. While it may seem time-consuming, sautéing or preheating some ingredients actually speeds up the total cooking time. Many foods, especially meats, get a flavor boost from a quick searing. And onions soften and caramelize during a sauté, making them taste much sweeter. To really kick up the flavor, deglaze the sauté pan with a half cup of wine or broth, scraping up the yummy brown bits stuck on the bottom, then transfer it all into the slow cooker. This extra work only adds about ten minutes to the prep time. But if these few minutes (plus an extra pan to wash) are too much in your busy morning, just skip it. Simply toss all the ingredients into the slow cooker, turn it on, and go about your business. The finished dish will still be delicious. Just not quite as delicious as it could have been.

In high altitude areas, liquids boil at lower temperatures than at sea level. As a result, cooking times and settings will have to be adjusted. Check for doneness after the maximum suggested cooking times, and cook for a longer time at possibly a higher setting than the recipe suggests.

Slow Cooker Safety

If the power goes out while you are not at home and you are unsure how long the cooker was off, throw away the food, even if it looks done. If you are at home during the power failure, finish cooking the ingredients immediately by some other means, such as a gas oven or cooktop or outside on the barbecue grill. But if the food was completely cooked before the power went out, the cooked food should remain safe for up to two hours in the cooker with the power off.

Never preheat an empty slow cooker or let it run on empty because extreme temperature changes may crack your crock. For the same reason, never pour cold food into a hot crock, and never refrigerate or immerse a hot crock in cold water.

Like all electrical appliances, care should be taken while using a slow cooker. The cord is short to prevent possible entanglements with another object; avoid using an extension cord.

Make sure the slow cooker fits comfortably on your countertop. Since the sides of a slow cooker can get very hot, allow at least six inches of clearance on all sides. Keep it from the edge of the counter, away from klutzy adults, small children, and large pets. Because heat rises, do not use the unit underneath a cabinet, or inside a cabinet.

Discard the cooker if the cord is cut or frayed. Unless you are an electrician, do not attempt to replace the cord yourself. To be safe, leave the unit unplugged when not in use.

ESSENTIAL

Unless there is a warm setting on your slow cooker, remove and serve the food immediately when done. After dinner, pack and refrigerate leftovers as soon as possible to prevent the growth of bacteria.

To help prevent baked-on food, lightly spray the bottom and sides of the slow cooker with vegetable oil or, more conveniently, with cooking spray.

Inspect the crock before each use, and discard if any cracks appear. Besides the danger of bacteria entering and flourishing in cracks, there is the danger of the crock shattering when heated.

Caring for Your Slow Cooker

Even with the use of cooking sprays, some foods just want to permanently bond to the crock. Avoid abrasive cleaners and steel wool pads. After the crock cools, place in the sink and fill with hot, soapy water. Let it soak for a half hour or so, then gently scrub with a sponge or plastic scrubbie. Rinse with hot water, then invert over a dish drainer and let dry.

Some crocks have dark interiors, which do a great job hiding stains. If you have stains on a lighter-color crock, soak in hot water with a cup of vinegar added, then rinse with hot water as above.

The exterior of the slow cooker, unless the directions for that model say otherwise, should never be immersed in water. Only surface clean it.

And the most important tip? Always read and follow the directions!

The Kosher Pantry

Since 1923, when the Orthodox Union created its famous OU logo to designate Heinz vegetarian beans as kosher and pareve, thousands of food items today are available certified as kosher. It is almost a certainty that every kitchen in America contains at least one food with a hechsher.

The following is a list of products often found in a kosher pantry. Many people unfamiliar with kosher products will be surprised to learn that most of the items on this list will be quite familiar, since formerly "exotic" food items have gone mainstream and are easily available at the local supermarket. Many of the staples listed are for today's kosher cook, who makes traditional comfort foods and incorporates international cuisines into everyday meals.

- Kasha
- Vegetarian bouillon
- Matzoh and matzoh meal
- Tapioca and cornstarch
- Dates
- Prunes (also known as dried plums), apricots and other dried fruit
- Pita bread
- Bagels
- Bread (usually pareve to avoid accidentally using a dairy with meat)
- Pearl barley
- Dried or canned beans
- Dried spices and herbs
- Pasta sauce (usually pareve to avoid unintentionally mixing a dairy with meat)

- Pasta and noodles in various widths and shapes
- Soba noodles
- Soy sauce
- Chili paste
- Olive oil
- Vegetable oil
- Balsamic vinegar
- White and/or cider vinegar
- Pareve "bacon bits"
- Cooking spray (usually pareve to avoid accidentally mixing milk with meat)
- Soy, coconut, almond, and rice milk—used as milk substitutes. Although dairy-free, some of these "milks" are produced on equipment that also processes dairy products. Look for a pareve hechsher to avoid combining milk and meat products.
- Couscous (both regular and Israeli style)
- Rice (such as long grain, basmati, and Arborio)
- Quinoa
- Farro—an ancient grain that lately has had a resurgence in popularity
- Olives—black, green, or both, depending on personal preference
- Kosher and table salt
- Canned tomatoes
- Kosher gelatin—vegetarian or fish-based. Some interpretations of kashrut allow any type of gelatin.
- Wine—although grapes are inherently kosher, winemaking must be supervised by religious Jews and produced according to kashrut in order to be kosher. Reform and most conservative interpretations allow any wine.
- Tofu—a pressed curd made from soy beans
- Meat analogs such as Morningstar Farms or textured vegetable protein (TVP) take the place of nonkosher varieties.
- Parsley—this book uses the flat Italian variety because it is much more flavorful than the curly variety.
- Hard cheeses—the production of ordinary hard cheese uses rennet, another animal-based product. Look for a kosher brand labeled with

a hechsher, where a vegetable-based rennet is used. Conservative and reform interpretations allow any American-made cheese.

- Margarine—some margarines contain dairy products. The margarine in a kosher kitchen will always be pareve to prevent the possibility of accidentally mixing a dairy margarine with meat. Recipes in this book use stick margarine.
- Kosher meats, poultry, and fish

Converting Recipes for the Slow Cooker

To avoid reinventing the wheel, first do a little investigating to see if a recipe similar to yours has already been adapted for the slow cooker. This cookbook is a great place to start.

If the original recipe calls for large pieces of meat, cut those pieces into individual serving sizes, or 1-inch cubes or strips. Large chunks of vegetables should be chopped or diced into similar-sized pieces as well.

Less liquid is lost to evaporation in a slow cooker, so start out with a little more than half of the liquid called for in the original recipe. For example, if a soup recipe calls for eight cups of water (or water to cover), start out with five cups. It's easier to add liquid afterward if the food seems too dry than to add too much liquid at the beginning and siphon out the excess later.

Similarly, because moisture and steam help in the cooking process, add a little liquid, such as water, broth, or juice (depending on the food) if none is listed in your recipe.

If too much liquid remains at the end of cooking time anyway, you have many options to fix it (besides just ignoring it). You can ladle the excess liquid out of the crock, or thicken the sauce by stirring in some cornstarch mixed with a little cold water. A third way to correct too much liquid is to grab the immersion blender and purée some or all of the ingredients. The purée will mix with and thicken the sauce. And, depending on the recipe, some cooks stir in up to an entire can of condensed soup, or (in the case of dairy food) some powdered milk.

Fresh herbs and spices lose their flavor with long cooking. Hold off adding fresh herbs and spices until at least thirty minutes before the end of cooking time. Conversely, the flavors of dried herbs and spices may become more pronounced or harsh from long cooking. Use about half of the dried herbs originally called for at the beginning of the cooking time; later on, taste and add more if necessary.

Milk and cheese tend to break down and separate. Substitute cream or evaporated milk, both of which can handle long cooking times. Wait to add cheese until about thirty to sixty minutes before the end of cooking time; or, add it at the start, then cook on the high setting.

ALERT

If the recipe you want to convert calls for stirring or basting the food, don't! Heat and moisture escape every time the lid is lifted; the cooking time can increase as much as thirty minutes with each peek. Besides, any evaporation will rise, condense on the lid, then drip back down on the food, essentially basting itself. Remember, the point of a slow cooker is that it can (and should!) be left alone.

Converting Cooking Times

To convert cooking times, the rule of thumb is for every thirty minutes of conventional cooking time, cook for four to six hours on low or two to four hours on high in the slow cooker. If the slow cooker is half to three-quarters full, assume it will be the longer cooking time. If the slow cooker is less than half full, be sure to check for doneness even before these time suggestions. It's difficult, but not impossible, to overcook food.

Browning

For recipes that might look bland and unappetizing without a brown crust, transfer the cooked food to a casserole dish and pop under the broiler for a minute or two for a quick browning. Another way is to first sear the meat in a skillet, then finish cooking in the slow cooker.

A way to camouflage the lack of a golden brown top is the use of garnishes. Depending on the recipe, parsley, green onions, shredded cheese, sliced fruit, or toasted nuts, coconut, or bread crumbs can hide plain-looking tops.

Rice

When converting a rice casserole recipe, keep in mind that rice, especially the long-grain varieties, generally break down and turn into an unpleasant mush from slow cooking. Add it instead toward the end of cooking time, or cook it separately and serve the slow-cooked food over the rice. The exceptions, of course, are short-grained rice, which can stand up to long cooking, and recipes such as rice pudding or kugel, in which the foods are cooked on high for a relatively short period of time. Congee, an Asian soup, actually benefits from breaking down during a long cooking, where a gruel-like consistency is part of its charm. Pasta dishes should be treated in a similar manner to rice dishes—cook pasta separately from other ingredients in a recipe, then combine before serving.

CHAPTER 2

Appetizers

Middle Eastern Eggplant Salad

Serve warm as a side dish, cold alongside mixed greens, or as a dip with toasted pita triangles.

INGREDIENTS | SERVES 6 AS A SIDE DISH, OR 12 AS A DIP

Cooking spray

2 (1-pound) eggplants, peeled and cubed

1 tablespoon olive oil

1 medium onion, peeled and diced

1 tablespoon tomato paste

2 cloves garlic, minced

1 lemon, juiced

2 teaspoons kosher salt

½ teaspoon black pepper

¼ cup sliced black olives

1. Lightly spray interior of a 4-quart slow cooker with cooking spray.

2. Combine all ingredients except the black olives in the slow cooker.

3. Cook on low for 4 hours or high for 2 hours, or until eggplant is very tender.

4. Gently mash mixture with a potato masher. Taste and add more salt and pepper if needed.

5. Transfer to a serving bowl. Cover and chill if serving cold. Just before serving, garnish with the sliced black olives.

Eggplant Caponata

Serve this on small slices of Italian bread as an appetizer or use as a filling in sandwiches or wraps.

INGREDIENTS | SERVES 8

2 (1-pound) eggplants
1 teaspoon olive oil
1 red onion, diced
4 cloves garlic, minced
1 stalk celery, diced
2 tomatoes, diced
2 tablespoons nonpareil capers
2 tablespoons toasted pine nuts
1 teaspoon red pepper flakes
¼ cup red wine vinegar

Caponata

Caponata is an eggplant spread thought to have originated in Sicily. It is usually made with vegetables such as eggplant, onion, celery, tomatoes, green olives, and yellow or white onions. It is traditionally served cold, making it perfect for hot summer days, but is enthusiastically welcomed by guests all year round.

1. Pierce the eggplants with a fork. Place into a 4- or 6-quart slow cooker and cook on high for 2 hours.

2. Allow to cool. Peel off the skin. Slice each in half and remove the seeds. Discard the skin and seeds.

3. Place the eggplant pulp in a food processor. Pulse until smooth. Set aside.

4. Heat the oil in a nonstick skillet. Sauté the onion, garlic, and celery for about 5 minutes, or until the onion has softened.

5. Add the eggplant and tomatoes. Sauté for 3 additional minutes.

6. Return the mixture to the slow cooker and add the capers, pine nuts, red pepper flakes, and vinegar. Stir. Cook on low for 30 minutes. Stir prior to serving.

Baba Gannouj

Baba Gannouj (also spelled ganoush) *is a very tasty Middle Eastern dip.*
Serve it chilled with toasted pita chips or as a vegetable dip.

INGREDIENTS | YIELDS 1½ CUPS

1 tablespoon olive oil
1 large eggplant, peeled and diced
4 cloves garlic, peeled and minced
½ cup water
3 tablespoons fresh parsley
½ teaspoon salt
2 tablespoons fresh lemon juice
2 tablespoons tahini
1 tablespoon extra-virgin olive oil

Tahini

Tahini is a paste made from sesame seeds. It is sold in cans or jars, but can easily be made by combining ¼ cup toasted sesame seeds, ¼ teaspoon kosher salt, and 1 teaspoon sesame or olive oil in a food processor. Thin if necessary by drizzling in water, a teaspoon at a time, while the processor is running. Store leftovers, covered, in the refrigerator for up to 5 days. Discard if it develops an "off" or rancid smell.

1. In a 4-quart slow cooker, add the olive oil, eggplant, garlic, and water and stir until coated. Cover and cook on high heat for 4 hours.

2. Strain the cooked eggplant and garlic and add to a food processor or blender along with the parsley, salt, lemon juice, and tahini. Pulse to process.

3. Scrape down the side of the food processor or blender container if necessary. Add the extra-virgin olive oil and process until smooth. Cover and chill before serving.

Caramelized Onion Dip

Caramelized onions give this dip an amazing depth of flavor.

INGREDIENTS | YIELDS ABOUT 2 CUPS

⅔ cup Caramelized Onions (see Chapter 10)
8 ounces reduced-fat cream cheese
8 ounces reduced-fat sour cream
1 tablespoon Worcestershire sauce
¼ teaspoon white pepper
⅛ teaspoon flour

1. Place all ingredients into a 1½- to 2-quart slow cooker.

2. Heat on low for 2 hours. Whisk before serving.

Make It Pareve

Make this recipe pareve by using Toffuti Better Than Cream Cheese (vegan cream cheese) and Tofutti Sour Supreme (vegan sour cream) instead of the dairy versions. Note: most brands of Worcestershire sauce contain fish (anchovies).

Party Sausage Bites

For a milder "bite," reduce the horseradish by half and substitute sweet sausages.

INGREDIENTS | YIELDS 32 SERVINGS

2 (12-ounce) packages Andouille sausages
1 cup packed brown sugar
½ cup ketchup
¼ cup prepared horseradish

1. Cut each sausage diagonally into 4 segments. Place sausages in a 4-quart slow cooker.

2. In a medium bowl, combine the brown sugar, ketchup, and horseradish; pour over sausages. Cover and cook on low for 4 hours. To serve, arrange on serving platter with decorative toothpicks.

Bean Dip

A football-watching party favorite! This dip tastes best hot or warm.
Serve with corn chips or tortilla chips.

2 (15-ounce) cans pinto beans, drained and rinsed

1½ cups water

1 tablespoon olive oil

1 small onion, peeled and diced

3 cloves garlic, minced

1 medium tomato, seeded and diced

1 teaspoon chipotle powder

½ teaspoon ground cumin

¼ cup packed fresh cilantro leaves and stems, finely chopped

1 teaspoon kosher salt, plus more to taste

1 cup grated Monterey jack or Cheddar cheese

1. In a 4-quart slow cooker, add the beans, water, olive oil, onion, and garlic. Cover and cook over low heat for 1 hour.

2. Using a potato masher, partly mash the bean mixture. Let about half remain chunky.

3. Uncover the slow cooker and stir in diced tomato, chipotle, cumin, cilantro, and kosher salt. Re-cover and cook for an additional 30 minutes. Taste and add more salt if needed.

4. Scoop out dip into a serving bowl. Top with grated cheese; let sit for 5 minutes for cheese to partially melt, then serve immediately.

How to Seed and Dice a Tomato

To seed a tomato, first take a paring knife and core out the green stem. Cut the tomato into quarters. Scoop out the interior from each piece. Then, holding a piece flat against the cutting board, slice from top to bottom into thin strips about ¼" in width, then crosscut across the strips.

Fabulous Fondue

For six servings, cut the recipe in half and prepare in a small (1½-quart) slow cooker. To make it easier for your guests to access the fondue and to ensure that it is maintained at the proper temperature to prevent the cheese from separating, transfer the prepared fondue to an electric fondue pot.

INGREDIENTS | SERVES 12

2 cloves of garlic, peeled and cut in half

2 cups evaporated milk

1 cup dry white wine or sparkling white grape juice

1 teaspoon hot pepper sauce, or to taste

¼ cup all-purpose flour

1 teaspoon dry mustard

4 cups Swiss cheese, cubed

4 cups Muenster cheese, cubed

Salt and freshly ground black pepper (optional)

Fabulous Fondue Serving Suggestions

Cheese fondue is traditionally served with bread cubes that are each pierced with a fondue fork and dipped into the fondue. Steamed or roasted asparagus spears, raw or cooked baby carrots, broccoli florets, cauliflower florets, cucumber or pickle slices, radishes, snow peas, and sweet bell pepper strips are also delicious dipped in a savory fondue sauce.

1. Rub the inside of a 4-quart slow cooker with the cut cloves of garlic. (For a stronger garlic flavor, leave the garlic in the cooker and use a slotted spoon to remove the pieces just before serving.) Add the milk, wine or sparkling grape juice, and hot pepper sauce to the slow cooker.

2. Add the flour and dry mustard to a large zip-top bag. Seal and shake to mix well. Add the cheese cubes to the bag; seal the bag and shake well to coat the cheese cubes in the flour. Pour the contents of the bag into the slow cooker and stir to combine. Cover and cook on low for 4 hours or until heated through and the cheese has melted.

3. Whisk the fondue to incorporate the melted cheese fully into the liquid. Taste for seasoning and add more hot sauce and/or salt and freshly ground pepper if desired.

Plum Sauce

Plum sauce is often served with egg rolls, but it's also delicious if you brush it on chicken or ribs; doing so near the end of the grilling time will add a succulent glaze to the grilled meat.

INGREDIENTS | YIELDS 4 CUPS

8 cups (about 3 pounds) plums, pitted and cut in half

1 small sweet onion, peeled and diced

1 cup water

1 teaspoon fresh ginger, peeled and minced

1 clove of garlic, peeled and minced

¾ cup granulated sugar

½ cup rice vinegar or cider vinegar

1 teaspoon ground coriander

½ teaspoon salt

½ teaspoon cinnamon

¼ teaspoon cayenne pepper

¼ teaspoon ground cloves

1. Add the plums, onion, water, ginger, and garlic into a 4-quart slow cooker; cover and, stirring occasionally, cook on low for 4 hours or until plums and onions are tender.

2. Use an immersion blender to pulverize the contents of the slow cooker before straining it, or press the cooked plum mixture through a sieve.

3. Return the liquefied and strained plum mixture to the slow cooker and stir in sugar, vinegar, coriander, salt, cinnamon, cayenne pepper, and cloves. Cover and, stirring occasionally, cook on low for 2 hours or until the sauce reaches the consistency of applesauce.

Sassy and Sweet Chicken Wings

For larger servings or to increase the number of servings, substitute 4 pounds of chicken drumettes (the meatiest pieces of the chicken wings) for the whole chicken wings.

INGREDIENTS | SERVES 12

1 cup ketchup

1 cup chili sauce

4 pounds chicken wings

1 (12-ounce) can Coca-Cola

1. In a small bowl, mix ketchup and chili sauce together to combine.

2. Add the chicken wings and ketchup mixture to a 5- or 6-quart slow cooker in alternating layers. Pour the cola over the chicken and ketchup mixture. Cover and cook on low for 6–8 hours.

3. Uncover the slow cooker and continue to cook on low until the sauce is thickened. To serve, reduce the heat setting of the slow cooker to warm.

Sticky Honey Wings

Making wings in the slow cooker is not only easy, it is a great way to keep wings warm throughout an entire party or game. Just switch the setting to warm after cooking and the wings will stay hot and sticky.

INGREDIENTS | SERVES 10

Cooking spray
3 pounds chicken wings, tips removed
¼ cup honey
¼ cup low-sodium soy sauce
½ teaspoon freshly ground pepper
2 tablespoons chili sauce
½ teaspoon garlic powder

1. Spray the inside of a 4-quart slow cooker with cooking spray. Layer the wings on the bottom.

2. In a small bowl, whisk together the honey, soy sauce, pepper, chili sauce, and garlic powder. Pour over the wings. Toss to coat with sauce.

3. Cook for 6–7 hours on low. Stir before serving.

The World of Chili Sauce

Chili sauce is a smooth, mild red sauce. A mixture of tomato purée and spices, it is most often used as a base for other sauces. Chili-garlic sauce is a mixture of coarsely ground chilies and garlic. It is robustly flavored and used frequently in soups, stir-fries, and dipping sauces.

Zesty Lemon Hummus

Serve this Middle Eastern spread with pita, vegetables, or falafel.

INGREDIENTS | SERVES 20

1 pound dried chickpeas, rinsed and drained

Water, as needed

3 tablespoons tahini

4 tablespoons lemon juice

2 teaspoons lemon zest

3 cloves garlic

½ teaspoon kosher salt, or to taste

¼ teaspoon white pepper, or to taste

Lemon Zest

Grate only the outer portion of the lemon skin, avoiding the bitter white pith underneath. My friend Juley passes along this tip: grate more than you need, then freeze the excess in a freezer-safe plastic bag (pressing out air before sealing) for up to 6 months. The natural oils in citrus zest prevent it from freezing solid, making it easy to measure out the amount needed.

1. In a 4-quart slow cooker, add the chickpeas and cover with water by several inches. Soak overnight.

2. The next day, drain the chickpeas and replace the water. Cover and cook on low for 8 hours. Drain, reserving the liquid.

3. In a food processor, place the cooked chickpeas, tahini, lemon juice, lemon zest, garlic, and salt and pepper. Pulse until smooth, adding the reserved liquid as needed to achieve the desired texture. Taste and add more salt and pepper if needed.

Fig and Ginger Spread

*This rich-tasting spread is great swirled into Greek yogurt or
served as a dip with strawberries and other fruit.*

INGREDIENTS | SERVES 25

2 pounds fresh figs

2 tablespoons minced fresh ginger

2 tablespoons lime juice

½ cup water

¾ cup sugar

1. Place all ingredients in a 2-quart slow cooker. Stir. Cook on low for 2–3 hours. Remove the lid and cook for an additional 2–3 hours until the mixture is thickened.

2. Pour into airtight containers and refrigerate for up to 6 weeks.

Traditional Apple Butter

The natural pectin in the apple peels helps thicken the butter.

INGREDIENTS | YIELDS ABOUT 3 CUPS

4 pounds Jonathan, McIntosh, or Rome apples
1 lemon
1⅓ cups light brown sugar, packed
1 cup apple cider
6" cinnamon stick (optional)

Wax On, Wax Off

Apples shipped long distances are usually coated with a thin layer of wax to preserve freshness. Although the total amount on each apple is minuscule (and therefore, even if the wax were to contain nonkosher elements the apple would still be considered kosher by most certifying agencies), to some consumers any amount is unacceptable. So in order to ensure that the apples haven't been waxed, purchase directly from an orchard or at a farmer's market.

1. Core and quarter the apples. Add to a 4- or 5-quart slow cooker.

2. Zest the lemon and squeeze out the juice into a small bowl.

3. Add the lemon zest, lemon juice, brown sugar, and cider to the slow cooker and stir to combine. Add the cinnamon stick if using. Cover and cook on low for 10 hours or until the apples are soft and tender.

4. Uncover and, stirring occasionally, cook on high for an additional 8–10 hours or until the mixture has reduced to about 3 cups.

5. If used, remove and discard the cinnamon stick. Use a spatula to press the apple butter through a large mesh strainer to remove the peel. Ladle the warm apple butter into hot, sterilized jars. Screw two-piece lids onto the jars. Allow to stand at room temperature for 8 hours; refrigerate for up to 6 months.

Vegetarian Cabbage Rolls

Even meat-eaters can't tell the difference! Serve these as a party appetizer or lunch.

INGREDIENTS | YIELDS 24–30 ROLLS

2 small heads of cabbage

2 (8-ounce) cans tomato sauce

2 tablespoons lemon juice

1 tablespoon sugar

1 (12-ounce) jar roasted, unsalted sunflower seeds

1 tablespoon vegetable oil

1 large Spanish (yellow) onion, finely diced

2 cups cooked long-grain rice

2 eggs

2 teaspoons kosher salt

¼ teaspoon freshly ground black pepper

Cooking spray, as needed

¼ cup raisins

Forget to Freeze the Cabbages Last Night?

Cut 12–15 large leaves from each cabbage. Place in a large pot containing a few inches of boiling water. Cover and let steam for 10 minutes. Drain in a colander. Allow to cool enough to handle, then proceed with the recipe.

1. The evening before, place the cabbages in the freezer and leave overnight.

2. The next morning, remove cabbages from freezer. Set aside to defrost enough to handle. Peel off 12–15 large leaves from each cabbage (as they defrost the leaves will soften) and cut off any heavy back membrane.

3. Meanwhile, in a 1-quart bowl, combine the tomato sauce, lemon juice, and sugar and set aside.

4. Pour sunflower seeds into a food processor and process in pulses until ground. Avoid overprocessing to prevent the ground seeds from becoming sunflower butter. Set aside.

5. Heat oil in a large skillet over medium heat. Add onion and sauté for 7–8 minutes or until lightly browned. Remove from heat and add rice, ground sunflower seeds, eggs, salt, and pepper. Mix well.

6. Place 1 cabbage leaf, cut side toward you, on a flat work surface. Put a heaping teaspoon of sunflower mixture near top of leaf. Fold over the top, then tightly fold in the sides. Tightly roll up and secure with a toothpick. Repeat until all the cabbage leaves are used up.

7. Spray the inside of a 4- to 6-quart slow cooker with cooking spray. Spread a thin layer of tomato sauce mixture on bottom. Arrange rolls on the sauce, toothpick side down. Sprinkle with raisins, then cover with remaining sauce. Cover and cook on low for 4–6 hours.

Stuffed Grape Leaves

Although there are many versions of stuffed grape leaves served across the Mediterranean, this version is inspired by Greece.

INGREDIENTS | SERVES 30

1 (16-ounce) jar grape leaves (about 60 leaves)

Cooking spray, as needed

¾ pound ground beef, chicken, or veal

1 shallot, minced

¾ cup cooked brown or white rice

¼ cup minced dill

½ cup lemon juice, divided use

2 tablespoons minced parsley

1 tablespoon dried mint

1 tablespoon ground fennel

¼ teaspoon freshly ground black pepper

⅛ teaspoon salt

2 cups water

Easy Greek-Style Dipping Sauce

In a medium bowl, stir together 1 cup pareve sour cream and 1 teaspoon each dried oregano, mint, thyme, dill weed, and white pepper. Stir in 3 tablespoons lemon juice. Refrigerate for 1 hour before serving. Refrigerate leftovers in an airtight container up to 2 days. If mixture separates, stir liquid back in before using.

1. Prepare the grape leaves according to package instructions. Set aside.

2. Spray a nonstick skillet with cooking spray. Sauté the meat and shallot until the meat is thoroughly cooked. Drain off any excess fat. Scrape into a large bowl and add the rice, dill, ¼ cup of the lemon juice, parsley, mint, fennel, pepper, and salt. Stir to incorporate all ingredients.

3. Place a grape leaf, stem side up, with the top of the leaf pointing away from you on a clean work surface. Place 1 teaspoon filling in the middle of the leaf. Fold the bottom toward the middle and then fold in the sides. Roll it toward the top to seal. Repeat with the other leaves.

4. Place the rolled grape leaves in two or three layers in a 4-quart slow cooker. Pour in the water and remaining lemon juice. Cover and cook on low for 4–6 hours. Serve warm or cold.

Coconut Chicken Fingers

Serve with Honey-Mustard Dipping Sauce.

INGREDIENTS | SERVES 8–10

Cooking spray

3 tablespoons fresh lemon juice

3 tablespoons fresh lime juice

3 tablespoons spicy brown mustard

½ cup plain toasted bread crumbs

½ cup unsweetened shredded coconut

½ teaspoon kosher salt

¼ teaspoon ground black pepper

¼ teaspoon curry powder

¼ teaspoon dried oregano

4 skinless, boneless chicken breasts, cut into 2" × 1" inch strips

¼ cup (½ stick) margarine, melted

1 recipe Honey-Mustard Dipping Sauce (see recipe in sidebar)

Honey-Mustard Dipping Sauce

Whisk together 3 tablespoons spicy brown mustard, 2 tablespoons honey, and 3 table-spoons mayonnaise until smooth. Cover and refrigerate until ready to use. Makes approximately ½ cup.

1. Spray the inside of a 4-quart slow cooker with the cooking spray. Set aside.

2. In a small bowl, whisk together the lemon juice, lime juice, and the mustard.

3. In another bowl, combine the bread crumbs, coconut, salt, pepper, curry powder, and oregano.

4. Dip the chicken strips in the mustard mixture, followed by the bread crumb mixture. Place in the prepared slow cooker. Drizzle the melted margarine over the chicken.

5. Cover and cook on high for 2–4 hours, or until the chicken fingers are fully cooked. Serve with Honey-Mustard Dipping Sauce alongside.

Eggplant Caviar

A simple yet tasty dip. Serve with toasted Italian bread slices.

INGREDIENTS | SERVES 8

2 medium-sized eggplants, peeled and cut across into ½" slices

½ cup plus 2 teaspoons kosher salt, divided

Cooking spray

¼ cup olive oil

1 small onion, peeled and diced

4 garlic cloves, minced

1 teaspoon ground black pepper

1 tablespoon red wine vinegar

1 loaf Italian bread, cut into ¼" slices and toasted

1. Place the eggplant slices in a colander in the sink. Use the ½ cup of the kosher salt to evenly salt both sides of eggplant slices. Let sit for 30 minutes, then rinse the slices and pat dry with paper towels. Cut into 1" chunks.

2. Spray the insides of a 4-quart slow cooker with the cooking spray. Add in the eggplant chunks. Stir in the olive oil, onion, garlic, remaining 2 teaspoons salt, and the pepper. Cover and cook on low for 6–8 hours, or until eggplant is very tender.

3. Mash eggplant mixture with a fork. Mix in red wine vinegar. Transfer to a serving bowl. Serve warm or chilled with toasted slices of Italian bread.

Black Bean Salsa

If making this addicting salsa in advance, add cilantro just before serving. Alternatively, this salsa can be served as a cool side dish for 8.

INGREDIENTS | SERVES 12 AS A DIP

1 cup dried black beans
Water, as needed
2 teaspoons salt
½ red pepper
½ green pepper
½ small red onion
½ packed cup cilantro, leaves and stems
1 lime, juiced (about 2 tablespoons juice)
2–4 tablespoons olive oil, depending on taste
1 teaspoon kosher salt, or to taste
2 drops Tabasco sauce, or to taste
Large bag of tortilla chips

Cilantro

Don't discard the cilantro stems! They are just as flavorful, if not more so, than the leaves. And unlike most fresh herbs, cilantro stems retain their flavor during long cooking times, making them perfect for slow cooker recipes. The stems can be tossed in at the beginning of a recipe; add the leaves just before serving.

1. Rinse the black beans in water. Place the beans in a container, then add water to cover by at least an inch; let soak overnight.

2. The next day, drain the water, rinse beans again, then add to a large pot and cover with water. Boil on high heat for 10 minutes, then drain.

3. Add black beans, enough fresh water to cover by 1 inch, and 2 teaspoons of salt to a 4-quart slow cooker. Cover and cook on low for 5–6 hours. Check the beans to see if they are tender after about 5 hours; continue cooking if necessary, checking every 30 minutes.

4. When the beans are done, drain in a colander; set aside to cool for 30 minutes.

5. Meanwhile, seed and finely chop the red and green pepper halves, the onion, and the cilantro.

6. Place beans in a large mixing bowl. Add the vegetables, lime juice, and 2 tablespoons olive oil. Sprinkle with salt and Tabasco sauce. Gently combine. Taste and add more oil and/or salt if necessary.

7. Transfer to a 2-quart serving bowl. Add cilantro just before serving. If not serving immediately, cover and refrigerate for up to a day. Remove from refrigerator 30 minutes before serving. Serve with tortilla chips.

Spinach-Artichoke Dip

For a different presentation, scrape cooked dip into broiler-safe dish. Top with ¼ cup of bread crumbs and heat under the broiler for 1–2 minutes or until bread crumbs just start to brown.

INGREDIENTS | SERVES 4

Cooking spray

1 tablespoon olive oil

2 cloves garlic, minced

1½ cups part-skim ricotta cheese

½ teaspoon thyme

1 teaspoon lemon zest

½ teaspoon cayenne pepper

1 (14-ounce) can artichoke hearts, drained and chopped

1 (10-ounce) package frozen spinach, thawed and drained well

¼ cup grated Parmesan cheese

½ teaspoon salt

¼ cup shredded mozzarella

Draining Frozen Spinach

Defrosted spinach contains a lot of water. Place defrosted spinach in a paper towel–lined colander over a bowl. Top with another paper towel and press down to extract as much water as possible.

1. Spray the inside of a 3- or 4-quart slow cooker with nonstick spray.

2. Heat the olive oil in a small nonstick skillet over medium heat. When hot, add the garlic and cook until fragrant and pale golden, about 1 minute. Remove the skillet from the heat and allow the garlic to cool while proceeding with next step.

3. In a large mixing bowl, combine the ricotta cheese, thyme, lemon zest, and cayenne pepper.

4. Add the artichokes, spinach, Parmesan, salt, and cooled garlic. Stir well to combine.

5. Transfer the artichoke mixture into the prepared cooker and sprinkle evenly with the mozzarella.

6. Cover and cook on high for 2 hours. Serve hot or warm.

CHAPTER 3

Breakfast and Brunch

Nutty Breakfast Pilaf

If you don't have fresh oranges, substitute ⅛ cup orange juice for the zest.

INGREDIENTS | SERVES 4

Baking spray
¼ cup chopped pecans
1 cup brown rice
½ cup golden raisins
1½ teaspoons grated orange zest
½ teaspoon cinnamon
1 (12-ounce) can evaporated milk
1½ cups water
¼ teaspoon salt
1 banana, cut up (optional)
1 cup blueberries, rinsed (optional)

Make It Pareve

Make this recipe pareve by substituting 2 cups soy, almond, or rice milk for the evaporated milk and by reducing the water to 1 cup.

1. Spray the inside of a 3- or 4-quart slow cooker with baking spray.

2. Heat a large saucepan over medium heat, then add the chopped pecans. Stir constantly for 1–2 minutes until pecans just begin to toast and smell nutty.

3. Immediately remove from heat and mix in rice. Spread mixture evenly over the bottom of the prepared slow cooker. Sprinkle with the raisins, orange zest, and cinnamon. Do not clean saucepan.

4. Combine the evaporated milk, water, and salt in the used saucepan. Bring just to a boil over medium heat. Pour the liquid carefully over the rice mixture.

5. Cover and cook on high for 2 hours or until liquid is totally absorbed. Turn off cooker.

6. Fluff pilaf with a fork, re-cover, and allow the rice to sit for 5 minutes. Serve hot with optional blueberries and/or bananas.

Almond and Dried Cherry Granola

Using the slow cooker virtually eliminates any chance of overcooking or burning the granola.

INGREDIENTS | SERVES 24

5 cups old-fashioned rolled oats
1 cup slivered almonds
¼ cup mild honey
¼ cup canola oil
1 teaspoon vanilla extract
½ cup dried tart cherries
¼ cup unsweetened flaked coconut
½ cup sunflower seeds

1. Place the oats and almonds into a 4-quart slow cooker. Drizzle with honey, oil, and vanilla. Stir the mixture to distribute the syrup evenly. Cook on high, uncovered, for 1½ hours, stirring every 15–20 minutes.

2. Add the cherries, coconut, and sunflower seeds. Reduce heat to low. Cook for 4 hours, uncovered, stirring every 20 minutes.

3. Allow the granola to cool fully, and then store it in an airtight container for up to 1 month.

French Toast Casserole

This recipe is great for breakfast, and it's a wonderful way to use bread that is slightly stale.

INGREDIENTS | SERVES 8

Nonstick spray
12 slices raisin bread
6 eggs
1 teaspoon vanilla extract
2 cups evaporated milk (regular, low-fat, or fat-free)
2 tablespoons dark brown sugar
1 teaspoon cinnamon
¼ teaspoon nutmeg

1. Spray a 4-quart slow cooker with the nonstick spray. Layer the raisin bread in the slow cooker.

2. In a small bowl, whisk the eggs, vanilla, evaporated milk, brown sugar, cinnamon, and nutmeg. Pour over the bread.

3. Cover and cook on low for 6–8 hours. Remove the lid and cook uncovered for 30 minutes or until the liquid has evaporated.

Challah French Toast Casserole

A delicious alternative to regular French toast.

INGREDIENTS | SERVES 8

Nonstick spray
½ loaf day-old challah, thickly sliced
¼ cup raisins
6 eggs
1 teaspoon vanilla extract
2 cups evaporated milk
3 tablespoons granulated sugar
1 teaspoon cinnamon
¼ teaspoon nutmeg
¼ teaspoon kosher salt

1. Spray a 4-quart slow cooker with nonstick spray. Layer the challah in the slow cooker, and sprinkle with the raisins.

2. In a small bowl, whisk the eggs, vanilla, evaporated milk, sugar, cinnamon, nutmeg, and salt. Pour over the challah and raisins.

3. Cover and cook on low for 6–8 hours. Remove the lid and cook uncovered for 30 minutes or until the liquid has evaporated.

Breakfast Quinoa with Maple, Walnuts, and Apples

Substitute fresh peeled, cored, and chopped apple for the dried apple. Add it just before serving.

INGREDIENTS | SERVES 4

Nonstick spray
1 cup quinoa, rinsed well
½ cup dried apples, chopped
½ cup chopped walnuts
¼ cup maple syrup
½ teaspoon cinnamon
¼ teaspoon nutmeg
¼ teaspoon salt
1 (12-ounce) can evaporated milk (regular, low-fat, or fat-free)
½ cup water

1. Spray the inside of a 3- or 4-quart slow cooker with nonstick spray.

2. Pour the quinoa into the prepared cooker and stir in the apples, walnuts, maple syrup, cinnamon, nutmeg, and salt.

3. Add the milk and water to a 2-quart saucepan. Place over medium heat and heat to a bare simmer. Stir into the quinoa mixture.

4. Cover and cook on high heat for 2 hours, then turn off. Let sit for about 5 minutes before serving.

Barley Porridge with Blueberries and Pecans

Dry-toasting the barley and pecans releases even more of their nutty flavors and is worth taking the extra couple of minutes. But if you are really short on time then skip this step.

INGREDIENTS | SERVES 4

Nonstick spray

1 cup pearl barley, rinsed

½ cup chopped pecan pieces

2 cups water

1 (12-ounce) can evaporated milk

¼ cup packed brown sugar

¼ teaspoon salt

1 pint fresh blueberries, rinsed

Barley

Although pearl barley is steam processed, which removes the outer layer of bran, this nutty and pleasantly chewy grain is still very healthy. One cooked cup of pearl barley contains 6 grams of dietary fiber, 4 grams of protein, less than 1 gram of fat, and many important vitamins and minerals. But if you are looking for a wheat-substitute, please note that barley does contain gluten.

1. Spray the inside of a 3- or 4-quart slow cooker with nonstick spray.

2. Heat a medium-sized frying pan over medium heat, then add the barley and chopped pecan pieces. Stir constantly for 1–2 minutes until the mixture just begins to toast and smell nutty.

3. Immediately remove from heat and place mixture in the prepared slow cooker.

4. Carefully pour in the water and milk.

5. Stir in the brown sugar and salt.

6. Cover and cook on low for 8–9 hours. Serve topped with blueberries.

Overnight Oatmeal

Wake up to the aroma of freshly cooked oatmeal.

INGREDIENTS | SERVES 6

Nonstick spray
2 cups old-fashioned rolled oats
2 (12-ounce) cans evaporated milk
½ cup raisins
¼ cup toasted walnut pieces
1 teaspoon cardamom
¼ teaspoon salt

1. Spray the inside of a 3- or 4-quart slow cooker with nonstick spray.

2. In a large bowl, stir together the oats, milk, raisins, walnut pieces, cardamom, and salt. Pour into the prepared cooker.

3. Cover and cook on low for 8–9 hours. Serve hot.

Cardamom

Cardamom is a sweet spice that goes perfectly with apples. If it is not available, substitute a teaspoon of apple pie spice or a mixture of ½ teaspoon cinnamon, ¼ teaspoon ginger, and a pinch each of cloves and nutmeg.

Cheese Grits

Top each individual bowl of grits with additional Cheddar cheese and place under the broiler until melted for an even tastier treat.

INGREDIENTS | SERVES 4

2 cups stone-ground grits
6 cups water
2 tablespoons butter
1 cup shredded Cheddar cheese
2 teaspoons kosher salt
¼ teaspoon black pepper
⅛ teaspoon cayenne pepper

1. Add all ingredients to a 4-quart slow cooker. Cover and cook on low heat for 6–9 hours.

Banana Walnut Frittata

You can add another flavor dimension to this dish by sprinkling some cinnamon to taste over the banana layers. Another option is to serve it with blueberry or strawberry syrup.

INGREDIENTS | SERVES 6

1 tablespoon unsalted butter

1 (1-pound) loaf bread, cut into ½ to ¾-inch cubes

1 (8-ounce) package cream cheese

2 ripe bananas

1 cup walnuts, coarsely chopped

12 large eggs

¼ cup maple syrup

1 cup milk or heavy cream

¼ teaspoon salt

Additional maple syrup for serving (optional)

Or, If You Prefer . . .

You can substitute 1 cup of blueberries, raspberries, or blackberries for the bananas and use toasted pecans instead of walnuts, or you could omit the nuts entirely.

1. At least 12 hours before you plan to begin cooking the frittata, coat the bottom and sides of a 4- or 5-quart slow cooker with the butter.

2. Place a third of the bread cubes (about 4 cups) in the bottom of the insert. Cut the cream cheese into ½ inch cubes and evenly spread half of them over the bread cubes. Slice 1 of the bananas, arrange the slices over the cream cheese layer, and sprinkle half of the walnut pieces over the banana. Add another 4 cups of bread cubes and create another cream cheese, banana, and walnut layer over the top of the bread. Add the remaining 4 cups of bread cubes to the cooker. Press the mixture down slightly.

3. Place the eggs in a small bowl and whisk until frothy. Whisk in the syrup, milk or cream, and salt. Pour over the bread in the insert. Cover and refrigerate for 12 hours.

4. After 12 hours, remove the insert from the refrigerator and place in the slow cooker. Cover and cook on low for 6 hours. Serve with warm maple syrup if desired.

Cheese Soufflé

Try this no-fuss version of soufflé at your next brunch.

INGREDIENTS | SERVES 8

8 ounces sharp Cheddar, shredded

8 ounces mozzarella, shredded

8 slices thin sandwich bread

Nonstick cooking spray

2 cups evaporated milk (regular, low-fat, or fat-free)

4 eggs

¼ teaspoon ground cayenne pepper

1. In a large bowl, mix the cheeses, and set aside.

2. Tear the bread into large pieces, and set aside.

3. Spray a 4-quart slow cooker with nonstick cooking spray. Alternately layer the cheese and bread in the insert, beginning and ending with bread.

4. In a small bowl, whisk together the evaporated milk, eggs, and cayenne. Pour over the bread and cheese layers. Cover and cook on low for 2–3 hours.

Spinach Quiche

This is an easy but festive dish that would be a perfect addition to brunch.

INGREDIENTS | SERVES 6

Nonstick cooking spray

¼ teaspoon ground cayenne pepper

½ teaspoon ground nutmeg

4 eggs

½ cup shredded low-fat sharp Cheddar

6 ounces baby spinach

1½ cups evaporated milk (regular, low-fat, or fat-free)

¼ cup diced green onion

2 slices sandwich bread, cut into ½ inch cubes

1. Spray a round 4-quart slow cooker with nonstick cooking spray.

2. In a small bowl, whisk together the cayenne, nutmeg, eggs, cheese, spinach, evaporated milk, and green onion.

3. Add the bread cubes in one layer on the bottom of the slow cooker. Pour the egg mixture over the top and cover. Cook for 2–3 hours on high or until the edges begin to pull away from the edge of the insert. Slice and lift out each slice individually.

Apple Cherry Granola Crisp

The use of both crisp and baking apples lends a pleasing combination of textures.

INGREDIENTS | SERVES 8

Cooking spray

4 crisp apples, such as Granny Smith, golden delicious, or Cortland

2 baking apples, such as gala, McIntosh, or pink lady

2 tablespoons fresh lemon juice

1 teaspoon ground cinnamon

¼ teaspoon ground cardamom

¼ cup granulated sugar

2 tablespoons cornstarch

1 cup Almond and Dried Cherry Granola (see the recipe in this chapter)

¼ cup firmly packed brown sugar

¼ cup (½ stick) unsalted butter or margarine, cubed

1 cup yogurt (optional)

Breakfast for Dessert?

Serve with ice cream or Tofutti for a yummy dessert.

1. Spray the inside of a 4-quart slow cooker with cooking spray.

2. Peel, core, and chop the apples into ½" cubes. Place in a large bowl and toss with the lemon juice.

3. In a small bowl mix together the cinnamon, cardamom, granulated sugar, and cornstarch. Add to the apple mixture; stir to combine. Transfer apple/spice mixture to prepared slow cooker.

4. In a medium bowl combine the granola with the brown sugar. Sprinkle evenly over the apple mixture. Arrange butter or margarine cubes on top. Cover and cook on high for 2½–3 hours. If mixture seems too liquidy, set cover ajar and cook on high for up to an additional half hour.

5. Serve warm with yogurt, if desired.

Hash Brown Casserole

Use vegetarian sausage links such as those from Morningstar Farms.

INGREDIENTS | SERVES 8

2 tablespoons unsalted butter

1 small onion, peeled and diced

1 small green pepper, seeded and diced

1 (8-ounce) package vegetarian sausage links

8 eggs

¼ cup milk, whole, low-fat, or skim

½ teaspoon kosher salt

¼ teaspoon ground black pepper

1 (30-ounce) bag plain frozen hash brown potatoes, defrosted

1 (8-ounce) package shredded Cheddar cheese

1. Melt butter in a small skillet over medium-high heat. Add the onion and green pepper. Cook, stirring frequently, until the onions soften, about 5 minutes.

2. Push the onions to the sides and add the vegetarian sausage links. Cook for about 3 minutes or until the sausages are browned on all sides. Transfer to a 4- or 6-quart slow cooker.

3. In a large bowl whisk together the eggs, milk, salt, and pepper. Add the hash browns and stir to completely coat the potatoes with the egg mixture, breaking up clumps, if any.

4. Pour the potato mixture over the onions and sausages. Sprinkle the cheese evenly on top. Cover and cook on high for 3–4 hours or until cheese has melted and eggs are set.

Shakshuka

Shakshuka is a Middle Eastern dish of eggs poached in a very spicy tomato sauce. Although it can be served at any meal, in Israel it is served for breakfast. This version adds a couple of potatoes for a very hearty first meal. Serve with pitas or a baguette.

INGREDIENTS | SERVES 4

1 tablespoon olive oil

1 large yellow onion, peeled and diced

2 large potatoes, peeled and cut into 1" chunks

1 red pepper, seeded and diced

4 garlic cloves, minced

1 teaspoon ground cumin

1 tablespoon sweet paprika

¼ teaspoon cayenne pepper

1 (28-ounce) can fire-roasted diced tomatoes, undrained

1 teaspoon kosher salt

4 eggs

¼ teaspoon ground black pepper

1 tablespoon parsley leaves, chopped (for garnish)

1. Heat the oil in a large skillet over medium-high heat. Add the onion and potatoes. Cook, stirring frequently, for about 5 minutes, or until the onions soften.

2. Add the red pepper and garlic. Continue to sauté for another 2 minutes.

3. Transfer mixture to a 4-quart slow cooker. Stir in remaining ingredients except the eggs, black pepper, and parsley. Cover and cook on low for 4 hours.

4. Carefully break the eggs on top of the tomato sauce. Do not stir in. Re-cover and continue to cook for another 10–15 minutes or until the eggs are poached to your preference. Sprinkle with the black pepper and parsley (if desired) before serving.

Pear, Apple, and Cranberry Pancake Topping

Add this festive topping to pancakes to make breakfast a real treat!

INGREDIENTS | SERVES 8

3 tart apples, thinly sliced

3 Bosc pears, thinly sliced

¾ cup fresh cranberries

1 tablespoon brown sugar

½ teaspoon ground ginger

½ teaspoon cinnamon

¼ teaspoon nutmeg

¼ teaspoon mace

1. Place all ingredients into a 3- or 4-quart slow cooker. Stir. Cook on low for 2 hours.

Crantastic!

Cranberries are a superfood. High in anti-oxidants and fiber, they are a welcome addition to both sweet and savory dishes. They are also naturally high in pectin, which means they'll thicken any dish.

Hot and Fruity Granola

With a little hot milk, granola becomes a warm, comforting breakfast.

INGREDIENTS | SERVES 6

Cooking spray

2 cups Almond and Dried Cherry Granola (see recipe in this chapter)

2 (12-ounce) cans evaporated milk

¼ teaspoon salt

2 apples (your favorite variety), peeled, cored, and diced

½ cup milk (whole, low-fat or skim) (for garnish)

1. Spray the inside of a 3- or 4-quart slow cooker with the cooking spray.

2. Stir together the granola, evaporated milk, and salt in the prepared slow cooker.

3. Cover and cook on low for 8–9 hours. Stir in the diced apple and milk, if desired, before serving.

Individual Spinach Florentine Cups

This dish can also be served as a light lunch. Serve alongside a chopped salad.

INGREDIENTS | SERVES 6

Cooking spray

2 cups cubed Italian bread, without crusts

1 (10-ounce) package frozen spinach, defrosted and squeezed dry

1 cup sliced fresh mushrooms

½ red pepper, seeded and finely diced

1 cup shredded sharp Cheddar cheese, divided

6 eggs

1 (12-ounce) can evaporated milk

1 teaspoon kosher salt

½ teaspoon sweet paprika

⅛ teaspoon ground black pepper

¼ cup thinly sliced scallions (for garnish)

1. Spray 6 small (4- or 5-ounce) ramekins with cooking spray. Divide the bread cubes, spinach, mushrooms, red pepper, and ½ cup of the Cheddar cheese evenly among the prepared ramekins.

2. In a small bowl, whisk together the eggs, evaporated milk, and salt. Pour evenly over the layers in the ramekins. Sprinkle with the remaining ½ cup cheese and the paprika.

3. Place the ramekins in an oval 6- or 7-quart slow cooker. Cover and cook on high for 2–2½ hours or until eggs are set. Sprinkle with black pepper and scallions, if using, before serving.

CHAPTER 4

Soups

Chicken Stock

Homemade chicken stock is much cheaper and tastier than store-bought.
Make a batch of the basic version below and freeze cup- or quart-sized portions
for up to 3 months. Defrost only the amount needed in a recipe.

INGREDIENTS | YIELDS 3 QUARTS

1 chicken carcass

2 carrots, cut into chunks

2 stalks celery, cut into chunks

2 onions, cut into chunks

2 parsnips, cut into chunks

1 head garlic

2 chicken wings

Water, as needed

Stock Options

Any leftover vegetables can be added to stock for extra flavor; fennel fronds, green onions, turnips, and red onion are all good choices. Depending on the recipe that the stock will be used in, adding items like dried chilies, ginger, or galangal root will customize the stock, making it an even better fit for the final product.

1. Place the carcass, carrots, celery, onions, parsnips, garlic, and wings into a 6-quart slow cooker.

2. Fill the slow cooker with water until it is 2 inches below the top. Cover and cook on low for 10 hours.

3. Strain into a large container. Discard the solids. Refrigerate the stock overnight.

4. The next day, scoop off any fat that has floated to the top. Discard the fat.

5. Refrigerate the stock for 2–3 days, or freeze up to 3 months.

Beef Broth

There is no added salt here since this broth is meant to be used in other recipes.

INGREDIENTS | YIELDS 7–8 CUPS

4 pounds meat beef bones (such as beef ribs, short ribs, or shank bones)

2 medium onions, peeled and quartered

2 carrots, peeled and coarsely chopped

2 celery stalks, coarsely chopped

3 garlic cloves, peeled and lightly crushed

1 bay leaf

8 cups water, heated to a simmer

1. Combine all ingredients in a 6- or 7-quart slow cooker. Cover and cook on low for 8–10 hours. Occasionally skim off any foam that may rise to the top.

2. Strain the broth to remove the solids. Let the meat cool, then save for another recipe. Store the broth in a covered container in the refrigerator for 2–3 days, or freeze for up to 3 months.

No-Beef Broth

Portobello mushrooms give this pareve soup a beefy, earthy taste.
Note: most Worcestershire sauce contains fish.

INGREDIENTS | YIELDS 4 CUPS

4 carrots, washed and cut into large pieces

2 large onions, peeled and quartered

1 celery stalk, chopped

2 cups fresh Portobello mushrooms, sliced

1 whole bulb garlic, crushed

1 tablespoon Worcestershire sauce

1 tablespoon brown sugar

6 cups water

1. In a 4-quart slow cooker, add all ingredients. Cover and cook on low heat for 8–10 hours.

2. Strain the broth to remove the vegetables. Store the broth in a covered container in the refrigerator for 2–3 days, or freeze for up to 3 months.

Vegetable Broth

A versatile vegetable broth can be used as the base for almost any soup or stew.
Note that it does not contain salt, so you must add that separately when using this broth in recipes.

INGREDIENTS | YIELDS 4 CUPS

2 large onions, peeled and halved

2 medium carrots, cleaned and cut into large pieces

3 stalks celery, cut in half

1 whole bulb garlic, crushed

10 peppercorns

1 bay leaf

6 cups water

1. In a 4-quart slow cooker, add all ingredients. Cover and cook on low heat for 8–10 hours.

2. Strain the broth to remove the vegetables. Store broth, tightly covered, in the refrigerator.

Storing Broth

Homemade broth can be stored in a covered container in the refrigerator for 2–3 days, or frozen for up to 3 months.

3-in-1 Soup (Mushroom-Barley Soup with Flanken)

*This soup was given its unusual name by a relative because it includes the soup,
the main course (flanken), and the side dish (the potatoes) all in one pot.
Lima bean-barley soup mix can substitute for the mushroom-barley soup mix.*

INGREDIENTS | SERVES 8

1 teaspoon vegetable oil

6 pieces flanken (short ribs)

8 cups water

1 (approx. 6-ounce) cellophane "tube" mushroom-barley soup mix, any brand

2 medium potatoes, peeled and quartered

1 teaspoon kosher salt, plus more to taste

Flanken

Flanken is also known by the name of "short ribs" or "Korean-style short ribs." The butcher creates flanken by cross-cutting a rack of beef ribs into strips about an inch wide. Sometimes the strips are then cut between the bones into individual pieces and packaged as riblets.

1. Heat oil in a skillet over medium-high heat. Add flanken and brown on all sides (about 2–3 minutes per side).

2. Transfer flanken to a 4- or 6-quart slow cooker. Carefully add water and the mushroom-barley soup mix (reserving the small seasoning packet). Cover and heat on low for 6–8 hours.

3. Uncover and add contents of small packet from soup mix along with potatoes. Re-cover and increase the heat to high for 30 minutes.

4. Stir in salt. Taste and add additional salt, if necessary. Ladle soup into bowls and serve. Serve flanken and potatoes as the entrée.

5. Let any remaining soup and flanken stand for 1 hour to cool down, then transfer to a covered pot or casserole; refrigerate for 8 hours or overnight. The following day, peel off and discard congealed layer of fat before reheating.

Chicken Soup with Lukshen (Noodles)

This recipe calls for fine egg noodles, but any variety of egg noodles work here.

INGREDIENTS | SERVES 8

1 small potato, peeled and diced

1 parsnip, cut into chunks

2 carrots, cut lengthwise then thinly sliced

1 small turnip, peeled and diced

1 stalk celery, diced

2 medium onions, cut into chunks

1 whole chicken (3–4 pounds), cut into quarters or eighths, most of skin removed

1 tablespoon fresh thyme leaves

2 teaspoons fresh rosemary leaves, minced

½ teaspoon whole black peppercorns

1 bay leaf

4 sprigs fresh dill

2 sprigs fresh parsley

1 teaspoon kosher salt, plus more to taste

8 cups water

1 (12–16-ounce) bag fine egg noodles

1. Place all ingredients except noodles into a 6-quart slow cooker in order listed. Cover and cook on low for 8–10 hours.

2. Use a slotted spoon to remove and discard parsley, dill, peppercorns, and bay leaf. Transfer chicken to a cutting board, and let cool enough to handle safely.

3. Meanwhile, add noodles to the slow cooker, cover, and continue to cook for another 15–20 minutes or until noodles are tender.

4. Discard skin of cooled chicken. Remove meat from the chicken bones and dice it; add 2 cups back to pot; freeze remaining diced chicken for future use. Discard bones.

5. Ladle soup into bowls and serve hot.

Make It Easy to Remove Spent Herbs and Peppercorns

Take a 7" or 8" square of cheesecloth and place peppercorns, bay leaf, dill, and parsley in the center. Put the corners together, twist, and tie with food-safe twine. Add your just-made packet, called a *bouquet garni*, to the soup before cooking. At the end of the cooking time simply pull out the bouquet garni and discard.

Aromatic Chicken Rice Soup

This Thai-influenced soup is wonderful when you're feeling under the weather.
It is also a great way to use up leftover chicken and that last box of rice from Chinese takeout.

INGREDIENTS | SERVES 8

2 quarts Chicken Stock (see recipe in this chapter)

2 carrots, peeled and diced

2 stalks celery, diced

2-inch piece of fresh ginger, peeled and minced (or 2 teaspoons ground ginger)

1 lime, juiced (about 2 tablespoons)

1 onion, peeled and finely diced

4 cloves garlic, minced

½ teaspoon kosher salt

½ teaspoon freshly ground pepper

½ cup minced cilantro

1½ cups cooked rice, any variety

2 cups diced cooked chicken

1. Place the stock, carrots, celery, ginger, lime juice, onion, garlic, salt, and pepper in a 4-quart slow cooker. Stir. Cook on low for 7–9 hours.

2. Stir in the cilantro, rice, and chicken. Cook on high for 15–30 minutes. Stir prior to serving.

Chicken Congee

Congee is a Chinese rice soup, cooked until the rice swells and
breaks down into an oatmeal-like consistency.

INGREDIENTS | SERVES 4

4 cups Chicken Stock (see recipe in this chapter)

1 cup water

½ cup uncooked long grain rice

1 teaspoon ground ginger

1 cooked chicken breast, shredded or thinly sliced

2 teaspoons soy sauce (or more to taste)

3 scallions, green parts thinly sliced or chopped

1. Combine chicken stock, water, rice, and ground ginger in a 4-quart slow cooker. Cover and cook on high for 2–3 hours or until rice breaks up and soup thickens.

2. Uncover and add chicken. Re-cover and continue to heat for another 30 minutes.

3. Uncover and stir in soy sauce. Taste and add more soy sauce if needed.

4. Ladle soup into bowls. Garnish with scallions. Serve hot.

Hot and Sour Soup

Adjust the spiciness of this soup by adding more or less chili paste, to taste.
Use plain dried mushrooms if kosher dried Chinese mushrooms are not available.

INGREDIENTS | SERVES 6

4 cups Vegetable Broth (see recipe in this chapter)

2 tablespoons soy sauce

2 tablespoons rice vinegar

1 teaspoon sesame oil

2 ounces dried Chinese mushrooms

½ cup canned bamboo shoots, sliced

4 ounces extra-firm tofu, cubed

1 tablespoon red chili paste

1 teaspoon white pepper

2 tablespoons cornstarch mixed with ¼ cup cold water

1. In a 4-quart slow cooker, add all ingredients except for the cornstarch mixture; cook on low for 6 hours.

2. Pour in the cornstarch mixture; stir, and cook on high heat for 20 additional minutes.

Pho Soup

This Vietnamese noodle soup is easy to make in the slow cooker.
Try it instead of vegetable soup on a cold night.

INGREDIENTS | SERVES 6

1 tablespoon coriander seeds

1 tablespoon whole cloves

6 star anise

1 cinnamon stick

1 tablespoon fennel seed

1 tablespoon whole cardamom

4-inch section of fresh ginger, peeled and sliced

1 onion, sliced

8 cups No-Beef Broth (see recipe in this chapter)

1 teaspoon soy sauce

8 ounces rice noodles

1 cooked chicken breast, thinly sliced or shredded

½ cup chopped cilantro

½ cup chopped Thai basil

2 cups mung bean sprouts

¼ cup sliced scallions

1. In a dry nonstick skillet, quickly heat the spices, ginger, and onion until the seeds start to pop, about 5 minutes. The onion and ginger should look slightly caramelized. Place the mixture in a cheesecloth packet and tie it securely with food-safe twine.

2. In a 4-quart slow cooker, place the cheesecloth packet. Add the broth, soy sauce, noodles, and chicken. Cover and cook on low for 4 hours.

3. Remove the cheesecloth packet after cooking. Ladle soup into bowls. Top with cilantro, basil, sprouts, and scallions.

Rice Noodles

Rice noodles are made from rice flour and water. They are sold in dry form and can usually be found in the Asian section of larger supermarkets. If you can't find kosher rice noodles in your area, substitute thin pasta.

Creamy Wild Mushroom Soup

Use margarine and soy or rice milk for a pareve alternative.

INGREDIENTS | SERVES 6

1 pound mixed wild mushrooms, sliced, divided

¼ cup (½ stick) unsalted butter

1 medium onion, peeled and diced

2 garlic cloves, minced

2 cups vegetable broth

2 cups water

2 teaspoons fresh thyme leaves

1 bay leaf

1 cup dry sherry

1 (15-ounce) can evaporated milk

1 teaspoon kosher salt

¼ teaspoon ground black pepper

½ cup minced fresh parsley leaves, chopped (for garnish)

2 tablespoons chopped chives (for garnish)

1. Coarsely chop ¼ cup of the sliced mushrooms and set aside.

2. Melt butter in a large skillet over medium-high heat. Add the diced onion and cook, stirring occasionally, until onions soften and start to brown, about 5–8 minutes. Add garlic and stir for an additional minute. Add remaining sliced mushrooms and cook for 5 more minutes, or just until mushrooms start to reduce and give off their liquid.

3. Transfer sautéed vegetables to a 4-quart slow cooker. Add in the vegetable broth, water, thyme, and bay leaf. Cover and cook on low for 4–6 hours.

4. Remove and discard the bay leaf. Stir in the sherry and evaporated milk. Set the cover ajar and cook for an additional 15 minutes to allow alcohol to evaporate.

5. Add the salt and black pepper. Taste and add additional salt and/or pepper if needed. Ladle into bowls and garnish with the chopped parsley leaves, chives, and the coarsely chopped mushrooms.

Southwestern Corn Chowder

The russet potatoes in this recipe will slowly break up during the cooking process and add to the creaminess of this pareve chowder.

INGREDIENTS | SERVES 4

¼ cup margarine

1 onion, diced

1 jalapeño, minced

1 cup diced tomato

2 medium russet potatoes, peeled and diced

2 (15-ounce) cans creamed corn

2 cups water

2 cups unsweetened soymilk or rice milk

1 teaspoon chili powder

1 teaspoon cumin

¼ teaspoon cayenne pepper

Salt and pepper, to taste

1. In a sauté pan over medium heat, melt the margarine; add the onion and jalapeño, and sauté for about 3 minutes.

2. In a 4-quart slow cooker, add all ingredients. Cover and cook on low heat for 6 hours.

Creamed Corn

Some creamed corn recipes don't get their creaminess from dairy products; it's from the milky substance that comes from the cob after the kernels are removed. Check the label for a pareve hechsher to be sure it is dairy-free.

Simple Split Pea Soup

Immersion blenders are hand-held blenders that can be used in the pot where food is cooked, which eliminates the need to transfer soup to a blender.

INGREDIENTS | SERVES 6

2 cups dried green split peas
Water, as needed
6 cups Vegetable Broth (see recipe in this chapter)
2 medium potatoes, peeled and diced
2 large carrots, chopped
3 stalks celery, chopped
2 cloves garlic, minced
1 teaspoon cumin
1 teaspoon thyme
1 bay leaf
1 teaspoon salt

1. Rinse the green split peas; soak overnight in enough water to cover them by more than 1". Drain.

2. In a 4-quart slow cooker, add all ingredients; cook on low heat for 6–8 hours.

3. Let the soup cool slightly, then remove the bay leaf. Process in a blender, or use an immersion blender, until smooth.

Moose Soup

Although moose is a kosher animal, kosher moose meat is unavailable in the United States. Feel free to substitute giraffe (also kosher) or the more easily accessible beef stew meat. But keep the name; picky kids might be intrigued enough to eat some without much coaxing.

INGREDIENTS | SERVES 6

2 carrots, peeled and cut into ¼" slices
2 parsnips, peeled and cut into ¼" slices
3 tablespoons vegetable oil
2 pounds moose (or beef stew) meat, diced
1 large onion, finely diced
1 jalapeño pepper, minced
1 rib celery, diced
2 cloves garlic, minced
10 cups water or beef broth
1 (16-ounce) can diced tomatoes, drained
2 cups cooked wild rice
1 teaspoon kosher salt, or to taste
¼ teaspoon black pepper, or to taste

1. Place carrots and parsnips in a 4- or 6-quart slow cooker. Set aside.

2. Heat the oil in a large skillet over medium-high heat. Working in batches, brown moose (or beef) cubes; add to slow cooker.

3. Add the onion, jalapeño, celery, and garlic to the skillet; sauté for 3 minutes, then add to slow cooker.

4. Pour the water or broth and remaining ingredients except the wild rice, salt, and pepper into the slow cooker. Cover and cook on low for 4–6 hours or until meat is tender.

5. Stir in the rice; add salt and pepper.

Minestrone Soup

Minestrone is a classic Italian vegetable soup. The zucchini and cabbage are added at the end for a burst of fresh flavor.

INGREDIENTS | SERVES 8

3 cloves garlic, minced

1 (15-ounce) can fire-roasted diced tomatoes

1 (28-ounce) can crushed tomatoes

2 stalks celery, diced

1 medium onion, diced

3 medium carrots, diced

3 cups Vegetable Broth (see recipe in this chapter)

2 (15-ounce) cans kidney beans, drained and rinsed

2 tablespoons tomato paste

2 tablespoons minced basil

2 tablespoons minced oregano

2 tablespoons minced Italian parsley

1½ cups shredded cabbage

¾ cup diced zucchini

1 teaspoon salt

½ teaspoon pepper

8 ounces small cooked pasta

1. In a 4-quart slow cooker, add the garlic, diced and crushed tomatoes, celery, onion, carrots, broth, beans, tomato paste, basil, and spices. Cover and cook on low heat for 6–8 hours.

2. Add shredded cabbage and zucchini and turn to high for the last hour.

3. Stir in the salt, pepper, and pasta before serving.

Suggested Pasta Shapes for Soup

Anchellini, small shells, hoops, alfabeto, or ditaletti are all small pasta shapes suitable for soup. For heartier soups, try bow ties or rotini. Thin rice noodles or vermicelli are better for Asian-style soups.

Italian Wedding Soup

This is a main-course soup that you can serve with garlic bread and a tossed salad.

INGREDIENTS | SERVES 4

1 pound frozen meatballs, thawed

6 cups Chicken Stock (see recipe in this chapter)

1 pound escarole or baby spinach, coarsely chopped

2 large eggs

Salt and freshly ground black pepper, to taste

1. Add the meatballs, broth, and escarole (reserve spinach, if using) to the slow cooker; cover and cook on low for 4 hours.

2. Use a slotted spoon to remove the meatballs to a serving bowl; cover and keep warm. Increase the setting of the slow cooker to high. Add spinach now if using. Cook uncovered while preparing next step.

3. Add the eggs, salt, and pepper to a small bowl; whisk to blend.

4. Stir the soup in the slow cooker in a circular motion, and then drizzle the egg mixture into the moving broth. Use a fork to separate the eggs into thin strands. Once the eggs are set, pour soup over the meatballs.

Scotch Broth

Scotch broth is not a broth in the traditional sense. Instead, it's the name of a barley soup.

INGREDIENTS | SERVES 4

2 leeks, white part only

4 lamb shoulder chops

⅓ cup pearl barley

1 large carrot, peeled and diced

1 stalk of celery, thinly sliced

2 medium potatoes, peeled and diced

6 cups water

Salt and freshly ground black pepper, to taste

Fresh parsley, minced (optional)

1. Dice the white part of the leeks; rinse well and drain. Add the leeks to the slow cooker along with the lamb chops, barley, carrot, celery, potatoes, water, salt, and pepper. Cover and cook on low for 6–8 hours or until the meat is tender and the potatoes are cooked through.

2. Transfer a lamb chop to each of 4 bowls and ladle the soup over the meat. Garnish with parsley if desired.

Tortilla Soup

Turn this dairy or pareve soup into a complete meal by adding pieces of cooked vegetarian chicken, such as Morningstar Farms Meal Starters Chik'n Strips or Gardein Seasoned Bites, available in larger supermarkets.

INGREDIENTS | SERVES 8

2 tablespoons olive oil

1 large onion, chopped

2 cloves garlic, minced

2 tablespoons soy sauce

7 cups Vegetable Broth (see recipe in this chapter)

12 ounces firm silken tofu, crumbled

2 cups tomato, diced

1 cup corn kernels

1 teaspoon chipotle powder

1 teaspoon cayenne pepper

2 teaspoons ground cumin

2 teaspoons salt

1 teaspoon dried oregano

10 small corn tortillas, sliced

8 ounces shredded Monterey jack cheese or vegan cheese, such as Daiya Mozzarella Style Shreds

1. In a sauté pan over medium heat, add the olive oil; sauté the onion until just soft, about 3 minutes. Add the garlic and sauté for an additional 30 seconds.

2. In a 4-quart slow cooker, add all ingredients except tortillas and cheese. Stir, cover, and cook on low heat for 4 hours.

3. While the soup is cooking, preheat oven to 450°F. Slice the corn tortillas into thin strips and place them on an ungreased baking sheet. Bake for about 10 minutes, or until they turn golden brown. Remove from heat and set aside.

4. After the soup has cooled slightly, use an immersion blender or regular blender to purée the soup.

5. Serve with cooked tortilla strips and 1 ounce of shredded cheese in each bowl of soup.

Chipotle Powder

Chipotle powder is made from ground chipotle peppers, a type of dried jalapeño. It brings a smoky spiciness to dishes, but can be replaced with cayenne pepper or chili powder.

Black Bean Soup

Don't throw out cilantro stems! They have as much flavor as the leaves.
For a dairy option, add a dollop of sour cream to each bowl just before serving.

INGREDIENTS | SERVES 6

2 tablespoons olive oil

2 cloves garlic, minced

1 green bell pepper, diced, divided

1 red bell pepper, diced, divided

1 red onion, diced, divided

2 (15-ounce) cans black beans, drained and rinsed

2 teaspoons cumin, minced

1 teaspoon chipotle powder

4 cups Vegetable Broth (see recipe in this chapter)

1 teaspoon kosher salt, or to taste

Frank's RedHot Sauce (optional, to taste)

¼ cup packed cilantro leaves and stems, chopped

1. In a sauté pan, heat the olive oil over medium heat, then sauté the garlic along with half each of the bell peppers and onion for 2–3 minutes.

2. Into a 4-quart slow cooker, add the sautéed vegetables, black beans, cumin, chipotle powder, and broth. Cover, and cook on low for 6 hours.

3. Using an immersion blender, process the soup so that most of the soup is smooth. Add salt and taste, adding more salt as necessary. Optionally, add a few drops of Frank's RedHot Sauce.

4. Ladle out the soup into bowls. Sprinkle each serving evenly with the cilantro and the remaining onion and peppers.

French Onion Soup

*With a little advanced planning, this weekend-type recipe
can be served during an otherwise busy weekday.*

INGREDIENTS | SERVES 4

½ tablespoon olive oil

4 cloves garlic, minced

1 cup Caramelized Onions (see Chapter 10)

1 teaspoon fresh thyme leaves, minced (or 1 tablespoon dried)

1 cup dry red kosher wine

4 cups No-Beef Broth or Vegetable Broth (see recipes in this chapter)

1 teaspoon kosher salt

¼ teaspoon black pepper

4 (1" thick) slices French bread

4 ounces Swiss cheese, thinly sliced

Kosher Wine

Although grapes are inherently kosher, kosher wine can only be created by Sabbath-observing Jews under strict supervision of a rabbi or mashgiach. A non-Jew involved in any step of wine production, from the moment the grapes enter the plant until the wine is bottled and sealed, renders the wine nonkosher. In addition, no animal products can be used in its production or as filters, and the wine must only be aged in either wooden barrels (new or previously used to store kosher wines) or in stainless steel tanks.

1. Heat the olive oil in a 4-quart slow cooker on high heat. Add the garlic and sauté for 1 minute.

2. Add the Caramelized Onions, thyme, red wine, broth, salt, and pepper. Cover and cook on low heat for 4 hours.

3. About 10 minutes before the soup has finished cooking, preheat the broiler. Place French bread slices on an ungreased cookie sheet and place under broiler for about 1 minute to lightly toast.

4. To serve, ladle the soup into 4 broiler-safe bowls. Place a slice of the toasted French bread on top of the soup. Divide Swiss cheese slices onto tops of bread. Place soup bowls under the broiler until the cheese has melted.

Beer-Cheese Soup

For the best results, use a pale ale in this recipe.

INGREDIENTS | SERVES 12

½ cup butter or margarine

½ white onion, diced

2 medium carrots, peeled and diced

2 ribs celery, diced

½ cup flour

3 cups Vegetable Broth (see recipe in this chapter)

1 (12-ounce) can or bottle of beer

3 cups milk

3 cups Cheddar cheese

½ teaspoon dry ground mustard

1 teaspoon kosher salt

1 teaspoon black pepper

1. In a sauté pan over medium heat, melt the butter or margarine, then sauté the onion, carrots, and celery until just softened, about 5–7 minutes. Add the flour and stir to form a roux. Let cook for 2–3 minutes.

2. In a 4-quart slow cooker, add the cooked vegetables and roux, then slowly pour in the broth and beer while whisking.

3. Add the milk, cheese, and dry mustard. Cover and cook on low for 4 hours.

4. Use an immersion blender to blend until smooth. Stir in salt and pepper. Taste and add more if needed.

Red Lentil and Vegetable Soup

*Red lentils have a milder taste than brown lentils. For a creamier option,
use an immersion blender to partially blend the lentils before adding the spinach.*

INGREDIENTS | SERVES 6

1 tablespoon olive oil

1 small onion, peeled and chopped

1½ teaspoons fresh ginger, peeled and minced

2 cloves garlic, minced

3 medium carrots, peeled and diced

1 teaspoon cumin

1 (14.5-ounce) can petite diced tomatoes, undrained

2 cups Vegetable Broth (see recipe in this chapter)

1 cup red lentils, rinsed, drained, and inspected to remove any dirt or debris

2 cups water

1 teaspoon kosher salt, plus more to taste

¼ teaspoon black pepper

1 (5-ounce) bag baby spinach leaves, rinsed and drained

1. In a sauté pan, heat the olive oil over medium heat, then sauté the onion for 5 minutes or until softened. Add the ginger, and garlic; sauté for an additional minute.

2. In a 4-quart slow cooker, add the sautéed mixture and all remaining ingredients. Cover, and cook on low for 6–8 hours. Add more salt, if necessary, to taste.

Kosher versus Table Salt

Named for its use in kashering meats. Kosher salt contains no additives, such as iodine. It has a larger grain and more surface area than table salt, allowing it to stick to food better. Because of its flakiness, a measure of kosher salt contains less salt by weight than the same measure of table salt. Use twice as much kosher salt when substituting for table salt.

Spring Vegetable Soup

Leave the skin on the squash and potatoes for a more rustic look and flavor.

INGREDIENTS | SERVES 6

½ red onion, diced

2 small zucchini, diced

2 small yellow squash, diced

4 small red potatoes, diced

3 carrots, peeled and diced

½ pound mushrooms, cleaned and quartered

1 cup green beans, cut into ½" pieces

6 cups Vegetable Broth (see recipe in this chapter)

1 (14-ounce) can diced tomatoes, undrained

1½ teaspoons kosher salt

½ teaspoon black pepper

6 green onions, green parts chopped

1. In a 4-quart slow cooker, add all ingredients except for salt, pepper, and green onions. Cover and cook on low for 6–8 hours.

2. Add salt and pepper; taste and add more of either, if needed.

3. Ladle soup into bowls. Garnish with chopped green onion just before serving.

Summer versus Winter Squash

Summer squash (such as zucchini) has a thin, edible skin and should be used within a few days of picking. Winter squash (such as pumpkin or butternut) has a tough, inedible skin and, stored carefully, can keep for months.

Potato-Leek Soup

If you'd like to omit the alcohol from this recipe, just add another ½ cup of broth.
Use margarine or olive oil instead of the butter for a pareve version.

INGREDIENTS | SERVES 6

2 tablespoons unsalted butter

2 small leeks, chopped (white and light green parts only)

3 large russet potatoes, peeled and diced

4 cups Vegetable Broth (see recipe in this chapter)

½ cup white wine

½ cup water

1 teaspoon salt

1 teaspoon pepper

¼ teaspoon dried thyme

1. In a sauté pan over medium heat, melt the butter, then add the leeks. Cook until softened, about 5 minutes.

2. In a 4-quart slow cooker, add the sautéed leeks, potatoes, broth, wine, water, salt, pepper, and thyme. Cover and cook over low heat for 6–8 hours.

3. Allow soup to cool slightly, then use an immersion blender or traditional blender to process until smooth.

Tomato Basil Soup

Use evaporated milk instead of the soymilk for a dairy alternative.

INGREDIENTS | SERVES 5

2 tablespoons margarine

½ onion, diced

2 cloves garlic, minced

1 (28-ounce) can whole peeled tomatoes, undrained

½ cup Vegetable Broth (see recipe in this chapter)

1 bay leaf

1 teaspoon salt

1 teaspoon pepper

½ cup unsweetened soymilk

¼ cup sliced fresh basil

1. In a sauté pan over medium heat, melt the margarine, then sauté the onion and garlic for 3–4 minutes.

2. In a 4-quart slow cooker, add the onion and garlic, tomatoes, broth, bay leaf, salt, and pepper. Cover and cook on low heat for 4 hours.

3. Allow to cool slightly, then remove the bay leaf. Process the soup in a blender or immersion blender.

4. Return the soup to the slow cooker, then add the soymilk and sliced basil, and heat on low for an additional 30 minutes.

Butternut Squash Soup

You can substitute an extra cup of vegetable broth for the white wine in this soup.

1 medium butternut squash, peeled and diced

1 russet potato, peeled and diced

1 large carrot, chopped

1 rib celery, sliced

1 onion, diced

4 cups Vegetable Broth (see recipe in this chapter)

1 cup white wine

1 bay leaf

¼ teaspoon dried thyme

1½ teaspoons salt

Pinch of nutmeg

1. In a 4-quart slow cooker, add all of the ingredients. Cover and cook over low heat for 6 hours.

2. Cool the soup slightly and remove the bay leaf. Process in a blender or with an immersion blender until the soup is completely smooth, about 30 seconds to 1 minute.

Vegetable Cuts

Sometimes rules are meant to be broken. Although vegetables will cook more evenly and look better when cut into same-size pieces, it is perfectly fine to save time by not chopping vegetables too perfect or too small for a dish that will be blended before serving.

Pumpkin Bisque

This simple soup is a perfect first course at a holiday meal or as a light lunch.

INGREDIENTS | SERVES 4

2 cups puréed pumpkin

2 cups water

1 cup coconut milk

¼ teaspoon ground nutmeg

2 cloves garlic, minced

1 onion, minced

1¼ teaspoon kosher salt, divided

½ cup hulled unsalted pumpkin seeds, for garnish

Make Your Own Pumpkin Purée

Preheat the oven to 350°F. Slice a pie pumpkin or an "eating" pumpkin into wedges and remove the seeds. Place the wedges on a baking sheet and bake until the flesh is soft, about 40 minutes. Scoop out the flesh and allow it to cool before puréeing it in a blender.

1. Place all ingredients except pumpkin seeds and salt into a 4-quart slow cooker. Stir. Cook on low for 8 hours.

2. Meanwhile, heat a small skillet or sauté pan over medium heat. Add pumpkin seeds and heat, stirring frequently, just until they become fragrant and lightly toasted, about 2–3 minutes. Immediately transfer seeds to a small bowl and toss with ¼ teaspoon salt.

3. Use an immersion blender or blend the bisque in batches in a standard blender until smooth. Add remaining salt and taste; add more if necessary. Serve hot, garnished with toasted pumpkin seeds.

Summer Borscht

Serve this cooling beet soup with a dollop of sour cream
or vegan sour cream. Try Tofutti's Sour Supreme.

INGREDIENTS | SERVES 6

3½ cups cooked beets, shredded

¼ cup onion, diced

½ teaspoon salt

1 teaspoon sugar

¼ cup lemon juice

½ tablespoon celery seed

2 cups Vegetable Broth (see recipe in this chapter)

2 cups water

1. In a 4-quart slow cooker, place all of the ingredients. Cover and cook on low for 6–8 hours, or on high for 4 hours.

2. Refrigerate the soup for 4 hours or overnight. Serve cold.

Can't Beat Beets

Beets, also known as beetroot, can be peeled, steamed, cooked, pickled, and shredded; they are good hot or cold. They are high in folate, vitamin C, potassium, and fiber. Although they have the highest sugar content of all vegetables, beets are very low in calories; one beet is only 35 calories.

Wild Rice and Portobello Soup

Any variety of rice will work in this soup. It's fine to substitute white rice or brown rice if that's all you have on hand.

INGREDIENTS | SERVES 4

½ yellow onion, diced

2 small carrots, peeled and diced

2 ribs celery, sliced

1 cup chopped Portobello mushroom

½ cup uncooked wild rice

4 cups Vegetable Broth (see recipe in this chapter)

1 bay leaf

1 sprig rosemary

1 teaspoon salt

½ teaspoon pepper

1. In a 4-quart slow cooker, add all ingredients. Cover and cook on low heat for 6 hours.

2. Remove the bay leaf and rosemary sprig before serving.

White Bean and Barley Soup

Cool soup to room temperature before refrigerating or freezing in order to save energy.

INGREDIENTS | SERVES 8

2 (15-ounce) cans great northern beans, drained and rinsed

½ cup pearl barley

1 small onion, diced

2 carrots, peeled and diced

2 cloves garlic, minced

¼ cup fresh parsley, chopped

2 sprigs fresh thyme (or ½ teaspoon dried)

6 cups No-Beef Broth (see recipe in this chapter)

2 teaspoons kosher salt

1. Add all the ingredients to a 4-quart slow cooker. Cover, and cook on low for 6–8 hours.

2. Remove the sprigs of thyme before serving.

Mulligatawny Soup

*Although the coconut milk gives this soup a very creamy taste,
it can be omitted. The soup will still be delicious.*

INGREDIENTS | SERVES 6–8

1 small yellow onion, peeled and finely diced

2 skinless and boneless chicken breasts, cut into ½" strips

1 medium tart apple such as Granny Smith, peeled, cored, and chopped

1 large carrot, peeled and diced

1 celery stalk, diced

½ small green pepper, seeded and diced

1 (15-ounce) can fire-roasted diced tomatoes, undrained

2 teaspoons curry powder

½ teaspoon ground ginger

¼ teaspoon ground nutmeg

1 bay leaf

½ teaspoon crushed red pepper flakes

4 cups Chicken Stock (see the recipe in this chapter)

1 (13.5-ounce) can coconut milk, optional

2 cups cooked rice

1 tablespoon fresh lime juice

1 teaspoon kosher salt, or to taste

¼ teaspoon ground black pepper, or to taste

¼ cup chopped cilantro leaves (for garnish)

1. Mix together first 13 ingredients (the onion through the Chicken Stock) in a 6- or 7-quart slow cooker. Cover and cook on high for 3–4 hours or on low for 6–8 hours. Discard bay leaf. Pour in the coconut milk if desired.

2. Stir in the rice, lime juice, salt, and pepper. Taste and add more salt and/or pepper if needed. If coconut milk was added, cover and cook on low for an additional 30 minutes. Serve garnished with the cilantro leaves if desired.

Origin of Mulligatawny Soup

The name Mulligatawny comes from the Tamil words for "pepper water." There are many versions as to the origins of Mulligatawny soup, but most people agree that it was created by Indian cooks to serve to the ruling British during the eighteenth century.

Russian Sweet and Sour Cabbage Soup

Regular paprika usually has very little taste and is best as a colorful garnish. Hungarian paprika has much more flavor. For this recipe, be sure to use the sweet variety, which might be simply labeled "Hungarian," not the one labeled "hot."

INGREDIENTS | SERVES 10

2 tablespoons olive oil

1 large onion, peeled and diced

1 carrot, peeled and chopped

1 large potato, peeled and diced

2 garlic cloves, minced

1 tablespoon sweet Hungarian paprika

1 head cabbage, thickly shredded (about 10 cups)

1 (14.5-ounce) can diced tomatoes, undrained

1 teaspoon sour salt

2 tablespoons granulated sugar

2 tablespoons raisins

2 teaspoons kosher salt, plus more if needed

¼ teaspoon ground black pepper, plus more if needed

8 cups Beef or Vegetable Broth (see recipes in this chapter)

¼ cup fresh lemon juice

1. Heat the olive oil in a large skillet over medium-high heat. Stir in onion, carrot, and potato; cook, stirring frequently, until the onion has softened, about 5 minutes.

2. Add the garlic and paprika; cook for 1 additional minute, stirring constantly.

3. Transfer vegetables into a 6- or 7-quart slow cooker. Stir in the remaining ingredients except lemon juice. Cover and cook for 6–8 hours or until cabbage is very tender.

4. Stir in the lemon juice. Taste and add more salt and pepper if needed before serving.

Sour Salt

Sour salt, also known as citric acid, is the naturally occurring acid found in citrus fruits. It is used to give cabbage soup its distinct, mildly sour taste. If sour salt is not available in the spice section of larger supermarkets, substitute a few tablespoons of apple cider vinegar.

CHAPTER 5

Chicken and Turkey

Chicken Cacciatore

Spend a few quick minutes in the morning preparing the ingredients.
The chicken will cook all day without help, ready and waiting for you by dinnertime.

INGREDIENTS | SERVES 4

Nonstick spray

2 tablespoons olive oil

1 small yellow onion, finely chopped

1 green bell pepper, finely chopped

1 teaspoon dried thyme (or 1½ tablespoons minced fresh)

3 garlic cloves, minced

2 cups sliced button mushrooms

1 (28-ounce) can crushed tomatoes

⅛ teaspoon black pepper

½ cup dry sherry (or dry white wine)

1 whole chicken, cut into quarters or eighths, most of the skin removed

¼ cup packed flat parsley leaves, chopped (for garnish)

Cacciatore

In Italian, *cacciatore* means "hunter." Food prepared in the cacciatore style therefore includes foods that might be gathered from the forests and fields: mushrooms, herbs, tomatoes and peppers. Sometimes wine is also added.

1. Spray the inside of a 4- or 6-quart slow cooker with the nonstick spray.

2. Heat the olive oil in a large skillet over medium heat. When hot, add the onion and bell pepper; cook until the vegetables are just tender, stirring occasionally, for 7 minutes.

3. Add the thyme, garlic, and mushrooms and cook until the mushrooms are almost cooked through, about 5 minutes.

4. Add the tomatoes, pepper, and white wine; bring the sauce to a simmer.

5. Pour about half the sauce into the prepared cooker. Arrange chicken parts over sauce, overlapping them to fit. Pour remaining sauce over chicken. Cover and cook on low for 4–6 hours or until chicken is cooked through. Garnish with parsley just before serving.

Chicken Makhani

Chicken Makhani is commonly known as Butter Chicken, a bit of a misnomer as the dish traditionally includes only a tablespoon or so of butter. This recipe uses margarine in place of the butter.

INGREDIENTS | SERVES 4

1 pound boneless, skinless chicken breasts or thighs

2 shallots, minced

2 cloves garlic, minced

½ knob ginger, minced

2 tablespoons lemon juice

2 teaspoons garam masala

1 teaspoon ground cumin

½ teaspoon ground cayenne pepper

½ teaspoon ground cloves

½ teaspoon fenugreek

¼ teaspoon salt

½ teaspoon ground black pepper

1 tablespoon margarine

1 tablespoon tomato paste

¾ cup pareve yogurt or sour cream

1. Place the chicken, shallots, garlic, ginger, lemon juice, spices, margarine, and tomato paste into a 4-quart slow cooker. Stir. Cook on low for 5 hours.

2. Stir in the pareve yogurt or sour cream. Serve immediately.

Moroccan Chicken

Serve this dish with couscous and mint tea for an authentic Moroccan meal.
If you are rushed for time, skip the sautéing; simply combine the ingredients in step 2
in a 2-quart saucepan and heat to a simmer before proceeding with the remaining steps.

INGREDIENTS | SERVES 4

Nonstick spray

1 tablespoon olive oil

1 large onion, finely chopped

1 teaspoon ground ginger (or 2 teaspoons minced fresh)

3 garlic cloves, minced

1 teaspoon ground coriander

2 teaspoons sweet paprika

2 bay leaves

½ cup raisins

½ cup dried apricots, halved

1 (10-ounce) can chicken broth, low-sodium preferred

1 chicken, cut up into quarters or eighths, most of the skin removed

2 tablespoons lemon juice

2 tablespoons chopped fresh parsley

1. Spray the inside of 4-quart slow cooker with the nonstick spray.

2. Heat the olive oil over medium-high heat in a medium saucepan. When hot, add the onion and cook until softened, about 5 minutes. Stir in the ginger, garlic, coriander, and paprika. Cook the vegetables for another minute, then add the bay leaves, raisins, dried apricots, and chicken broth; bring the mixture to a simmer.

3. Pour about a third of the sauce into the prepared cooker. Arrange the chicken on top of the sauce, overlapping the pieces if necessary to fit. Pour remaining sauce over the chicken. Cover and cook on low for 3 hours or until chicken is cooked through.

4. Uncover and stir in the lemon juice and parsley. Remove bay leaves. Serve hot.

Sweet and Spicy Pulled Chicken

Make this recipe after breakfast and it will be ready by lunchtime.

INGREDIENTS | SERVES 4

1¾ pounds boneless, skinless chicken thighs

¼ cup chili sauce

¼ cup balsamic vinegar

2 tablespoons ginger preserves

2 tablespoons pineapple juice

2 tablespoons lime juice

1 teaspoon ground cayenne

½ teaspoon ground chipotle powder

½ teaspoon hot paprika

1 jalapeño pepper, seeded and minced

3 cloves garlic, minced

1 teaspoon hot sauce

1. Place all ingredients in a 4-quart slow cooker. Cook on low for 3½ hours, or for 1½ hours on low and then turn up the heat to high for an additional hour.

2. When done, the meat should shred easily with a fork. Thoroughly shred the chicken. Toss to coat the meat evenly with the sauce.

Chicken Chili

A tasty alternative to beef chili. Save leftover barbecued or roasted chicken from another meal to use here.

INGREDIENTS | SERVES 4

½ cup onion, diced

½ cup bell pepper, diced

1 cup shredded roasted chicken

2 cloves garlic, minced

1 (15-ounce) can kidney beans, rinsed and drained

2 cups Vegetable Broth (see Chapter 4)

1 tablespoon chili powder

½ tablespoon chipotle powder

½ tablespoon cumin

1 teaspoon thyme

1 tablespoon oregano

1 (15-ounce) can diced tomatoes, drained

1 tablespoon tomato paste

1 tablespoon cider vinegar

2 teaspoons salt

1. In a 4-quart slow cooker, add all ingredients. Cover and cook on low heat for 5 hours.

Chicken Meatballs in Tropical Sauce

This is a festive appetizer for a party! Serve leftovers with hot cooked rice for a quick and easy meal.

INGREDIENTS | SERVES 15

Nonstick spray

Sauce

1 tablespoon vegetable oil
1 onion, minced
1 tablespoon minced jalapeño pepper
1 tablespoon grated fresh ginger
1 cup pineapple juice
⅓ cup packed dark brown sugar
¼ cup teriyaki sauce
¼ cup ponzu sauce
3 tablespoons lime juice
1 tablespoon cornstarch
4 cups frozen pineapple chunks

Meatballs

2 pounds ground chicken breast
1 teaspoon ground ginger
½ cup bread crumbs
1 egg
¼ cup minced onion
2 cloves garlic, minced

1. Spray the inside of 4-quart slow cooker with nonstick spray.

2. Heat the oil over medium-high heat in a 3- or 4-quart saucepan. When hot, add the onion, jalapeño, and ginger. Cook, stirring often, until the onion becomes translucent, about 5 minutes.

3. Add the pineapple juice, brown sugar, teriyaki sauce, and ponzu sauce. Mix the lime juice together with the cornstarch and whisk into the sauce. Stir in the pineapple chunks and bring the sauce to a boil.

4. While sauce is heating, mix the chicken, ground ginger, bread crumbs, egg, minced onion, and garlic together in a large bowl. Form the mixture into 1" balls and place in prepared cooker. Pour sauce over meatballs. Cover and cook on low for 4–6 hours or until meatballs are no longer pink in the center.

Teriyaki Chicken

With the use of packaged chicken nuggets, this is a very simple dish to make.
Serve this dish with hot cooked rice and a green salad.

INGREDIENTS | SERVES 6

1 pound frozen chicken nuggets, defrosted

5–6 ounces teriyaki sauce

1 teaspoon hot sauce

1. In a 4-quart slow cooker, combine all ingredients and cook over low heat for 1 hour. Serve hot.

Thai-Influenced Braised Chicken Thighs

A flavorful poaching liquid ensures a flavorful chicken thigh.
If shallots are not available in your area, add another garlic clove.

INGREDIENTS | SERVES 4

4 boneless, skinless chicken thighs

3 tablespoons soy sauce

3 tablespoons chicken or vegetable broth

3 tablespoons lime juice

1 knob ginger, minced (or 1 teaspoon ground ginger)

1 shallot, thinly sliced

2 cloves garlic, thinly sliced

¼ teaspoon white pepper

1. Place all ingredients into a 4-quart slow cooker. Cook on high for 2½ hours. Discard the cooking liquid before serving.

Goan Chicken Curry

This Indian dish is made easily in the slow cooker. Try it over rice or with some naan.

INGREDIENTS | SERVES 10

1 teaspoon canola oil

2 medium onions, diced

4 cloves garlic, minced

3 pounds boneless, skinless chicken thighs, cubed

1 tablespoon minced fresh ginger

2 cups toasted unsweetened coconut

1 teaspoon ground cinnamon

¼ teaspoon ground nutmeg

½ teaspoon ground cloves

½ teaspoon salt

1 teaspoon cumin seeds

1 teaspoon black mustard seeds

2 tablespoons red pepper flakes

1½ cups water

1. In a large nonstick skillet, heat the oil. Add the onions and garlic and sauté them for 3 minutes.

2. Place all ingredients in a 6-quart slow cooker. Stir. Cover and cook for 6–8 hours on low. Stir before serving.

How to Toast Coconut

Preheat the oven to 350°F. Arrange shredded coconut in a single layer on a cookie sheet. Bake for 10–15 minutes or until light golden brown. Stir the coconut and check it frequently to prevent burning. Remove it from the oven and allow it to cool before using.

Indian Chicken with Chickpea Sauce

Serve over rice to soak up the delicious sauce.

INGREDIENTS | SERVES 4

Nonstick spray

1 tablespoon olive oil

2 medium onions, finely chopped

3 garlic cloves, minced

1 teaspoon ground ginger

½ teaspoon turmeric

2 teaspoons sweet paprika

2 teaspoons curry powder

1 (12-ounce) can chicken broth, low-sodium preferred

1 (14.5-ounce) can chickpeas, drained and rinsed

⅓ cup packed fresh cilantro leaves, coarsely chopped

4 boneless, skinless chicken breasts

Hot cooked rice

Handling Poultry

Salmonella is a type of bacteria that can cause abdominal upset and fever if it is not killed first by cooking or by proper sanitation. According to the USDA, kashering meat reduces Salmonella contamination by 80 percent. But to be absolutely safe, keep poultry refrigerated until ready to use and wash all work surfaces, utensils, and your hands with hot soapy water before and after handling poultry.

1. Spray the inside of a 4- or 5-quart slow cooker with nonstick spray.

2. Heat the oil over medium-high heat in a large skillet. When hot, add the onions and cook, stirring frequently, for about 5 minutes or until they begin to brown.

3. Add the garlic, ginger, turmeric, paprika, and curry powder; stir continuously for 1 minute or until fragrant. Add the chicken broth, and chickpeas; bring the mixture to a boil.

4. Once the sauce has reached a boil, mash some of the chickpeas with the back of a wooden spoon or potato masher to help thicken sauce. Add the cilantro and remove from the heat.

5. Place the chicken in the prepared cooker. Pour the chickpea mixture over the chicken.

6. Cover and cook on high for 2–3 hours or low for 4–6 hours. If sauce is too thin, uncover and continue to cook on high for another 30 minutes. Serve over hot cooked rice.

Jambalaya

Kosher sausage comes in many varieties. Try Andouille or Mexican chorizo styles for even more heat.

INGREDIENTS | SERVES 8

1 tablespoon vegetable oil

1 medium yellow onion, peeled and diced

1 small green bell pepper, finely chopped

1 small red bell pepper, finely chopped

2 garlic cloves, minced

1 (12-ounce) package sweet Italian sausages, cut on the diagonal into ¼" slices

3 skinless, boneless chicken breasts (approximately 1½ pounds), cut into ½" wide strips

1 teaspoon kosher salt

¼ teaspoon cayenne pepper

¼ teaspoon black pepper

1 bay leaf

1 (15-ounce) can diced tomatoes, drained

2 cups chicken broth

4 cups cooked rice

¼ loosely packed cup parsley leaves (for garnish)

1. Heat oil in a large skillet over medium-high heat. Add onion and bell peppers and sauté, stirring frequently, for 5 minutes or until onion begins to brown. Add garlic and stir for another 30 seconds.

2. Transfer vegetables to the slow cooker. Add sausage slices to the skillet. Let brown without stirring for 2 minutes each side.

3. Transfer sausage slices to the slow cooker. Top with chicken, then add remaining ingredients except rice and parsley.

4. Cover and cook on low for 6–8 hours or on high for 3–4 hours. Discard bay leaf. Serve over rice, garnished with parsley leaves.

Orange Chicken

Serve this Asian-style dish with rice and steamed broccoli.

INGREDIENTS | SERVES 4

2 tablespoons soy sauce

2 tablespoons spiced ginger preserves or orange marmalade

1 teaspoon ground ginger (if orange marmalade is used)

½ cup freshly squeezed orange juice

1 large orange, cut into ⅛-inch thick slices

3 boneless, skinless chicken breasts (about 1 pound)

Cooking with Boneless Skinless Chicken Breasts

Boneless skinless breasts are a low-fat source of protein, but it can be tricky to use them in the slow cooker. They are best when used raw in a recipe with a short cooking time to avoid any chance of drying out. Cooked, they hold up well when added toward the end of a longer-cooking recipe such as a soup, stew, or chili.

1. In a small bowl, whisk together the soy sauce, preserves, ginger (if using), and orange juice.

2. Arrange the orange slices along the bottom of a 4-quart slow cooker. Top with the chicken breasts. Pour the sauce over the chicken. Cook for 3 hours on low or until the chicken is thoroughly cooked.

Chicken Meatballs in Italian Tomato Sauce

Sautéing the garlic directly in the slow cooker makes this recipe a snap to put together.

INGREDIENTS | SERVES 4

12 frozen chicken meatballs

1 tablespoon vegetable oil

2 cloves garlic, minced

1½ tablespoons minced basil

1 medium onion, minced

2 (15-ounce) cans fire-roasted tomatoes, undrained

1 teaspoon crushed red pepper flakes

1 teaspoon kosher salt

1. Defrost the meatballs according to package instructions.

2. Meanwhile, pour oil into a 4-quart slow cooker. Add garlic and set cooker on high. Stir continuously until garlic becomes very fragrant, 2–3 minutes.

3. Add the remaining ingredients except salt. Stir. Cook on low for 3–6 hours. Stir in salt and taste; add more salt if needed.

Slow-Roasted Chicken with Potatoes, Parsnips, and Onions

Chicken made in the slow cooker is very tender. The onions add a lot of flavor with no added fat needed.

INGREDIENTS | SERVES 6

4 medium onions, sliced

1 whole roasting chicken (5 or more pounds)

6 large red-skin potatoes, halved

4 parsnips, diced

1 teaspoon kosher salt

½ teaspoon black pepper

A Snippet about Parsnips

Parsnips have a mild flavor and a texture that is well suited to extended cooking times. Always peel off the bitter skin before cooking. If parsnips are not available, carrots are an acceptable substitute.

1. Cover the bottom of a 6- to 7-quart slow cooker with half of the onions.

2. Place the chicken, breast side up, on top of the onions.

3. Cover the chicken with the remaining onions.

4. Arrange the potatoes and parsnips around the chicken.

5. Cover and cook on low for 8 hours or until the chicken has an internal temperature of 165°F as measured using a food thermometer. Discard the chicken skin. Sprinkle the salt and pepper evenly over the chicken and vegetables before serving.

Tuscan Chicken

This simple dish is perfect served over warm white beans.

INGREDIENTS | SERVES 4

1 pound boneless, skinless chicken breasts

4 cloves garlic, minced

1 shallot, minced

2 tablespoons white wine vinegar

1 tablespoon lemon juice

1 tablespoon minced fresh rosemary

1 cup Chicken Stock (see Chapter 4)

1. Place all ingredients into a 4-quart slow cooker. Stir. Cook on low for 4 hours or until the chicken is fully cooked.

South African–Style Chicken

South African cuisine is a blend of foods from the many nations that ruled it over the centuries.

INGREDIENTS | SERVES 6

Cooking spray

6 boneless, skinless chicken breasts

½ cup barbecue sauce

½ cup chicken broth

1 medium onion, diced

½ cup dried apricots, halved

½ cup golden raisins

1 tablespoon curry powder

1 teaspoon coriander

½ teaspoon ground cinnamon

2 garlic cloves, minced

3 cups cooked couscous

1. Lightly spray inside of a 4-quart slow cooker with cooking spray. Place chicken in slow cooker in a single layer, overlapping to fit if necessary.

2. In a medium bowl, combine the remaining ingredients except the couscous, and pour over chicken. Cover and cook on low for 8 hours. Serve over couscous.

Basque-Style Chicken

Basque cooking traditionally uses bell peppers, rice, and spices.
Omit the cayenne pepper to reduce the heat.

INGREDIENTS | SERVES 6

Cooking spray

2 tablespoons vegetable oil

2 medium onions, peeled and thinly sliced into rings

2 cloves garlic, peeled and minced

1 large red bell pepper, seeded and cut into ½"-thick strips

1 yellow, green, or orange bell pepper, seeded and cut into ½"-thick strips

1 teaspoon smoked paprika

1 teaspoon dried thyme

1 chicken, cut into eighths

2 tablespoons red wine vinegar

½ cup Chicken Stock (see Chapter 4)

1 (12-ounce) package chorizo-style sausages, cut into ¼" slices

1 (15-ounce) can diced tomatoes, drained

¼ teaspoon cayenne pepper (optional)

1 teaspoon kosher salt, if needed

¼ teaspoon black pepper, if needed

3 cups cooked rice

¼ cup parsley leaves, chopped (for garnish)

1. Lightly grease the inside of a 6-quart slow cooker with cooking spray.

2. Heat the oil in a large skillet over medium-high heat. Add the onions, garlic, bell peppers, paprika, and thyme to skillet and sauté frequently until vegetables soften, 7–8 minutes.

3. Transfer vegetables to the slow cooker. Return skillet to the stovetop and add the chicken. Lightly brown the chicken, about 2 minutes per side (chicken will not be cooked through).

4. Place the chicken over the vegetables in the slow cooker. Stir in the wine vinegar, broth, chorizo, and diced tomatoes. Cover and cook on low for 7–8 hours (or on high for 3–4 hours), until chicken is cooked through and juices run clear when pierced with a knife.

5. Stir in cayenne pepper, if using. Taste and stir in salt and pepper, if needed. Serve chicken over rice. Ladle on sauce and garnish with parsley.

Pineapple Teriyaki Drumsticks

Serve this crowd-pleasing favorite as a hearty appetizer.
Pair leftovers with steamed rice for a great lunch.

INGREDIENTS | SERVES 12

12 chicken drumsticks

1 (8-ounce) can pineapple slices in juice, undrained

¼ cup teriyaki sauce

1 teaspoon ground ginger

¼ cup hoisin sauce

1. Arrange the drumsticks in a single layer on a broiling pan. Broil for 10 minutes on high, flipping the drumsticks once halfway through the cooking time.

2. Drain the juice from the pineapple into a 4- or 6-quart slow cooker, reserving pineapple rings. Add the teriyaki sauce, ginger, and hoisin sauce. Stir to combine.

3. Cut the reserved pineapple rings in half. Add them to the slow cooker.

4. Add the drumsticks to the slow cooker and stir to combine. Cover and cook on low for 4–6 hours.

Spicy Buffalo Nuggets with Ranch Dressing

*Serve this crowd-pleasing appetizer with the nondairy
Ranch Dressing featured with this recipe.*

INGREDIENTS | SERVES 6

½ stick (¼ cup) margarine, cut up

1 tablespoon hot sauce, such as Frank's RedHot Sauce

1 tablespoon white vinegar

1 teaspoon garlic powder

1 pound frozen fully cooked chicken nuggets, defrosted

Ranch Dressing

1 cup mayonnaise

½ cup pareve sour cream

½ teaspoon salt

½ teaspoon black pepper

½ teaspoon garlic powder

1½ tablespoons dried parsley

1 tablespoon chopped fresh chives (optional)

1 teaspoon dried dill

¼ teaspoon sweet paprika

1 teaspoon lemon juice

½ teaspoon Worcestershire sauce

1. Place margarine in a small bowl and microwave for 30 seconds, or until almost melted. Remove from microwave and stir until melted completely.

2. Add the hot sauce, vinegar, and garlic powder; stir well.

3. In a 4-quart slow cooker, add about a third of the sauce. Arrange chicken nuggets over sauce. Pour remaining sauce over nuggets. Cover and cook on low for 1 hour.

4. While nuggets are cooking, make the ranch dressing. Stir mayonnaise and sour cream together until completely blended. Stir in remaining dressing ingredients. Chill for at least 30 minutes before serving.

5. Serve the chicken nuggets with the ranch dressing.

Cornish Hens in Plum Sauce

Serve hens with rice and broccoli.

INGREDIENTS | SERVES 4

Nonstick spray

1 cup Plum Sauce (see Chapter 2)

2 tablespoons soy sauce

1 teaspoon ground ginger

1 teaspoon Chinese five-spice powder

2 Cornish hens

2 green onions, green parts thinly sliced (for garnish)

Toasted sesame seeds (for garnish)

For a Crispier Skin

If you like a crispier skin on Cornish hens, after the hens have finished cooking, transfer to a greased broiling pan and place under the broiler for 3–5 minutes.

1. Spray the inside of a 6-quart slow cooker with nonstick spray.

2. In a medium bowl, mix the plum sauce, soy sauce, ginger, and five-spice powder.

3. Place hens in the prepared slow cooker, breast side down. Brush with half the plum sauce mixture. Cover and cook on low for 4 hours.

4. Brush with remaining sauce. Re-cover and continue to cook for another 2–4 hours, or until juices run clear when pierced with a knife. Serve hens garnished with green onions and/or sesame seeds, if desired.

Cornish Hens in Cider Sauce with Potatoes

This is an easy one-pot dinner. The baking apples should break down and "melt" into the sauce.

INGREDIENTS | SERVES 4

Nonstick spray

1 large yellow onion, peeled and quartered

4 potatoes, peeled and cut into large chunks

2 large baking apples, peeled, cored, and cut into small chunks

2 Cornish hens

2 cups apple cider or apple juice

1 teaspoon dried thyme

½ teaspoon kosher salt

½ teaspoon ground black pepper

1. Spray the inside of a 6-quart slow cooker with nonstick spray. Layer in the diced onions, potatoes, and apple chunks. Place the Cornish hens on top, breast sides down.

2. Pour cider or juice over hens and sprinkle with thyme, salt, and pepper.

3. Cover and cook on low for 6–8 hours, or until juices run clear when pierced with a knife.

4. Spoon accumulated juices over hens and vegetables before serving.

Almond Apricot Turkey Bread Pudding

This is a tasty and unusual way to use up leftover Thanksgiving turkey.

INGREDIENTS | SERVES 8

Nonstick spray
1 tablespoon olive oil
½ cup diced sweet onion
½ cup diced celery
10 cups stale bread cubes
1½ cups diced cooked turkey
1 cup slivered almonds
½ cup chopped dried apricots
6 eggs
3 cups chicken broth
3½ cups almond milk
2 teaspoons curry powder
1 teaspoon thyme
1 teaspoon kosher salt
¼ teaspoon ground black pepper

1. Spray the inside of a 6-quart slow cooker with the nonstick spray.

2. Heat the olive oil in a medium skillet over medium-high heat. When hot, add the onion and celery and cook, stirring occasionally, until the vegetables have softened, 7–10 minutes.

3. Place the bread cubes in the prepared cooker. Sprinkle the celery, onion, turkey, almonds, and apricots over the bread cubes and toss them together lightly with your hands.

4. In a large bowl, mix together the eggs, chicken broth, almond milk, curry, thyme, salt, and pepper. Pour evenly over the bread cubes.

5. Cover and cook on high for 2–4 hours or until all the liquid has been absorbed.

Cranberry Turkey Meatballs

Serve this easy appetizer at your next holiday party straight from the slow cooker. This recipe can also be made with chicken.

INGREDIENTS | SERVES 12

28 ounces frozen, precooked turkey meatballs (about 24 meatballs)

¼ cup chili sauce

2 (14–16 ounce) cans whole-berry cranberry sauce

1½ packed tablespoons dark brown sugar

1 tablespoon ginger preserves

Simple Homemade Turkey or Chicken Meatballs

In a small bowl, combine 1 pound ground turkey or chicken, ½ cup bread crumbs, ½ teaspoon each salt and pepper, ⅛ teaspoon nutmeg, and 1 minced shallot. Form into 1½" balls. Broil for 10 minutes or until cooked through.

1. Defrost the meatballs according to package instructions. Mix together the chili sauce, cranberry sauce, brown sugar, and preserves in a large bowl.

2. Pour half of the sauce into the bottom of a 4-quart slow cooker. Place the meatballs on top. Pour the remaining sauce over the meatballs. Cook on low for 4 hours or on high for 2 hours.

Wild Rice–Stuffed Turkey Breast Cutlets

All this hearty dish needs is a side of steamed vegetables to make it a complete meal.

INGREDIENTS | SERVES 4

1 onion, sliced

4 ounces button mushrooms, sliced

1 cup cooked wild rice

1 tablespoon fresh parsley leaves, minced

1 teaspoon thyme leaves

½ tablespoon finely minced fresh basil leaves

1 teaspoon minced fresh rosemary leaves

¼ teaspoon black pepper

2 cloves garlic, minced

4 turkey breast cutlets (about 1 pound)

½ cup Chicken Stock (see Chapter 4)

1. Place the onion and mushrooms on the bottom of a 4-quart slow cooker.

2. In a large bowl, mix together the wild rice, parsley, thyme, basil, rosemary, black pepper, and garlic. Divide the rice mixture into four portions. Place a single portion in the center of each turkey cutlet. Roll, rice side in, and secure with a toothpick or kitchen twine. Place on top of the onions and mushrooms in the slow cooker. Pour the Stock over top.

3. Cook on low for 4 hours.

Turkey and Gravy

Season with your choice of Mrs. Dash Garlic & Herb, Onion & Herb, Original Blend, or Table Blend seasoning. For more servings, increase the size of the turkey breast; if necessary, increase the cooking time so the turkey reaches an internal temperature of 170°F.

INGREDIENTS | SERVES 8

1¾ cups turkey or chicken broth

2 stalks celery

1 large carrot

1 medium onion, peeled and quartered

1 (3-pound) boneless turkey breast

1 teaspoon Mrs. Dash Seasoning Blend

2 tablespoons Madeira wine (optional)

¼ cup (Wondra) instant flour

Salt and freshly ground black pepper, to taste

Or, If You Prefer . . .

If you don't have instant flour on hand, you can instead strain the turkey broth into a bowl or large measuring cup. Melt ¼ cup margarine in a large nonstick skillet and whisk ¼ cup all-purpose flour into the margarine. Slowly whisk the broth into the resulting roux; bring to a boil, stirring constantly, and cook until thickened.

1. Add the broth to the slow cooker. Cut each celery stalk in half. Scrub and cut the carrot into four pieces. Add the celery, carrot, and onion to the slow cooker. Nestle the turkey breast on top of the vegetables, and sprinkle the seasoning blend over it. Cover and cook on low for 8 hours.

2. Remove the turkey breast to a serving platter; cover and keep warm.

3. Strain the pan juices through a cheesecloth-lined colander set over a large nonstick skillet, squeezing the vegetables in the cheesecloth to release the juices.

4. Transfer ¼ cup of the broth to a bowl and mix it together with the Madeira and instant flour; stir until the flour is dissolved. Bring the broth to a boil over medium-high heat. Whisk the flour mixture into the broth, stirring constantly until the gravy is thickened and coats the back of a spoon. Taste for seasoning, and add salt and pepper if needed. Slice the turkey and pour the gravy over the top of the slices, or serve the gravy on the side.

Turkey in Onion Sauce

This is an African-inspired dish. Serve it over cooked rice.

INGREDIENTS | SERVES 8

5 large onions, peeled and thinly sliced
4 cloves of garlic, peeled and minced
¼ cup fresh lemon juice
1 teaspoon salt
¼ teaspoon cayenne pepper
4 turkey thighs, skin removed
Freshly ground black pepper, to taste

1. Add the onions, garlic, lemon juice, salt, and cayenne pepper to a 5- or 6-quart slow cooker; stir to combine. Nestle the turkey thighs into the onion mixture. Cover and cook on low for 8 hours.

2. Remove the turkey thighs and allow to cool enough to remove the meat from the bone. Leave the cover off of the slow cooker and allow the onion mixture to continue to cook until the liquid has totally evaporated. (You may raise the setting to high to speed things up if you wish. Just be sure to stir the mixture occasionally to prevent the onions from burning.)

3. Stir the turkey meat into the onion mixture. Taste for seasoning and add pepper if desired. For more heat, add additional cayenne pepper, too.

CHAPTER 6

Beef, Veal, and Lamb

Indoor "Barbecued" Brisket Sliders

Because of the salt already in the barbecue sauce, bouillon, and soy sauce, no extra salt is needed.

INGREDIENTS | SERVES 8

Cooking spray

2 tablespoons vegetable oil

1 large onion, diced

3 garlic cloves, minced

1 (2- to 3-pound) brisket, trimmed of excess fat

½ cup barbecue sauce

3 tablespoons chili sauce

1 tablespoon chili powder

1 tablespoon soy sauce

1 teaspoon powdered beef bouillon

1 teaspoon cinnamon

1 teaspoon ground cumin

½ teaspoon pepper

16 pareve dinner rolls, split horizontally

1 cup coleslaw, drained

1. Lightly spray the inside of a 6-quart slow cooker with cooking spray.

2. Heat vegetable oil in a large skillet over medium heat. Add onion and garlic and stir frequently for 3–4 minutes or until onions just start to brown. Push to the sides and add brisket. Let sear for 4 minutes, then carefully use tongs to turn brisket over. Let sear for another 4 minutes.

3. Transfer brisket and onions to prepared slow cooker.

4. In a medium bowl, stir together the barbecue sauce, chili sauce, chili powder, soy sauce, bouillon, cinnamon, cumin, and pepper. Pour mixture over brisket. Cover and cook on low for 7–8 hours or until brisket is very tender.

5. Transfer the brisket to a cutting board. Use two forks to shred the meat.

6. Skim any excess fat from the sauce. Return shredded meat to the cooker and stir to combine.

7. To serve, divide meat among dinner rolls. Top evenly with the drained coleslaw.

Apple-Mustard Beef Brisket

Serve Apple-Mustard Beef Brisket with a crusty bread and a tossed salad with honey-mustard dressing. If you wish, you can add some peeled and quartered root vegetables (carrots, parsnips, or turnips) to the cooker, too.

INGREDIENTS | SERVES 8

1 (3-pound) beef brisket

1 large yellow onion, peeled and quartered

2 large cloves of garlic, peeled and minced

4 large cloves of garlic, peeled and left whole

1 (10-ounce) jar apple jelly

3 tablespoons Dijon mustard

Salt and freshly ground pepper, to taste

¾ teaspoon curry powder

⅓ cup dry white wine

1 cup apple juice

1 cup water

2 apples (optional)

1. Add all ingredients to 5- or 6-quart slow cooker in the order given. If using apples, peel, core, and slice them and put them in a layer on top of the meat. Cover and cook on low for 8 hours or until meat is tender.

Delayed Satisfaction

Brisket will become even more moist and tender if you allow it to cool in the broth, so this makes a good dish to make the day before. To reheat it, bake it for 45 minutes at 325°F. Baste it with some additional sauce and put it under the broiler for a few minutes to allow the meat to develop a glaze.

Beef Cholent

Cholent mixes are convenient, but buying the beans and barley separately is much more economical.

INGREDIENTS | SERVES 6

½ cup lima beans

½ cup navy beans

1 cup pearl barley

1 small onion, chopped

1 carrot, peeled and cut into 1" pieces

1 pound flanken ribs

2 medium or large potatoes, peeled and cut into large chunks

1 teaspoon sweet paprika

1 teaspoon garlic powder

4 cups water, plus more if needed

2 teaspoons kosher salt

½ teaspoon black pepper

1. Place lima beans, navy beans, and barley in a fine mesh drainer. Rinse several times in cold water and drain.

2. In a 6-quart slow cooker, place ingredients in the following order: chopped onion, carrot, flanken, prepared beans and barley, potatoes, paprika, garlic powder, and water.

3. Cover and cook on low for 12–26 hours. Check and add water at any time if cholent looks too dry. If there is too much liquid at the end of the cooking time, uncover and let cook for an additional 30 minutes. Add salt and pepper. Taste and add additional salt and pepper if needed.

Cholent

Cholent (CHUH-lent) is a stew traditionally assembled and set over a low flame just before Shabbat began at sundown Friday night, and left to cook overnight and on through the entire next day until after sundown, when Shabbat is over. Since work (which includes lighting a flame or turning on an oven) is prohibited during this seventh day of rest, this dish allows observant Jews to have a warm meal on Saturday night at a reasonable hour.

Sephardic Cholent

*The ingredients and spices may vary depending upon local customs,
but all Sephardic cholents contain eggs cooked in their shells.*

INGREDIENTS | SERVES 6–8

Cooking spray
2 tablespoons olive oil
2 large onions, chopped
4 cloves garlic, coarsely chopped
3 pounds flanken ribs
2 (15-ounce) cans chickpeas, drained and rinsed
3 large sweet potatoes, peeled and cut into 1" chunks
2 teaspoons ground cumin
1 teaspoon turmeric
1 teaspoon cinnamon
1 tablespoon paprika
½ teaspoon kosher salt
¼ teaspoon black pepper
3 tablespoons honey
Pinch of saffron threads, crushed
1 cup chicken broth
6 uncooked whole eggs

1. Spray the inside of a 6-quart slow cooker with the cooking spray.

2. Heat oil in a large skillet over medium-high heat. Add onions and cook, stirring frequently, until they soften and just start to turn brown, about 8 minutes. Add garlic; stir for 30 seconds, then push mixture to the sides. Add flanken and let sear for 3 minutes without disturbing. Carefully turn flanken and sear again for 3 minutes.

3. Transfer flanken and onions into prepared slow cooker and top with chickpeas and sweet potatoes. Sprinkle in the cumin, turmeric, cinnamon, paprika, salt, and pepper. Drizzle in the honey.

4. In a small bowl, mix the saffron into the broth and pour into slow cooker.

5. Nestle the eggs in the center of the slow cooker. Cover and cook on low for 8–12 hours.

Red Wine Beef Stew

A little bit of wine goes a long way in flavoring this simple one-crock meal.

INGREDIENTS | SERVES 6

⅓ cup red wine

½ cup water

4 red skin potatoes, quartered

3 carrots, cut into thirds

2 bulbs fennel, quartered

2 rutabagas, quartered

1 onion, sliced

4 cloves garlic, sliced

3 pounds beef stew meat, cut into 2" cubes

½ teaspoon kosher salt

½ teaspoon freshly ground black pepper

1. Pour the wine and water into a 4-quart slow cooker. Add the potatoes, carrots, fennel, rutabagas, onion, and garlic. Stir.

2. Arrange stew meat evenly over vegetables. Sprinkle with salt and pepper. Cover and cook on low for 8 hours.

Flanken Ribs in Spicy Tomato Sauce

Reduce Tabasco sauce to a few drops to tone down the "heat."

INGREDIENTS | SERVES 4

2 pounds flanken ribs

1 (28-ounce) can tomato sauce

½ cup water

⅛ cup Worcestershire sauce

2 tablespoons brown sugar

1 teaspoon Tabasco sauce

1 teaspoon salt

¼ teaspoon black pepper

1 lemon, juiced

1 tablespoon soy sauce

¼ cup parsley leaves

1. Add all ingredients except parsley leaves to a 4-quart slow cooker. Cover and cook on low heat for 6 hours. Sprinkle on parsley evenly just before serving.

Beef Bourguignon

For a complete fine-dining experience, serve Beef Bourguignon over noodles with a salad.

INGREDIENTS | SERVES 8

2 tablespoons vegetable oil

1 large yellow onion, peeled and diced

3 cloves of garlic, peeled and minced

1 (3-pound) boneless chuck roast, trimmed of fat and cut into 1" cubes

16 ounces fresh mushrooms, cleaned and sliced

2 tablespoons tomato paste

2 cups beef broth or water

4 cups burgundy

½ teaspoon thyme

1 bay leaf

Salt and freshly ground black pepper, to taste

1 large yellow onion, peeled and thinly sliced

½ cup margarine, softened (optional)

½ cup all-purpose flour (optional)

1. Heat oil in a large nonstick skillet over medium-high heat. Add the onion to the skillet and sauté for 5 minutes or until it is transparent. Stir in the garlic, sauté for 30 seconds, and then transfer the onion mixture to the slow cooker. Cover the cooker.

2. Add the beef cubes to the skillet and brown the meat over medium-high heat for 5 minutes. Transfer the meat to the slow cooker. Cover the cooker.

3. Add half of the sliced mushrooms to the skillet; stir-fry for 5 minutes or until the mushroom liquids have evaporated; transfer to the slow cooker and replace the cover.

4. Add the tomato paste to the skillet and sauté for 3 minutes or until the tomato paste just begins to brown. Stir in the broth or water, scraping the bottom of the pan to remove any browned bits and work them into the sauce. Remove the pan from the heat and stir in the burgundy, thyme, bay leaf, salt, and pepper; stir to combine. Pour into the slow cooker. Add the remaining mushrooms and sliced onions to slow cooker. Cover and cook on low for 8 hours.

5. Optional: To thicken the sauce, use a slotted spoon to transfer the meat, cooked onions, and mushrooms to a serving platter; cover and keep warm. In a small bowl, mix the margarine together with the flour to form a paste; whisk in some of the pan liquid a little at a time to thin the paste. Strain out any lumps. Increase the heat of the cooker to high. When the pan liquids begin to bubble around the edges, whisk in the flour mixture. Cook, stirring constantly, for 15 minutes or until the sauce has thickened enough to coat the back of a spoon. Pour over the meat, mushrooms, and onions on the serving platter.

Brisket Tzimmes

If there's room in the slow cooker, at the beginning of Step 3 you can add a 1-pound bag of thawed frozen cut green beans along with the sweet potatoes.

INGREDIENTS | SERVES 8

1 (3-pound) beef brisket

1 large yellow onion, peeled and diced

Salt and freshly ground black pepper, to taste

2 stalks celery, diced

1 large carrot, peeled and diced

1 (12-ounce) box pitted prunes (dried plums)

1 tablespoon dried or freeze-dried parsley

3 cups beef broth

3 tablespoons fresh lemon juice

¼ teaspoon ground cloves

1 teaspoon ground cinnamon

1 tablespoon honey

2 tablespoons white or white wine vinegar

4 large sweet potatoes, peeled and quartered

1. Add the brisket, onion, salt, pepper, celery, carrot, prunes, and parsley to a 5- or 6-quart slow cooker.

2. In a large bowl, mix the broth, lemon juice, cloves, cinnamon, honey, and vinegar together and then pour over the meat. Cover and cook on low for 6 hours or until the meat is cooked through.

3. Add the sweet potatoes. Cover and cook on low for another 2 hours or until the brisket and sweet potatoes are tender.

4. Use a slotted spoon to move the vegetables and meat to a serving platter. Tent with foil or otherwise cover and keep warm. Allow the meat to rest for 15 minutes before you carve it, slicing it against the grain.

A Touch More Cinnamon?

Taste the broth at the end of Step 2. That's the ideal time to add more ground cloves and cinnamon to taste if you think it could use more.

Barbecue Meatloaf

This recipe assumes you're using commercial barbecue sauce, which is usually thicker than homemade sauce. The brown sugar sprinkled over the top of the meatloaf helps caramelize the sauce.

INGREDIENTS | SERVES 8

2 pounds lean ground beef

½ pound lean ground veal

2 large eggs

1 large yellow onion, peeled and diced

Salt and freshly ground pepper, to taste

1½ cups quick-cooking oatmeal

1 teaspoon dried parsley

1½ cups barbecue sauce

1 tablespoon brown sugar

Mrs. Dash Extra Spicy Seasoning Blend, to taste (optional)

1. In a large bowl, add the ground beef, ground veal, eggs, onion, salt, pepper, oatmeal, parsley, and 1 cup of the barbecue sauce; mix well with your hands. Form into a loaf to fit the size (round or oval) of your slow cooker.

2. Line the slow cooker with two pieces of heavy-duty aluminum foil long enough to reach up both sides of the slow cooker and over the edges, crossing one piece over the other. Place a piece of nonstick foil the size of the bottom of the slow cooker crock inside the crossed pieces of foil (or a slow cooker liner) to form a platform for the meatloaf. (This is to make it easier to lift the meatloaf out of the slow cooker.)

3. Put the meatloaf over the top of the nonstick foil. Spread the remaining ½ cup of barbecue sauce over the top of the meatloaf. Sprinkle the brown sugar and Mrs. Dash Extra Spicy Seasoning Blend, if using, over the top of the barbecue sauce. Cover and cook on low for 8 hours or until the internal temperature of the meatloaf registers 165°F.

4. Lift the meatloaf out of the slow cooker and place it on a cooling rack. Allow it to rest for 20 minutes before transferring it to a serving platter and slicing it.

Cottage Pie with Carrots, Parsnips, and Celery

Cottage Pie is similar to the more familiar Shepherd's Pie, but it uses beef instead of lamb.

INGREDIENTS | SERVES 6

1 large onion, diced

3 cloves garlic, minced

1 carrot, diced

1 parsnip, diced

1 stalk celery, diced

1 pound lean ground beef

1½ cups beef stock

½ teaspoon hot paprika

½ teaspoon crushed rosemary

1 tablespoon Worcestershire sauce

½ teaspoon dried savory

⅛ teaspoon salt

¼ teaspoon freshly ground black pepper

1 tablespoon cornstarch and 1 tablespoon water, mixed (if necessary)

¼ cup minced fresh parsley

2¾ cups plain mashed potatoes

1. In a large nonstick skillet, sauté the onion, garlic, carrot, parsnip, celery, and beef until the ground beef is browned, about 5 minutes. Drain off any excess fat and discard it. Place the mixture into a round 4-quart slow cooker.

2. Add the stock, paprika, rosemary, Worcestershire sauce, savory, salt, and pepper. Stir.

3. Cook on low for 6–8 hours. If the meat mixture still looks very wet, create a slurry by mixing together 1 tablespoon cornstarch and 1 tablespoon water. Stir this into the meat mixture.

4. In a medium bowl, mash the parsley and potatoes using a potato masher. Spread on top of the ground beef mixture in the slow cooker. Cover and cook on high for 30–60 minutes or until the potatoes are warmed through.

Save Time in the Morning

Take a few minutes the night before cooking to cut up any vegetables you need for a recipe. Place them in an airtight container or plastic bag and refrigerate until morning. Measure any dried spices and place them in a small container on the counter until needed.

Pastrami

New York–style pastrami is peppercorn-crusted smoked corned beef that is sometimes steamed before serving. Smoked paprika will impart a subtle smoky flavor. For a more intense smoked flavor, use liquid smoke, too.

INGREDIENTS | SERVES 12

1 (4-pound) corned beef brisket

2 large onions, peeled and sliced

2 cloves of garlic, peeled and minced

2 tablespoons pickling spice

1½ cups water

1 tablespoon black peppercorns, crushed

¾ teaspoon freshly grated nutmeg

¾ teaspoon ground allspice

2 teaspoons smoked paprika

¼ teaspoon liquid smoke (optional)

Deli-Style Pastrami Sandwich

Pile thin slices of pastrami on a slice of deli rye slathered with mustard. Top with another slice of rye bread. Serve with a big, crisp kosher dill pickle.

1. Trim any fat from the corned beef brisket. Add the brisket, onions, garlic, pickling spice, and water to a 5- or 6-quart slow cooker. Cover and cook on low for 8 hours. Turn off the cooker and allow the meat to cool enough to handle it.

2. Preheat the oven to 350°F.

3. In a small bowl, add the crushed (or cracked) peppercorns, nutmeg, allspice, paprika, and liquid smoke (if using) and mix well. Rub the peppercorn mixture over all sides of the corned beef.

4. Place beef on a roasting pan; roast on the middle shelf for 45 minutes. Let the meat rest for 10 minutes, then carve by slicing it against the grain or on the diagonal.

Swiss Steak

*Pound each steak thin between two pieces of plastic wrap
before coating with flour. Serve Swiss Steak over mashed potatoes.*

INGREDIENTS | SERVES 6

½ cup all-purpose flour
1 teaspoon salt
¼ teaspoon freshly ground black pepper
6 (6-ounce) beef minute steaks
2 tablespoons vegetable oil
2 teaspoons margarine
½ stalk celery, finely diced
1 large yellow onion, peeled and diced
1 cup beef broth
1 cup water
1 (1-pound) bag baby carrots
Steak sauce, to taste (optional)

1. Add the flour, salt, pepper, and minute steaks to a 1-gallon plastic bag; seal and shake to coat the meat.

2. Add the oil and margarine to a large skillet over medium-high heat. After margarine melts and begins to bubble, add the steaks and brown them for 5 minutes on each side (you might have to brown them in batches). Transfer the steaks to a 5- or 6-quart slow cooker.

3. Add the celery to the skillet and sauté while you add the onion to the plastic bag; seal and shake to coat the onion in flour. Add the flour-coated onions to the skillet and, stirring constantly, sauté for 10 minutes or until the onions are lightly browned.

4. Add the beef broth to the skillet and stir to scrape up any browned bits clinging to the pan. Add the water and continue to cook until the liquid is thickened enough to lightly coat the back of a spoon. Pour into the slow cooker. Add the carrots. Cover and cook on low for 8 hours.

5. Transfer the meat and carrots to a serving platter. Taste the gravy for seasoning, and add steak sauce to taste if desired. Serve gravy alongside or over the meat and carrots.

Chili con Corn Chips

For a fun way to serve the chili, serve directly from the chip bag! Slit open the bag lengthwise along the center and across near both ends. Fold back the flaps and pour the chili directly over the chips.

INGREDIENTS | SERVES 4–6

1 tablespoon vegetable oil

1 medium onion, diced

1 pound lean ground beef

1 (15-ounce) can diced tomatoes, drained

½ red pepper, finely diced

½ green pepper, finely diced

1 tablespoon chili powder

1 teaspoon ground coriander

1 teaspoon ground cumin

1 teaspoon dried oregano

2 teaspoons kosher salt

¼ teaspoon black pepper

Large bag Fritos corn chips, divided

8 ounces grated pareve plain or pepper jack cheese (optional)

1. Heat oil in a large skillet over medium-high heat. Add onion and cook, stirring occasionally, for 5–8 minutes or until softened and starting to brown. Transfer to a 4- or 5-quart slow cooker and set aside.

2. Add ground beef to skillet. Break up beef and stir until no pink remains. Drain off grease, then add meat and remaining ingredients except Fritos and cheese to slow cooker. Stir, then cover and cook on low for 6–8 hours.

3. Crush ¼ cup of Fritos and stir them into chili. Cover and continue to cook another 15 minutes.

4. Place remaining Fritos on serving platter. Ladle chili over Fritos. Top with grated pareve cheese, if desired. Serve immediately.

"Creamy" Swedish Meatballs

Serve leftover meatballs over medium or wide egg noodles.

INGREDIENTS | SERVES 20

Cooking spray

Meatballs

2 thin slices white sandwich bread, torn into ½ inch pieces

½ cup soymilk

2 pounds lean ground beef

2 cloves garlic, minced

1 egg

¼ teaspoon salt

¼ teaspoon allspice

⅛ teaspoon nutmeg

Sauce

1 tablespoon olive oil

⅓ cup all-purpose flour

3 cups low-sodium chicken broth

1½ cups pareve nondairy creamer such as Rich's

¼ teaspoon allspice

⅛ teaspoon nutmeg

¼ teaspoon salt

¼ teaspoon white pepper

Nondairy Creamer

Some nondairy creamers contain casein, which is a milk derivative; check the fine print for a pareve hechsher. Rice milk or almond milk can substitute for the nondairy creamer.

1. Preheat the oven to 400°F. Line 2 rimmed baking sheets with foil and spray each lightly with nonstick spray.

2. To make the meatballs, place the bread pieces into a large bowl. Pour in the soymilk and let the bread soak for a minute. Add the meat, garlic, egg, salt, allspice, and nutmeg. Using clean hands, mix it all together just until combined.

3. Form the mixture into 1" balls and divide balls evenly between the baking sheets. Bake the meatballs until they just begin to color, 10–15 minutes. Drain the meatballs on paper towel–lined plates, then transfer to the slow cooker.

4. To make the sauce, while the meatballs are cooking, heat the oil over medium heat in a 3-quart saucepan. When melted, add the flour and stir to combine. Slowly stream in the chicken broth, whisking constantly to avoid lumps. Whisk in the pareve nondairy creamer, allspice, nutmeg, salt, and pepper. Simmer until the mixture thickens slightly, then remove from heat.

5. Pour sauce over meatballs. Cover and cook on low for 2–4 hours.

Barbecue Meatballs

Enjoy these meatballs as a party appetizer or use them as the filling in a hearty sub.

INGREDIENTS | YIELDS 12 MEATBALLS

1 (18-ounce) bottle barbecue sauce

2 teaspoons onion powder

1 teaspoon garlic powder

1 (32-ounce) package pre-cooked meatballs (beef or chicken), such as Of Tov

1. In a medium-sized mixing bowl, combine barbecue sauce, onion powder, and garlic powder.

2. Pour about 1 cup of sauce into a 4-quart slow cooker. Add the meatballs.

3. Pour remaining barbecue sauce over meatballs. Cover and cook on high for 1 hour.

Better-Than-Takeout Mongolian Beef

This homemade version of the Chinese takeout favorite is lower in fat and sodium.
Serve it over rice and sprinkle with diced green onion before serving.

INGREDIENTS | SERVES 6

3 pounds lean beef roast, extra fat removed

3 cloves garlic, grated

1 knob peeled fresh ginger, grated, or 1 teaspoon ground ginger

1 medium onion, thinly sliced

½ cup water

½ cup low-sodium soy sauce

2 tablespoons balsamic vinegar

2 tablespoons hoisin sauce

1 tablespoon five-spice powder

1 tablespoon cornstarch

1 teaspoon red pepper flakes

1 teaspoon sesame oil

1. Place all ingredients in a 4-quart slow cooker. Cover and cook for 5 hours on low or until the meat is thoroughly cooked through and tender.

2. Remove the roast to a cutting board. Slice thinly and return it to the slow cooker. Cook for an additional 20 minutes on high. Stir the meat and the sauce before serving.

Cincinnati Chili

Cincinnati chili is native to the state of Ohio and is typically eaten over spaghetti or on hot dogs.

INGREDIENTS | SERVES 4

1 tablespoon vegetable oil

1 onion, chopped

3 cloves garlic, minced

1 pound ground beef

1 cup tomato sauce

1 cup water

2 tablespoons red wine vinegar

2 tablespoons chili powder

½ teaspoon cumin

½ teaspoon ground cinnamon

½ teaspoon sweet paprika

½ teaspoon ground cinnamon

1 tablespoon light brown sugar

1 tablespoon unsweetened cocoa powder

1 teaspoon hot pepper sauce

16 ounces cooked spaghetti

1. Heat oil in a large skillet over medium-high heat. Add onion and garlic. Sauté for about 3–4 minutes, or until onions start to soften.

2. Push everything to the sides of the pan, then add the ground beef. With a wooden spoon, break up meat, then cook, stirring occasionally, until meat is browned and no pink remains.

3. Pour off grease, then add meat to a 4-quart slow cooker. Top with all ingredients except for the spaghetti. Cover and cook on low heat for 5 hours.

4. Serve the chili over the spaghetti.

Semi-Spicy Beef Chili

Fire-roasted tomatoes give the chili wonderful flavor without kicking up the spiciness level.

INGREDIENTS | SERVES 4

1 tablespoon vegetable oil

1 medium onion, peeled and diced

2 cloves garlic, minced

1 chili in adobo sauce, finely diced

1 pound lean ground beef

2 (14.5-ounce) cans fire-roasted diced tomatoes

2 teaspoons chili powder

1 teaspoon ground cumin

Pinch cayenne pepper

Pareve shredded pepper jack "cheese" (optional)

Chili in Adobo Sauce

Chili in adobo sauce gives this chili a smoky flavor, but has a bit of spiciness. For a milder chili, omit and instead substitute 1 teaspoon adobo chili powder for all the chili powder.

1. Heat oil in a large skillet over medium-high heat. Add onion and garlic. Sauté for about 3–4 minutes, or until onions start to soften. Stir in the chili in adobo sauce.

2. Push everything to the sides of the pan, then add the ground beef. With a wooden spoon, break up meat, then cook, stirring occasionally, until meat is browned and no pink remains.

3. Pour off grease, then add meat to a 4-quart slow cooker. Drain 1 can of tomatoes and discard liquid. Add the drained tomatoes, the remaining can of tomatoes and their liquid, chili powder, cumin, and cayenne pepper to the slow cooker.

4. Cover and cook on low for 4–6 hours.

5. Divide chili among 5 dishes and serve hot, topped with pareve "cheese" if desired.

Moroccan-Style Lamb Stew

It is a Moroccan custom to serve sweetened mint tea several times a day and especially to guests.

INGREDIENTS | SERVES 6

Cooking spray
½ cup chicken broth
1 pinch saffron threads, lightly crushed
2 pounds lamb stew meat, cut into 1" cubes
1 medium onion, diced
¼ cup golden raisins
½ cup dried apricots, cut into halves
½ teaspoon ground ginger
1 teaspoon ground cinnamon
1 teaspoon kosher salt
¼ teaspoon black pepper
3 cups cooked couscous
4 tablespoons toasted slivered almonds (for garnish)

1. Lightly spray inside of a 6-quart slow cooker with cooking spray.

2. In a heat-safe bowl, mix the chicken broth with the crushed saffron threads. Heat the mixture for 30 seconds in a microwave at full power.

3. Place the lamb, onion, raisins, and apricots in the prepared slow cooker. Sprinkle with the remaining spices. Pour the broth mixture over spices. Cover and cook on low for 8–10 hours.

4. Serve over couscous and garnish with almonds, if desired.

Saffron

Saffron is the dried stigma of a crocus flower cultivated in the Mediterranean and the Middle East. It is the world's most expensive spice, taking about 5,400 flowers to produce one ounce of saffron. Luckily, a little goes a long way!

Stuffed Cabbage

This is the traditional version of a wonderful dish to serve to guests. Although there is some advance preparation to do, you will have plenty of time to clean up before your guests arrive.

INGREDIENTS | SERVES 4

Water, as needed

1 large head cabbage

1 teaspoon margarine

½ cup sliced onions

1 (28-ounce) can whole tomatoes in purée

½ cup minced onions

1 egg

1½ cups cooked long-grain rice

½ tablespoon garlic powder

½ tablespoon sweet paprika

1 pound lean ground beef

1. Bring a large pot of water to a boil. Meanwhile, using a knife, make 4 or 5 cuts around the core of the cabbage and remove the core. Discard the core and 2 layers of the outer leaves. Peel off 6–8 large whole leaves. Place the leaves in a steamer basket and allow them to steam over the boiling water for 7 minutes. Allow the leaves to cool enough to handle. Dice the remaining cabbage to equal ½ cup.

2. In a nonstick skillet, melt margarine. Add sliced onions and diced cabbage, and sauté until the onions are soft, about 5 minutes.

3. Add the tomatoes. Break up tomatoes into small chunks using the back of a spoon. Simmer for about 10–15 minutes. Ladle a third of the sauce over the bottom of a 4-quart slow cooker.

4. In a medium-sized bowl, add the minced onions, egg, rice, spices, and beef and mix to distribute all ingredients evenly.

5. Place a cabbage leaf with the open side up and the stem part facing you on a clean work area. Add about ¼ cup filling to the leaf, toward the stem. Fold the sides together, and then pull the top down and over the filling to form a packet. It should look like a burrito. Repeat until all the filling is gone.

6. Arrange the cabbage rolls, seam side down, in a single layer in the slow cooker. Ladle about half of the remaining sauce over the rolls and repeat with a second layer. Ladle the remaining sauce over the rolls. Cover and cook on low for up to 10 hours.

Shredded Beef for Sandwiches

*Due to the long cooking time, you might want to prepare the meat late
the night before serving so it will be ready to eat for lunch.*

INGREDIENTS | SERVES 16

4 pounds boneless beef roast, excess fat removed

1 onion, chopped

3 cloves garlic, chopped

1 teaspoon sweet paprika

1 teaspoon chili powder

½ teaspoon celery seed

½ teaspoon dried tarragon

½ teaspoon dried mustard

½ teaspoon freshly ground black pepper

¼ teaspoon salt

1 tablespoon hot sauce

1 tablespoon hickory liquid smoke

½ cup water

1. Place all ingredients into a 6- to 7-quart slow cooker. Cook on low for 10–12 hours. The meat should be easily shredded with a fork.

2. Remove the meat from the slow cooker to a plate. Shred with a fork. Mash the contents of the slow cooker with a potato masher. Return the beef to the slow cooker and stir to distribute the ingredients evenly.

Ask the Butcher

If the beef sitting on the shelf of the local store is too fatty, ask the butcher to cut a fresh, leaner cut. You won't have to do fat removal at home, which can be tricky depending on the cut of meat. The butcher can also suggest lean beef alternatives to fattier cuts.

Potato Lasagna • Chapter 8

Mock Chopped "Liver" • Chapter 15

Kichel Cake • Chapter 14

Beanie Weenies • Chapter 11

Challah French Toast Casserole • Chapter 3

Barbecue Meatballs • Chapter 6

Shakshuka • Chapter 3

Warm Rice Pudding • Chapter 13

Middle Eastern Eggplant Salad • Chapter 2

Pareve Palak Paneer • Chapter 9

Sticky Honey Wings • Chapter 2

Marinara Sauce • Chapter 12

Salmon with Lemon, Capers, and Rosemary • Chapter 7

Vegetarian Cholent with Kishke • Chapter 11

Chili con Corn Chips • Chapter 6

Chanukah Carrot "Coins" • Chapter 15

Sweet Potatoes with Coconut Milk • Chapter 10

Breakfast Quinoa with Fruit • Chapter 14

Mocha Truffles 3 Ways • Chapter 13

Zesty Lemon Hummus • Chapter 2

Barbecue Ribs

At the end of the 8-hour cooking time, the meat will be tender and falling off of the bones. You can stretch this recipe to 8 servings if you serve barbecue beef sandwiches instead of 4 servings of beef. Add potato chips and coleslaw for a delicious, casual meal.

INGREDIENTS | SERVES 4

1 cup barbecue sauce
½ cup orange marmalade
½ cup water
3 pounds beef ribs

1. Add the barbecue sauce, marmalade, and water to a 5- or 6-quart slow cooker. Stir to mix. Add the ribs, ladling some of the sauce over the ribs. Cover and cook on low for 8 hours. To thicken the sauce, if desired, use a slotted spoon to remove the meat and bones; cover and keep warm.

2. Skim any fat from the sauce in the cooker; increase the heat setting to high and cook uncovered for 15 minutes or until the sauce is reduced and coats the back of a spoon.

Beef Biryani

Biryani is an Indian one-pot meal that is well spiced but not spicy.

INGREDIENTS | SERVES 6

1 pound London broil, cut into ¼ inch thick strips
1 tablespoon minced fresh ginger
½ teaspoon ground cloves
½ teaspoon ground cardamom
½ teaspoon ground coriander
½ teaspoon freshly ground black pepper
½ teaspoon cinnamon
½ teaspoon cumin
¼ teaspoon salt
2 cloves garlic, minced
1 onion, minced
1 cup pareve yogurt or sour cream
1 cup frozen peas
1½ cups cooked basmati or brown rice

1. Place the beef, spices, garlic, and onion into a 4-quart slow cooker. Stir. Cook on low for 7–8 hours.

2. About 30 minutes before serving, stir in the pareve yogurt, peas, and rice. Cook for 30 minutes. Stir before serving.

Tavas

Tavas is a simple Greek lamb stew named for the crock in which it is traditionally cooked. Since it is usually cooked at a low temperature for many hours, this dish is perfect for the slow cooker.

INGREDIENTS | SERVES 4

Cooking spray

1 large onion, peeled and thinly sliced

2 (15-ounce) cans diced tomatoes, undrained

2 pounds lamb shoulder, cut into 1" cubes

1 tablespoon olive oil

1 tablespoon cumin seeds, lightly crushed

1 teaspoon kosher salt

¼ teaspoon black pepper

2–3 cups cooked brown or white rice

¼ cup parsley leaves (for garnish)

1. Spray the inside of a 4- or 6-quart slow cooker with cooking spray. Add all ingredients except the rice and parsley and stir. Cover and cook on low for 6–8 hours.

2. If sauce is not thickened, uncover and cook for an additional 30 minutes. Serve over rice and garnish with the parsley.

Unstuffed Cabbage

Give this a quick sauté at breakfast, then ignore until dinner time.

INGREDIENTS | SERVES 4

1 tablespoon olive oil

1 pound ground beef

1 (12-ounce) bag coleslaw mix

1 small onion, peeled and diced

1 (28-ounce) can diced tomatoes, undrained

1 cup uncooked long-grain rice

3 garlic cloves, minced

1 tablespoon sweet Hungarian paprika

2 tablespoons lemon juice

1 teaspoon kosher salt

¼ teaspoon ground black pepper

1. Heat the oil in a large skillet over medium-high heat. Add ground beef; break up chunks using the back of a spoon. Sauté for about 4–5 minutes or until no pink remains. Drain and add to a 4-quart slow cooker. Stir in the remaining ingredients.

2. Cover and cook on low for 6–8 hours. Taste and add additional salt and pepper, if needed.

Lamb in Curry Sauce

The ingredients list seems long, but once the onions and garlic
are sautéed the entire recipe comes together quickly.

INGREDIENTS | SERVES 4

1 tablespoon vegetable oil

1 medium onion, peeled and diced

1 clove garlic, minced

Cooking spray

1 large potato, peeled and diced

2 carrots, peeled and julienned

2 teaspoons curry powder

½ teaspoon ground turmeric

2 teaspoons ground cumin

1 teaspoon cinnamon

1 teaspoon kosher salt

¼ teaspoon ground black pepper

1" piece fresh ginger, peeled and grated
(or 1 teaspoon ground ginger)

2 packages (about 3 pounds total) lamb
shoulder, cut into 2" pieces

1 (10- to 12-ounce) can coconut milk
(regular or light)

1 cup water

2 cups cooked rice, any variety

¼ cup packed coriander leaves

1. Heat the vegetable oil in a large skillet. Add the onion and garlic. Sauté for 5 minutes or until onions just start to brown. Remove from heat and set aside.

2. Spray the inside of a 6-quart slow cooker with cooking spray. Add potato, carrots, onion mixture, and spices; stir to combine.

3. Arrange lamb on top of vegetables. Pour in the coconut milk and the water. Cover and cook on low for 8–9 hours.

4. Serve the lamb over rice. Ladle the curried sauce over lamb and garnish with cilantro leaves.

Coconut Milk

Coconut milk is the water extracted from grated coconut. It can substitute in many recipes where cow's milk or cream is used. Since coconut milk has a tendency to harmlessly separate in storage, shake the can prior to opening.

Picadillo

Picadillo is the Cuban equivalent of Sloppy Joes. Serve these over rice.

1. Heat the oil in a large skillet over medium-high heat. Add the onion. Cook, stirring frequently, for about 5 minutes, or until the onions soften. Add the green pepper and garlic. Continue to sauté for another 2 minutes.

2. Push everything to the sides of the pan, then add the ground beef. With a wooden spoon, break up meat, then cook, stirring occasionally, until meat is browned and no pink remains, about 5 minutes.

3. Pour off grease, then transfer meat mixture to a 4-quart slow cooker. Stir in remaining ingredients except the rice.

4. Cover and cook on low for 4–6 hours. Serve over rice.

And Now for Something a Little Different

Tired of the same old taco or burrito filling? Replace their meat fillings with Picadillo!

Veal Marengo

This long-braised dinner is perfect for the slow cooker. Serve over rice.

INGREDIENTS | SERVES 12–16

Cooking spray

2 tablespoons olive oil

4 large onions, chopped (about 3–4 cups)

4 garlic cloves, minced

4 pounds boneless veal, cut into 1½" cubes

½ cup dry white wine

1 cup Beef Broth (see Chapter 4)

3 ounces (½ of a small can) tomato paste

1 teaspoon kosher salt

½ teaspoon black pepper

1 pound white mushrooms, sliced

½ cup lightly packed fresh parsley leaves, coarsely chopped

What Is a Marengo?

Napoleon's chef has been credited with first creating chicken Marengo to celebrate Napoleon's victory at the Battle of Marengo in 1800. Nowadays, veal is also used to create this slow-cooked dish.

1. Spray the inside of a 7-quart slow cooker with cooking spray.

2. Heat oil in a large skillet over medium-high heat. Add the onions and cook, stirring frequently, until onions soften, about 5 minutes. Add the garlic and stir for another 30 seconds.

3. Push the onion mixture to the sides of the pan and add veal cubes in batches, letting them sear for about 2 minutes per side. Transfer onion mixture and veal, as it finishes browning, into prepared slow cooker.

4. In a small bowl, mix together the wine, beef broth, tomato paste, salt, and pepper, and pour over the veal.

5. Cover and cook on low for 5–6 hours, or until the veal is tender. Add mushrooms and continue to cook for another 30 minutes. Turn off slow cooker. Add parsley. Cover and let sit for 5 minutes before serving.

Moo Shu Beef

Another Chinese takeout favorite!

INGREDIENTS | SERVES 4

1 pound ground beef

2 tablespoons soy sauce

2 tablespoons hoisin sauce

1 (12- to 16-ounce) bag coleslaw mix

8 flour tortillas, wrapped in foil and warmed in a 200°F oven

½ cup plum sauce (ready-made or from Chapter 2)

1. Break up beef into a 4-quart oval slow cooker. Mix in soy sauce and hoisin sauce. Cover and cook on low for 2 hours.

2. Stir in coleslaw mix. Cover and cook for an additional 1 hour, or until coleslaw is wilted.

3. To serve, place a tortilla on a dinner plate. Spoon some plum sauce down the center. Place about ¼ cup of the meat mixture on the lower half of the tortilla. Fold up the lower third of the tortilla to cover meat. Fold over the sides, then roll up tightly. Serve 2 wraps per person.

Short Ribs in Ginger Chutney Sauce

Chutney is a condiment made from fruit and/or vegetables. Mango chutney, such as Major Grey's, uses a sweet-sour mixture that includes mango, raisins, and lime juice.

INGREDIENTS | SERVES 4

Cooking spray

2 pounds short ribs

¼ cup mango chutney

1 teaspoon ground ginger

½ teaspoon kosher salt

¼ teaspoon black pepper

2 tablespoons lemon juice

¼ cup fresh parsley leaves, chopped, for garnish

1. Lightly spray the inside of a 6-quart slow cooker with the cooking spray. Arrange the short ribs in the cooker, overlapping if necessary.

2. In a medium bowl, whisk the chutney, ginger, salt, pepper, and lemon juice together; pour over ribs.

3. Cover and cook on low heat for 6–8 hours or until short ribs are tender. Sprinkle on parsley just before serving.

CHAPTER 7

Fish

Almond-Stuffed Flounder

Making this dish in the slow cooker lets you layer the fish and stuffing rather than stuffing and rolling the fillets. You can substitute sole for the flounder. Serve with warm dinner rolls, a tossed salad, and cooked wild rice.

INGREDIENTS | SERVES 4

Nonstick spray

4 (4-ounce) fresh or frozen flounder fillets

1 cup (4 ounces) grated Swiss cheese

½ cup slivered almonds

1 tablespoon freeze-dried chives (optional)

Sweet paprika, to taste

¼ cup dry white wine (optional)

1 tablespoon unsalted butter

½ cup grated carrot

1 tablespoon all-purpose flour

¼ teaspoon dried tarragon

Sea salt, to taste

White pepper, to taste

1 cup evaporated milk

1. Spray the inside of a 4-quart slow cooker with nonstick spray.

2. Rinse the fish and pat dry with paper towels. Lay 2 fillets flat in the slow cooker. Sprinkle the grated cheese, almonds, and chives (if using) over the fillets. Place the remaining fillets on top. Sprinkle paprika over the fish fillets. Pour the wine around the fish.

3. Add the butter and carrots to a microwave-safe bowl or measuring cup. Cover and microwave on high for 1 minute; stir and microwave on high for 1 more minute. Stir in the flour, tarragon, salt, and pepper. Whisk in the evaporated milk. Cover and microwave on high for 1 minute. Pour the sauce over the fish.

4. Cover and cook on low for 2 hours or until the fish is cooked through, the cheese is melted, and the sauce is thickened. Turn off the slow cooker and let rest for 15 minutes.

5. To serve, use a knife to cut through all layers into four wedges. Spoon each wedge onto a plate (so that there is fish and filling in each serving). Sprinkle with additional paprika before serving if desired.

Étouffée

Serve this kosher version of the famous Creole dish over cooked rice.

INGREDIENTS | SERVES 6

2 tablespoons vegetable oil

1 large onion, peeled and diced

6 scallions

2 stalks celery, finely diced

1 green bell pepper, seeded and diced

1 jalapeño, seeded and diced

2 cloves of garlic, peeled and minced

3 tablespoons tomato paste

3 (15-ounce) cans diced tomatoes

Salt, to taste

½ teaspoon dried basil

½ teaspoon dried oregano

½ teaspoon dried thyme

¼ teaspoon cayenne pepper

1 package shrimp-style or crabmeat-style surimi

2 teaspoons cornstarch

1 tablespoon cold water

Hot sauce, to taste

Surimi

Surimi is a paste made from fish that is shaped, cooked, and colored to resemble other seafood, such as shrimp or crab. Be sure to check for a hechsher since some brands of surimi have treif (nonkosher) seafood products added for flavoring.

1. Add the oil and onion to the slow cooker. Clean the scallions and chop the white parts and about 1" of the greens. Add to the slow cooker along with the celery, green bell pepper, and jalapeño. Stir to coat the vegetables in the oil. Cover and cook on high for 30 minutes or until the vegetables are soft.

2. Stir in the garlic and tomato paste. Cover and cook on high for 15 minutes.

3. Stir in the tomatoes, salt, basil, oregano, thyme, and cayenne pepper. Reduce the heat setting of the slow cooker to low; cover and cook for 6 hours.

4. Stir in the surimi. Increase the heat setting to high, cover, and cook for 15 minutes.

5. In a small bowl, add the cornstarch and water. Stir to mix. Remove any lumps if necessary. Uncover the slow cooker and stir in the cornstarch mixture. Cook and stir for 5 minutes, or until the mixture is thickened and the cornstarch flavor is cooked out. Stir in hot sauce, to taste.

Ginger-Lime Salmon

The slow cooker does all the work in this recipe, creating a healthy yet impressive dish that requires virtually no hands-on time.

INGREDIENTS | SERVES 12

1 (3-pound) salmon fillet, bones removed
¼ cup minced fresh ginger
¼ cup lime juice
1 lime, thinly sliced
1 onion, thinly sliced

Cracked!

Before each use, check your slow cooker for cracks. Even small cracks in the glaze can allow bacteria to grow in the ceramic insert. If there are cracks, replace the insert or the entire slow cooker.

1. Place the salmon skin side down in a 6- to 7-quart slow cooker. Pour the ginger and lime juice over the fish. Arrange the lime slices and then the onion in single layers over the fish.

2. Cook on low for 3–4 hours or until the fish is fully cooked and flaky. Remove the skin before serving.

Halibut in White Wine Sauce

You can omit the wine in the sauce and replace it with more evaporated milk. Then, when you taste the sauce for seasoning before you pour it over the fish, whisk in a little white wine vinegar and mayonnaise.

INGREDIENTS | SERVES 4

Nonstick spray
2 (12-ounce) packages frozen halibut fillets, thawed
¼ cup unsalted butter
2 tablespoons all-purpose flour
1 tablespoon sugar
¼ teaspoon sea salt
⅓ cup dry white wine
⅔ cup evaporated milk
Fresh dill (optional)
Lemon wedges (optional)

1. Treat the inside of a 4-quart slow cooker with nonstick spray. Rinse the halibut and pat dry with paper towels. Place them in the slow cooker.

2. Melt the butter in a small saucepan. Stir in the flour, sugar, and salt. When well blended, whisk in the wine and evaporated milk. Cook and stir for 5 minutes (allowing the sauce to boil for at least 1 minute), or until thickened. Taste for seasoning and add additional salt if needed.

3. Pour the sauce over the fish. Cover and cook on high for 3 hours or until the fish is opaque and flakes easily with a fork. Garnish with fresh dill and lemon wedges if desired.

Salmon Loaf

If you're using saltine crackers, add dill pickles to Salmon Loaf. If you prefer butter style crackers, use sweet pickles. Serve it as you would meatloaf, topped with Creamy Dill Sauce (see sidebar) instead of gravy.

INGREDIENTS | SERVES 4

2 (7½-ounce) cans red sockeye salmon, drained, skin removed

¼ cup crackers, finely crushed

1 small onion, peeled and minced

1 large egg

2 tablespoons mayonnaise

1 tablespoon fresh lemon juice

1 tablespoon fresh parsley, minced

1 tablespoon fresh dill, chopped

½ teaspoon freshly ground black pepper

2 tablespoons pickles, finely minced (optional)

Creamy Dill Sauce

Melt 1 tablespoon unsalted butter in a nonstick skillet over medium heat. Whisk in 1 tablespoon flour, ¼ teaspoon sea salt, and ¼ teaspoon freshly ground black pepper. Slowly whisk in 1 cup milk and 2 tablespoons minced fresh dill. Stirring constantly, bring to a boil and boil for 1 minute; lower heat and simmer and stir until the mixture is thick enough to coat the back of a spoon. Serve over the Salmon Loaf.

1. In a large bowl, add the salmon, crackers, onion, egg, mayonnaise, lemon juice, parsley, dill, pepper, and pickles, if using. Gently mix with a fork until evenly combined.

2. Place two long pieces of heavy-duty aluminum foil across each other in the insert of the slow cooker. Press into the insert and top with a piece of nonstick foil shaped to hold the salmon loaf. Use your hands to shape the salmon loaf and place it on top of the nonstick foil.

3. Cover the slow cooker, tucking the ends of the heavy-duty foil under lid. Cook on low for 6–8 hours or on high for 3–4 hours or until the salmon loaf is cooked through and set.

4. Turn off the slow cooker, remove the lid, and let the salmon loaf stand for 15 minutes. Use the heavy-duty foil as handles to lift the loaf out of the slow cooker.

5. Transfer the loaf to a serving plate. Slice and serve with Creamy Dill Sauce if desired.

Asian-Style Mahi-Mahi

This recipe works well with any thick cut of fish like halibut or salmon.

INGREDIENTS | SERVES 4

4 tablespoons (½ stick) unsalted butter, divided
1 medium onion, thinly sliced into rings
4 portions mahi-mahi fillets (about 1½ pounds total)
2 tablespoons soy sauce
3 tablespoons white wine
2 cups cooked white or brown rice
1 tablespoon fresh lemon juice
2 teaspoons sesame seeds, for garnish

1. Grease the bottom of a 4- or 6-quart slow cooker with 1 tablespoon of the butter. Separate and scatter onion rings in cooker. Arrange mahi-mahi fillets in a single layer over the onion rings.

2. In a saucepan, melt remaining butter and combine it with the soy sauce and wine. Pour over fillets. Cover and cook on high for 3–4 hours or until fillets are opaque and flake easily with a fork.

3. Serve mahi-mahi over rice. Discard onions. Stir lemon juice into remaining sauce; spoon sauce over fish. Garnish with sesame seeds, if desired.

Salmon with Lemon, Capers, and Rosemary

Salmon is very moist and tender when cooked in the slow cooker.

INGREDIENTS | SERVES 2

2 salmon steaks, about 1" thick each
⅓ cup white wine
2 tablespoons lemon juice
4 thin slices fresh lemon
1 tablespoon nonpareil capers
½ teaspoon minced fresh rosemary
½ teaspoon kosher salt

1. Place the salmon on the bottom of a 2- or 4-quart slow cooker. Pour the wine and lemon juice over the fish. Arrange the lemon slices in a single layer on top of the fish. Sprinkle with capers, rosemary, and salt.

2. Cook on low for 2 hours. Discard lemon slices prior to serving.

The Easy Way to Debone a Fish

A pair of needle-nose pliers easily removes bones from fish, especially those tiny ones. Just grab and pull!

Sea Bass with Mango Salsa

The buttery flavor of sea bass is enhanced by the olive oil.

INGREDIENTS | SERVES 4

Cooking spray

4 sea bass fillets

2 tablespoons olive oil, divided

1 ripe mango, peeled and finely diced

¼ cup finely diced red onion

1 baby red pepper, finely chopped (optional)

6–8 sprigs cilantro leaves, finely chopped

1 tablespoon fresh lime juice

¼ teaspoon kosher salt

¼ teaspoon coarsely ground black pepper

1. Lightly coat the inside of a 4-quart slow cooker with cooking spray. Arrange fillets in a single layer on the bottom of the cooker. Drizzle 1 tablespoon of the olive oil over the fillets. Cook on low for 3–4 hours or until fish flakes easily with a fork.

2. Meanwhile, in a small mixing bowl, mix the remaining olive oil with the remaining ingredients. Refrigerate until ready to use.

3. Carefully lift cooked fillets onto a serving platter. Spoon mango salsa over fillets and serve immediately.

Other Uses for Mango Salsa

Leftover mango salsa can be served as a very easy appetizer! Spoon into store-bought mini-phyllo cups and garnish with a cilantro leaf before serving.

Sea Bass with Tofu and Garlic Sauce

If kosher black bean and garlic sauce is not available, substitute with hoisin sauce.

INGREDIENTS | SERVES 4

Cooking spray

4 sea bass fillets

1 tablespoon olive oil

2 garlic cloves, minced

1 teaspoon ground ginger

2 tablespoons black bean and garlic sauce

2 tablespoons soy sauce

1 teaspoon granulated sugar

⅛ teaspoon black pepper

8 ounces extra-firm tofu, drained and diced

3–4 scallions, green parts thinly sliced for garnish

1. Lightly coat the inside of a 4-quart slow cooker with cooking spray. Arrange fillets in a single layer on the bottom of the cooker.

2. In a medium bowl, whisk together the oil, garlic, ginger, black bean and garlic sauce, soy sauce, sugar, and black pepper. Use a spoon to gently mix in the tofu. Pour over the fish. Cook on low for 3–4 hours or until fish flakes easily with a fork. Transfer fish to covered dish; keep warm.

3. Increase heat to high and cook sauce uncovered for 15 minutes. Serve fish with sauce, garnished with sliced scallions if desired.

Slow Cooker Fish

To avoid overcooking, be sure to use fish that is of a firm variety and is at least 1" thick. Salmon steak, sea bass, cod, halibut, and mahi-mahi are excellent examples of fish that can be easily cooked in a slow cooker.

Poached Salmon with Lemon-Parsley Sauce

Salmon steaks are usually cut thicker than most fish fillets, plus they're a firmer fish, so it takes longer to poach them. You can speed up the poaching process a little if you remove the steaks from the refrigerator and put them in room temperature water during the 30 minutes of Step 1.

INGREDIENTS | SERVES 4

1 tablespoon unsalted butter

4 thin slices sweet onion

2 cups water

4 (6-ounce) salmon steaks

Kosher salt, to taste

1 lemon

2 tablespoons extra-virgin olive oil

2 teaspoons fresh lemon juice

½ teaspoon Dijon mustard

Freshly ground white or black pepper, to taste (optional)

1 tablespoon fresh flat leaf parsley leaves, minced

Salmon Salad

Triple the amount of lemon-parsley sauce and toss two-thirds of it together with 8 cups of salad greens. Arrange 2 cups of greens on each serving plate. Place a hot or chilled salmon steak over each plate of the dressed greens. Spoon the remaining sauce over the fish.

1. Use the butter to grease the bottom and halfway up the sides of the slow cooker. Arrange the onion slices over the bottom of the slow cooker, pressing them into the butter so that they stay in place. Pour in the water. Cover and cook on high for 30 minutes.

2. Place a salmon steak over each onion slice. Salt to taste. Thinly slice the lemon; discard the seeds and place the slices over the fish. Cover and cook on high for 45 minutes or until the fish is opaque.

3. Transfer the (well-drained) fish to individual serving plates or to a serving platter.

4. In a small bowl, add the oil, lemon juice, mustard, and white or black pepper, if using; whisk to combine. Immediately before serving the salmon, fold in the parsley. Evenly divide the sauce among the salmon steaks.

Tuna with Garlic Butter in Foil

Be careful when opening each packet, as the escaping steam can cause severe burns.

INGREDIENTS | SERVES 8

½ cup (1 stick) unsalted butter, softened
4 minced garlic cloves
1 teaspoon salt
2 tablespoons minced fresh Italian parsley leaves
Cooking spray
8 (6-ounce) tuna steaks
1 lemon, thinly sliced

1. In a small bowl, whisk together butter, garlic, salt, and parsley. Set aside.

2. Lightly spray 8 large pieces of aluminum foil with cooking spray. Place 1 tuna steak on each piece of foil. Divide the butter mixture evenly and spread over the tuna steaks. Top with the lemon slices. Fold up two edges and crimp together, allowing a little space for steam to expand. Fold up the ends and crimp together as well.

3. Place packets in a 6-quart slow cooker. Cook on high for 2 hours.

CHAPTER 8

Dairy

Meatless Moussaka

For a pareve version, use a nondairy cream cheese such as Tofutti Better Than Cream Cheese.

INGREDIENTS | SERVES 8

¾ cup dry brown or yellow lentils, rinsed and drained

2 large potatoes, peeled and diced

1 cup water

1 stalk celery, finely diced

1 medium sweet onion, peeled and diced

3 cloves of garlic, minced

½ teaspoon salt

¼ teaspoon ground cinnamon

Pinch freshly ground nutmeg

¼ teaspoon freshly ground black pepper

¼ teaspoon dried basil

¼ teaspoon dried oregano

¼ teaspoon dried parsley

1 medium eggplant, diced

12 baby carrots, each cut into 3 pieces

1 (14½-ounce) can diced tomatoes, undrained

1 (8-ounce) package cream cheese, softened

1. Add the lentils, potatoes, water, celery, onion, garlic, salt, cinnamon, nutmeg, pepper, basil, oregano, and parsley to a 4-quart slow cooker. Stir. Top with eggplant and carrots.

2. Cover and cook on low for 6 hours, or until the lentils are cooked through.

3. Stir in tomatoes and add dollops of cream cheese over lentil mixture. Cover, and cook on low for an additional 30 minutes.

Welsh Rarebit

Welsh Rarebit can be served as a party dip or spooned over toast points and then dusted with paprika. It's also good served as part of a breakfast buffet, spooned over scrambled eggs or egg-topped English muffins.

INGREDIENTS | SERVES 8

2½ cups dark beer or ale

2 tablespoons unsalted butter

Hot sauce, to taste

Worcestershire sauce, to taste

2 pounds (4 cups) medium or sharp Cheddar cheese, grated

2 tablespoons all-purpose flour

2 teaspoons dry mustard

2 large eggs

Sweet paprika (optional)

Leftover Welsh Rarebit

Refrigerate leftover Welsh Rarebit in a covered container for up to a week. Reheat slowly (so the cheese doesn't separate) and serve over steamed vegetables or as a baked potato topper.

1. Pour 2 cups of the beer, butter, hot sauce, and Worcestershire sauce into the slow cooker. Cook uncovered on high for 30 minutes.

2. Put half of the grated cheese and all of the flour in a zip-top bag. Shake well to coat the cheese with flour, adding as much of the cheese to the bag as will fit and still allow room to mix it with the flour. Add all of the cheese-flour mixture and remaining cheese to the slow cooker. Cover and cook on low for 1 hour or until cheese is melted.

3. In a medium bowl, add the dry mustard and the eggs; whisk to combine. Whisk the remaining ½ cup of beer into the egg mixture and then slowly stir the egg mixture into the slow cooker. Cover and cook on low for 30 minutes.

4. To serve, reduce the heat setting of the slow cooker to warm. Dust servings with paprika if desired.

Zucchini Onion Casserole

For added fiber and protein, sneak in ½ cup of ground walnuts and mix them into the bread crumbs.

INGREDIENTS | SERVES 8

Cooking spray
2½ cups thinly sliced sweet onion
2½ cups sliced zucchini
2 medium-large sliced ripe red tomatoes
10 leaves fresh basil, finely chopped
1 tablespoon dried rosemary
½ teaspoon salt
¼ teaspoon pepper
2 cups croutons
1 cup shredded Cheddar cheese

1. Spray a 3- or 4-quart slow cooker with nonstick cooking spray.

2. Arrange half of each of the sweet onion, zucchini, and tomatoes along the bottom of the cooker. Sprinkle evenly with all the basil and rosemary, and half of the salt and pepper.

3. Scatter half of the croutons over the seasoned vegetables, then half of the Cheddar cheese over the croutons.

4. Repeat the layering with the remaining vegetables, salt, and pepper. Sprinkle the remaining croutons and Cheddar cheese on top.

5. Cover and cook on high for 2–4 hours. Serve hot.

Broccoli and Cheese Strata

You may substitute a firm white or whole wheat bread or stale challah.

INGREDIENTS | SERVES 6

Cooking spray
2 tablespoons olive oil
1 small onion, finely chopped
2 garlic cloves, minced
1 (10-ounce) box frozen broccoli, thawed and chopped
5 large eggs
1 (12-ounce) can evaporated milk
½ teaspoon salt
¼ teaspoon pepper
2 teaspoons Worcestershire sauce
1 baguette, cubed (about 4 cups)
½ cup shredded Cheddar cheese
¼ cup grated Parmesan cheese

1. Spray the inside of a 4- or 6-quart slow cooker with cooking spray.

2. Heat the olive oil in a small nonstick skillet over medium heat and sauté the onion for 5 minutes or until softened. Add garlic and continue to sauté for another 30 seconds.

3. Remove the pan from the heat and stir in the broccoli. Allow the mixture to cool while proceeding with the next step.

4. In a large bowl, whisk together the eggs, milk, salt, pepper, and Worcestershire sauce. Stir in the bread cubes, Cheddar and Parmesan cheeses, and cooled broccoli.

5. Pour the mixture into the prepared cooker. Cover and heat on high for 2 hours. Serve hot.

Rice and Vegetable Casserole

Vegetables are layered with a rice and egg mixture in this easy and delicious vegetarian entrée. Use brown rice for a healthy alternative.

INGREDIENTS | SERVES 8

1½ tablespoons olive oil, divided
2 medium onions, chopped
1 (10-ounce) package sliced mushrooms
2 red bell peppers, chopped
1 jalapeño pepper, minced
4 cups cooked brown rice
1½ cups milk
2 eggs
½ cup low-fat sour cream
1 cup shredded mozzarella cheese
½ cup shredded Cheddar or Colby cheese

1. Grease a 4- or 6-quart slow cooker with ½ tablespoon of olive oil and set aside.

2. Heat remaining olive oil in a large saucepan over medium-high heat. When hot, add the onions and mushrooms and cook, stirring occasionally, for 3 minutes. Add the bell peppers and jalapeño and cook for 3–4 minutes longer until vegetables are crisp-tender.

3. In a large bowl, combine the rice, milk, eggs, sour cream, mozzarella cheese, and Cheddar cheese. Layer half of this mixture in the prepared cooker. Top the rice mixture with the vegetables, then spread the remaining rice mixture over the top.

4. Cover and cook on high for 3–4 hours. Serve hot.

Beet Salad with Blue Cheese and Walnuts

Beets can stain hands bright red. Wear rubber gloves while removing the skins.

INGREDIENTS | SERVES 8

6 medium beets (about 2 bunches), cleaned and trimmed

4 tablespoons olive oil, divided

8 cups spring or baby salad greens

¼ cup balsamic vinegar

½ teaspoon kosher salt

¼ teaspoon coarsely ground black pepper

½ cup crumbled blue cheese

⅓ cup toasted walnut pieces

Instead of Walnuts . . .

Toasted pecans can replace walnuts in recipes for a delicious option. Both contain protein, unsaturated fat (the "good" kind), fiber, vitamins, and minerals. Use just enough to add flavor, since pecans and walnuts also contribute a lot of calories.

1. Place the beets in a 4-quart slow cooker. Toss with 2 tablespoons of the olive oil.

2. Cover and cook on high for 3–4 hours or until beets are easily pierced with a fork. Place the hot beets on a chopping board. Let cool enough to handle, then remove and discard skins. Slice each beet into 8 wedges. Divide salad greens among 8 plates. Evenly top with beet wedges.

3. In a small bowl, whisk together the remaining olive oil with the balsamic vinegar, salt, and pepper. Pour over the salad. Sprinkle evenly with the crumbled blue cheese and toasted walnuts before serving.

Greek-Style Mushroom Burritos

*Next time you make the mushrooms, cook up a double batch
and save some to quickly put together this easy lunch.*

INGREDIENTS | SERVES 4

1 pound Portobello mushrooms, cleaned and sliced

2 garlic cloves, minced

1 tablespoon plus 1 teaspoon olive oil, divided

½ cup feta cheese, drained and crumbled

2 teaspoons balsamic vinegar

½ teaspoon kosher salt

¼ teaspoon black pepper

1 teaspoon dried oregano

4 flour or whole wheat burrito-size tortillas

1 cup shredded lettuce

2 Roma tomatoes, seeded and diced

1 cup tzatziki sauce (see sidebar), (optional)

1. Mix the mushrooms, garlic, and 1 tablespoon of the olive oil in a 4-quart slow cooker. Cover and cook on low for 2–4 hours. Uncover and cook on low for another 30 minutes or until excess moisture evaporates.

2. Meanwhile, in a large bowl mix together the cheese, remaining 1 teaspoon of olive oil, balsamic vinegar, salt, black pepper, and oregano. Set aside, covered, in the refrigerator.

3. Spoon the hot cooked mushrooms evenly over the tortillas. Top with the cheese mixture. Cover with the lettuce and tomatoes and top with tzatziki sauce, if desired. Roll up burrito-style and serve immediately.

Tzatziki Sauce

Stir together 1 (6-ounce) cup plain Greek yogurt (low-fat or fat-free), 1 tablespoon fresh lemon juice, 1 small cucumber (peeled, seeded and finely diced), 1 teaspoon kosher salt, 1 tablespoon finely chopped fresh dill, and ⅛ teaspoon ground black pepper. Store, covered in the refrigerator, for at least 1 hour and up to 3 days. Pour off any liquid that may rise to the surface before using.

Mexican Lasagna

*This is a very hearty dairy meal that even meat-eaters will enjoy. As an option,
one or all of the salsa verde layers can be replaced with additional enchilada sauce.*

INGREDIENTS | SERVES 8

1 tablespoon olive oil

1 (15-ounce) can fire-roasted diced tomatoes, drained

1 medium-sized onion, peeled and diced

4 cloves garlic, minced

1 tablespoon chili powder

2 teaspoons paprika, sweet or smoked

½ tablespoon ground cumin

1 (15-ounce) can black beans, drained and rinsed

1 cup sliced black olives

2 cups cooked rice

1 (12- to 16-ounce) jar roasted (medium) or regular (mild) salsa verde

1 (12-count) package corn tortillas

2 (8-ounce) packages shredded Cheddar cheese

1 cup Enchilada Sauce (see Chapter 9)

1 (12-ounce) bag frozen corn, defrosted

½ cup chopped cilantro leaves (for garnish)

½ cup sour cream (for garnish)

Salsa Verde

Salsa verde is a green salsa made with tomatillos, a popular Mexican fruit used as a vegetable. Tomatillos resemble small green tomatoes.

1. Heat oil in a large skillet over medium-high heat. Add the tomatoes, onion, and garlic. Cook, stirring frequently, for 5 minutes until onions are softened. Add the chili powder, paprika, and cumin. Stir for 1 minute. Stir in the black beans, olives, and cooked rice. Remove from heat and set aside.

2. Spread half of the jar of salsa verde in the bottom of a 6-quart slow cooker. Place 2 or 3 tortillas over the sauce, overlapping or tearing the tortillas as necessary to fit.

3. Spread half of the rice mixture over the tortillas. Sprinkle half of the cheese over the rice.

4. Place another layer of tortillas on top of the cheese. Pour all of the enchilada sauce evenly over the tortillas. Pour all the corn evenly over the sauce, followed by the remaining rice mixture. Add a final layer of tortillas over the rice mixture. Pour the remaining salsa verde evenly over the tortillas, using the back of a spoon to spread the sauce, followed by the remaining cheese.

5. Cover and cook on high for 2½–3 hours, or until the cheese has completely melted and the sauce is bubbling. Sprinkle on the cilantro and garnish with sour cream, if desired.

Potato Lasagna

Try this unique recipe for a delicious change of pace for lunch or dinner.

INGREDIENTS | SERVES 8

1 (15-ounce) container ricotta cheese

4 ounces grated Parmesan cheese

1 (16-ounce) package shredded mozzarella or Cheddar cheese

2 eggs, lightly beaten

¼ teaspoon ground black pepper

1 teaspoon dried basil

½ teaspoon dried oregano

4 cups Marinara Sauce, divided (see Chapter 12)

6 large Yukon gold potatoes (about 3 pounds), peeled and thinly sliced

1. In a large bowl, combine the 3 cheeses, eggs, pepper, basil, and oregano. Set aside.

2. Spread about ⅓ cup of marinara sauce into the slow cooker to cover the bottom with a thin layer. Top with a third of the sliced potatoes, overlapping if necessary. Spread half of the cheese mixture on top of the potatoes. Spoon a third of the remaining sauce over the cheese.

3. Layer another third of the potatoes over the sauce. Top with the remaining cheese mixture and another third of the sauce. Layer the remaining potatoes over the sauce and top with remaining sauce, making sure that all the potatoes are coated.

4. Cover and cook on high for 3–4 hours until the potatoes are tender.

Cheesy Tuna Casserole

The title may be cheesy, but the taste is delicious!

INGREDIENTS | YIELDS 4 SERVINGS

Cooking spray

1 (12-ounce) package wide egg noodles

2 (5- to 6-ounce) cans tuna packed in water, drained (reserve liquid)

1 (6-ounce) can French fried onions (such as French's), divided

1 (14-ounce) can cream of mushroom soup, undiluted

½ cup evaporated milk

½ cup Vegetable Broth (see Chapter 4)

1 (4-ounce) can sliced mushrooms, drained

1 (8-ounce) package Cheddar cheese

½ cup grated Parmesan cheese

½ cup frozen peas, defrosted

A Crispier Topping

If you like a crunchier topping, sprinkle the last half of the French fried onions on top just after mixing in the peas.

1. Spray the inside of a 4-quart slow cooker with the cooking spray. Add half of the egg noodles into the slow cooker.

2. Using a fork, break up tuna in a bowl. Mix in half of the can of French fried onions. Add tuna mixture on top of the noodles.

3. Cover tuna with remaining egg noodles. Combine cream of mushroom soup, evaporated milk and vegetable broth; pour evenly over noodles. Top with mushrooms and sprinkle evenly with the cheeses. Top with remaining French fried onions. Cook on low for 5 hours.

4. Gently mix in the peas. Cover and cook on low for an additional 15 minutes.

Lentil Vegetable Stew with Cheese

Let this stew simmer all day, then add the baby spinach a few minutes before serving. The spinach will gently wilt to perfection.

INGREDIENTS | SERVES 4

Nonstick spray

1 tablespoon olive oil

3 medium carrots, peeled and diced

1 small onion, peeled and diced

2 cups fresh cauliflower florets, rinsed and coarsely chopped

1 sweet potato, peeled and cut into 1" cubes

1 cup brown lentils, rinsed, drained, and inspected to remove any dirt or debris

½ teaspoon ground ginger

2 tablespoons soy sauce

¼ teaspoon black pepper

1½ cups Vegetable Broth (see Chapter 4)

1 (5-ounce) bag baby spinach leaves, rinsed and drained

½ cup grated Parmesan cheese

1. Spray a 4-quart slow cooker with nonstick spray.

2. Heat the olive oil in a large skillet over medium-high heat. When hot, add the carrots and onion. Cook, stirring frequently, for 5 minutes or until the onions soften.

3. Add the cauliflower and sweet potatoes. Cook for 3–4 minutes longer, stirring frequently until vegetables are crisp-tender. Add the sautéed vegetables to the prepared slow cooker.

4. Stir in the lentils, ginger, soy sauce, black pepper, and vegetable broth. Cover and cook on low for 6–8 hours.

5. Turn off cooker. Stir in the spinach, cover, and let sit for 15 minutes to allow spinach to wilt.

6. Ladle stew into bowls and sprinkle with Parmesan cheese just before serving.

Eggplant Parmesan

Smaller eggplants are less likely to be bitter than larger ones.

2 medium-sized eggplants, peeled and cut into ½" slices

½ cup plus ½ teaspoon kosher salt, divided

3¼ cups Marinara Sauce (see Chapter 12), divided

½ cup plain toasted bread crumbs

½ teaspoon dried oregano

1 teaspoon dried basil

¼ teaspoon ground black pepper

1 large egg, lightly beaten

½ cup grated Parmesan cheese

1 (12-ounce) package mozzarella cheese, shredded

4 large basil leaves, chopped (for garnish)

Eggplant Gender

Select an eggplant with a smooth blossom end. It is most likely a male, with less seeds than a female eggplant (with an indented end).

1. Place the eggplant slices in a colander in the sink. Use the ½ cup of kosher salt to evenly salt both sides of each eggplant slice. Let sit for 30 minutes, then rinse the slices and pat dry with paper towels.

2. Meanwhile, coat a 4-quart slow cooker with ¼ cup of the marinara sauce. Set aside.

3. In a medium bowl, combine the bread crumbs, oregano, basil, remaining ½ teaspoon kosher salt, and the black pepper.

4. Place the beaten egg in a medium bowl. Dip each eggplant slice into the beaten egg, then into the bread crumb mixture.

5. Layer a third of the eggplant slices in the prepared slow cooker. Top with a third each of the Parmesan cheese, the mozzarella cheese, and a cup of the marinara sauce. Repeat layering two more times.

6. Cover and cook on low for 4–5 hours or until the eggplant is tender. Sprinkle with fresh basil before serving, if desired.

Spicy Bean Burritos

Adobo chilies in sauce make these vegetarian burritos very spicy.
Lower the heat by reducing or omitting either the chilies or the adobo sauce.

½ red pepper, seeded and diced

½ green pepper, seeded and diced

2 cups Vegetarian Refried Beans (see Chapter 11)

1 (15-ounce) can black beans, rinsed and drained

1 cup frozen corn, defrosted

1 cup salsa or taco sauce

2 chipotle chilies in adobo sauce (from 7-ounce can), chopped

2 teaspoons adobo sauce (from same can)

1 (8-ounce) package shredded Cheddar or taco blend cheese, divided

8 burrito-size flour tortillas

½ cup sour cream (for garnish)

4 scallions, green parts thinly sliced (for garnish)

1. In a 4-quart slow cooker, stir together the diced red and green peppers, refried beans, black beans, corn, salsa, chilies, adobo sauce, and 1 cup of the cheese. Cover and cook on low for 3–4 hours, stirring after 2 hours.

2. Spread a layer of the bean mixture down the center of each tortilla, leaving about an inch margin on each end.

3. Sprinkle the remaining cheese over the bean mixture. Spread a dollop of sour cream and sprinkle with scallions, if desired. Fold margin ends over, then roll up each burrito and serve immediately.

Frozen Chilies

Leftover adobo chilies and their sauce can be frozen for later use. Place them in a freezer-safe plastic bag, making sure the chilies are in a single layer, then seal. Next time, it will be easy to break off the amount of chilies (and sauce) needed without having to defrost the entire bag.

Sweet Potato Enchiladas

This is an unusual yet delicious vegetarian version of a favorite Mexican dish.
To tone down the spiciness, omit the jalapeño peppers.

INGREDIENTS | SERVES 8

2½ tablespoons olive oil, divided

1 onion, chopped

3 garlic cloves, minced

2 jalapeño peppers, seeded and minced

2 cups Vegetarian Refried Beans (see Chapter 11)

1 tablespoon chili powder

1 teaspoon ground cumin

½ teaspoon salt

⅛ teaspoon pepper

1 (20-ounce) can sweet potatoes, drained and chopped

1½ cups salsa, divided

12 (10-inch) flour tortillas

2½ cups shredded Cheddar cheese, divided

2 cups Enchilada Sauce (see Chapter 9)

1. Grease the inside of a 4- to 6-quart slow cooker with ½ tablespoon of the olive oil.

2. In a large skillet, heat remaining olive oil over medium heat. When hot, add the onion. Cook, stirring occasionally, until the onions are softened, about 5 minutes. Add the garlic and jalapeños and stir for another minute.

3. Add the refried beans, chili powder, cumin, salt, and pepper; bring the mixture to a simmer. Add the sweet potatoes and ½ cup salsa; remove from the heat.

4. Place the tortillas on a clean work surface. Divide the sweet potato mixture among them; top each with 2 tablespoons of Cheddar cheese. Roll up, enclosing the filling.

5. In a medium bowl, combine the remaining 1 cup salsa with the enchilada sauce and mix well. Place ½ cup sauce in the prepared cooker. Top with the enchiladas, then pour the remaining sauce evenly over the enchiladas.

6. Cover and cook on high for 1–2 hours. Uncover and top with the remaining 1 cup cheese. Cover and continue cooking for another hour. Serve immediately.

Tuna Corn Chowder

The sherry is a luxurious touch for this light, one-bowl lunch. Serve the chowder with crusty bread.

INGREDIENTS | SERVES 4

2 (5-ounce) cans solid white tuna packed in water, undrained

4 medium potatoes, peeled and cut into ½" chunks

1 small onion, peeled and diced

1 (20-ounce) bag frozen corn, defrosted

3 cups water, heated to a simmer

2 teaspoons kosher salt, plus more to taste

¼ teaspoon ground black pepper, plus more to taste

1 (12-ounce) can evaporated milk

½ cup frozen peas and carrots, defrosted

¼ cup dry sherry (optional)

¼ cup chopped Italian parsley leaves (for garnish)

¼ cup imitation bacon chips, such as Bacos (for garnish)

1. Place the tuna in a 4-quart slow cooker. Break up the tuna with a fork. Stir in the potatoes, onion, corn, and water. Cover and cook on low for 4–6 hours.

2. Stir in the salt, pepper, evaporated milk, peas, carrots, and the sherry if using. Cover and cook on low for an additional 30 minutes. Taste and add additional salt and pepper if needed.

3. Garnish with parsley leaves and imitation bacon chips, if using, before serving.

CHAPTER 9

Vegetarian and Vegan

Mediterranean Vegetable Stew

Try serving this stew with large pieces of pita bread and a scoop of hummus.

2 tablespoons extra-virgin olive oil

4 garlic cloves, chopped

1 red onion, chopped

1 red bell pepper, seeded and chopped

1 eggplant, chopped

1 (15-ounce) can artichokes, drained and chopped

⅓ cup kalamata olives, pitted and chopped

2 (15-ounce) cans diced tomatoes

4 cups Vegetable Broth (see Chapter 4)

1 teaspoon red pepper flakes

½ teaspoon dried oregano

½ teaspoon dried parsley

1 teaspoon salt

½ teaspoon pepper

1. In a 4-quart slow cooker, add all ingredients. Cover and cook on low heat for 4–6 hours.

Preparing Eggplant

Some people salt eggplant prior to cooking in order to remove bitterness, but this step is not really needed. The skins can be removed, but this also is not necessary. Eggplants, called aubergines in almost all other parts of the world, can be boiled, steamed, sautéed, stir-fried, deep-fried, braised, baked, grilled, broiled, and microwaved.

White Bean Cassoulet

The longer you cook this cassoulet, the creamier it gets.

INGREDIENTS | SERVES 8

1 pound dried cannellini beans

2 cups boiling water

1 ounce dried porcini mushrooms

2 leeks, sliced

1 teaspoon canola oil

2 parsnips, diced

2 carrots, diced

2 stalks celery, diced

½ teaspoon ground fennel

1 teaspoon crushed rosemary

1 teaspoon dried chervil

⅛ teaspoon cloves

¼ teaspoon salt

¼ teaspoon freshly ground black pepper

2 cups Vegetable Broth (see Chapter 4)

Using Dried Beans

Dried beans must be soaked overnight and boiled for at least 10 minutes before being added to a slow cooker, if you prefer to use them over canned beans.

1. The night before making the soup, place the beans in a 4-quart slow cooker. Fill with water to 1" below the top of the insert. Soak overnight.

2. Drain the beans and return them to the slow cooker.

3. In a heat-proof bowl, pour the 2 cups of boiling water over the dried mushrooms and let them soak for 15 minutes.

4. Slice only the white and light green parts of the leeks into ¼" rounds. Cut the rounds in half.

5. In a nonstick skillet, heat the oil; add the parsnip, carrots, celery, and leeks. Sauté for 1 minute, just until the color of the vegetables brightens.

6. Add the vegetables to the slow cooker along with the spices. Add the mushrooms, their soaking liquid, and the broth; stir.

7. Cook on low for 8–10 hours.

Chili con "Carne"

Try this vegan alternative to the standard ground beef in this fast recipe.

INGREDIENTS | SERVES 4

½ cup onion, diced

½ cup bell pepper, diced

1 (12-ounce) package frozen veggie burger crumbles

2 cloves garlic, minced

1 (15-ounce) can kidney beans, rinsed and drained

2 cups Vegetable Broth (see Chapter 4)

1 tablespoon chili powder

½ tablespoon chipotle powder

½ tablespoon cumin

1 teaspoon thyme

1 tablespoon oregano

2 cups fresh tomatoes, diced

1 tablespoon tomato paste

1 tablespoon cider vinegar

2 teaspoons salt

1. In a 4-quart slow cooker, add all ingredients. Cover and cook on low heat for 5 hours.

Vegan Beef

There are many brands of vegetarian ground beef on the market. Try Boca Ground Crumbles, Gimme Lean Ground Beef Style or Morningstar Farms Crumbles for a prepackaged option. Or try using dehydrated textured vegetable protein (TVP).

Southwest Vegetable Chili

Southwest cuisine is similar to Mexican food and includes a wide variety of peppers, such as the jalapeños, bell peppers, chipotle, and chili powder found in this recipe.

INGREDIENTS | SERVES 4

1 (28-ounce) can diced tomatoes

1 (15-ounce) can red kidney beans

1 medium onion, diced

1 green bell pepper, seeded and diced

1 red bell pepper, seeded and diced

1 zucchini, chopped

1 squash, chopped

¼ cup pickled jalapeños, chopped

⅛ cup chili powder

2 tablespoons garlic powder

2 tablespoons cumin

1 teaspoon chipotle powder

⅛ teaspoon dried thyme

1 teaspoon salt

¼ teaspoon black pepper

1. In a 4-quart slow cooker, add all ingredients. Cover and cook on low heat for 5 hours.

Sweet Potato Chili

Sweet potatoes are great sources of fiber and beta carotene, making this chili healthy and delicious.

INGREDIENTS | SERVES 4

1 red onion, diced

1 jalapeño, seeded and minced

3 cloves garlic, minced

1 (15-ounce) can black beans, drained

1 sweet potato, peeled and diced

3 tablespoons chili powder

1 tablespoon sweet paprika

1 teaspoon dried oregano

1 teaspoon ground cumin

½ teaspoon chipotle powder

1 (28-ounce) can diced tomatoes, drained

2 cups Vegetable Broth (see Chapter 4)

1 teaspoon salt

¼ teaspoon black pepper

Juice from 1 lime

¼ cup cilantro, chopped

1. In a 4-quart slow cooker, add all ingredients except the lime juice and cilantro. Cover and cook on low heat for 8 hours.

2. When the chili is done cooking, mix in the lime juice and garnish with the cilantro.

What Is Chili Powder?

Chili powder is made from grinding dried chilies, and may be created from a blend of different types of chilies or just one variety. The most commonly used chilies are red peppers and cayenne peppers.

Lentil Chili

Before using dried lentils, rinse them well and pick through to remove any debris or undesirable pieces.

INGREDIENTS | SERVES 6

1 cup brown lentils, uncooked

1 onion, diced

3 cloves garlic, minced

4 cups Vegetable Broth (see Chapter 4)

¼ cup tomato paste

1 cup carrots, chopped

1 cup celery, chopped

1 (15-ounce) can diced tomatoes, drained

2 tablespoons chili powder

½ tablespoon sweet paprika

1 teaspoon dried oregano

1 teaspoon cumin

1 teaspoon salt

¼ teaspoon black pepper

1. In a 4-quart slow cooker, add all ingredients. Cover and cook on low heat for 8 hours.

Israeli Couscous with Chickpeas

Queen Esther, the heroine of Purim, was said to have eaten a vegetarian diet, including beans such as chickpeas, to avoid breaking kashrut.

INGREDIENTS | SERVES 8

1 tablespoon olive oil

1 cup Israeli couscous

2 (15-ounce) cans chickpeas, drained and rinsed

1 cup water

2 teaspoons kosher salt

1 teaspoon black pepper

½ teaspoon ground cumin

½ teaspoon ground coriander

5 cloves garlic, minced

¼ cup parsley leaves, chopped (for garnish)

1. Heat the oil in a small skillet over medium heat. Sauté the couscous until it starts to brown, about 4–5 minutes.

2. Transfer couscous to a 4-quart slow cooker. Add all remaining ingredients except parsley. Cover and cook on low heat for 4 hours. Sprinkle with parsley leaves, if desired, before serving.

Spicy Tofu and Vegetables

Tofu gets virtually all its flavor from the sauce that surrounds it.
Be sure to purchase the regular variety. Silken tofu will easily break up while stirring.

INGREDIENTS | SERVES 4–6

Cooking spray

2 medium onions

1 medium carrot

3 garlic cloves, minced

¼ cup hoisin sauce

2 tablespoons rice wine vinegar

1 tablespoon soy sauce

2 teaspoons Sriracha sauce

2 teaspoons ground ginger

¼ teaspoon five-spice powder

2 tablespoons brown sugar

1 (1-pound) package extra-firm tofu, drained well and sliced into ½" cubes

3 cups cooked brown or white rice

1 tablespoon toasted sesame seeds (for garnish)

1. Lightly spray the inside of a 4-quart slow cooker with cooking spray.

2. Peel onions. Cut each in half, then thinly slice. Peel carrot, then thinly slice on the diagonal. Place in prepared slow cooker.

3. In a small mixing bowl stir together remaining ingredients except the tofu, rice, and sesame seeds. Pour into the slow cooker and mix with the vegetables.

4. Add the tofu and gently stir until tofu is completely coated with the sauce. Cover and cook on low for 5 hours or on high for 2½–3 hours.

5. Ladle tofu and vegetables over cooked rice. Sprinkle evenly with sesame seeds, if desired.

Curried Lentils

Serve this Indian-style dish with hot brown or white rice. It can also be served with plain yogurt or sour cream as garnish or on the side. Reduce the amount of jalapeños or omit completely if they are too spicy for your taste.

INGREDIENTS | SERVES 6

2 teaspoons butter

1 large onion, thinly sliced

2 cloves garlic, minced

2 jalapeños, diced

½ teaspoon red pepper flakes

½ teaspoon ground cumin

1 pound yellow lentils

6 cups water

½ teaspoon salt

½ teaspoon ground turmeric

4 cups chopped fresh spinach

For a Pareve Alternative

Make this dish pareve by substituting margarine for the butter. Garnish with pareve yogurt or sour cream on the side in place of their dairy versions.

1. Heat the butter in a sauté pan. Sauté the onion slices until they start to brown, about 8–10 minutes.

2. Add the garlic, jalapeños, red pepper flakes, and cumin. Sauté for 2–3 minutes.

3. Add the onion mixture to a 4-quart slow cooker.

4. Sort through the lentils and discard any rocks or foreign matter, then rinse and drain. Add the lentils to the slow cooker. Stir in the water, salt, and turmeric.

5. Cover and cook on high for 2½ hours.

6. Add the spinach and stir. Cook on high for an additional 15 minutes.

Stuffed Eggplant

This easy pareve dish is a complete meal in itself.

INGREDIENTS | SERVES 2

1 (1-pound) eggplant
½ teaspoon olive oil
2 tablespoons minced red onion
1 clove garlic, minced
⅓ cup cooked brown or white rice
1 tablespoon fresh parsley
¼ cup corn kernels
¼ cup diced crimini mushrooms
1 (15-ounce) can diced tomatoes with onions and garlic

1. Preheat oven to 375°F.

2. Slice the eggplant into 2 equal halves, lengthwise. Use an ice cream scoop to take out the seeds. Place on a baking sheet, skin side down. Bake for 8 minutes. Allow to cool slightly.

3. Heat the oil in a small skillet. Sauté the onion and garlic until softened, about 5 minutes.

4. In a medium bowl, stir the onions, garlic, rice, parsley, corn, and mushrooms. Divide evenly among the wells in the eggplant.

5. Pour the tomatoes onto the bottom of a 4- or 6-quart slow cooker. Place the eggplant halves side by side on top of the tomatoes. Cook on low for 3 hours.

6. Remove the eggplants and plate. Drizzle with tomato sauce.

Enchilada Sauce

Despite its spicy-sounding name, Mexican chili powder is really quite mild.
This very easy sauce can replace smooth taco sauce in most recipes.

INGREDIENTS | YIELDS ABOUT 2 CUPS

1 tablespoon olive oil

1 tablespoon cornstarch

3 tablespoons Mexican chili powder

2 teaspoons dried oregano

2 teaspoons ground cumin

1 (6-ounce) can tomato paste

1 tablespoon sugar

1 teaspoon salt, plus more to taste

2 cups Vegetable Broth (see recipe Chapter 4)

1. Combine all ingredients in a 4-quart slow cooker. Cover and cook on low for 2 hours. Stir. Leave uncovered; increase heat to high and cook, stirring occasionally, for 15–30 minutes or until sauce is reduced to desired thickness. Taste and add more salt if needed.

Chipotle Tomato Sauce

Try this spicy Southwestern take on the classic Italian tomato sauce on pasta, or in place of salsa in burritos or tacos.

INGREDIENTS | SERVES 6

3 cloves garlic, minced

1 onion, minced

1 (28-ounce) can crushed tomatoes

1 (14-ounce) can diced tomatoes, undrained

3 chipotle peppers in adobo sauce, minced

1 teaspoon dried oregano

1 tablespoon minced cilantro

½ teaspoon freshly ground black pepper

1. Place all ingredients into a 4-quart slow cooker. Cook on low for 8–10 hours. Stir before serving.

Know Your Slow Cooker

When using a new or new-to-you slow cooker for the first time, pick a day when someone can be there to keep tabs on it. In general, older slow cookers cook at a higher temperature than new models, but even new slow cookers can have some differences. It is a good idea to know the quirks of a particular slow cooker so food is not overcooked or undercooked. Tweak cooking times accordingly.

Seitan Bourguignon

Seitan Bourguignon is a pareve adaptation of the French classic Boeuf Bourguignon.

INGREDIENTS | SERVES 6

2 tablespoons olive oil

1 pound cooked seitan, cut into 2" cubes

2 carrots, sliced

1 onion, sliced

1 teaspoon salt

2 tablespoons flour

2 cups red wine

2 cups No-Beef Broth (see Chapter 4)

1 tablespoon tomato paste

2 cloves garlic, minced

½ teaspoon dried thyme

1 bay leaf

¼ teaspoon pepper

1 tablespoon margarine

18 whole pearl onions, peeled

2 cups button mushrooms, sliced

Seitan

Seitan is made from wheat gluten and is often used as a vegetarian substitute for all types of meat. It's one of the easiest meat substitutes to cook with at home.

1. Heat the olive oil in a sauté pan over medium heat. Sauté the seitan, carrots, and onion until soft, about 7 minutes. Stir in the salt and flour.

2. In a 4-quart slow cooker, add the vegetables and roux. Whisk in the red wine and No-Beef Broth, then add all remaining ingredients.

3. Cover and cook on low heat for 6–8 hours.

Cranberry Walnut Brussels Sprouts

Even a Brussels sprouts hater will love this! The combination of cranberries and walnuts makes this a perfect Thanksgiving side dish.

INGREDIENTS | SERVES 6

1 pound Brussels sprouts, trimmed and quartered

2 tablespoons olive oil

2 tablespoons water

½ teaspoon salt

¼ teaspoon pepper

¼ cup dried cranberries

¼ cup walnuts, chopped

1. Place all ingredients in a 2-quart slow cooker; stir until the olive oil coats the other ingredients.

2. Cover and cook on high heat for 2½ hours.

Thai Tofu Coconut Curry

Try this easy curry over brown rice instead of the usual white rice.

INGREDIENTS | SERVES 6

12 ounces extra-firm tofu

¼ cup unsweetened shredded coconut

¼ cup water

4 cloves garlic, minced

1 tablespoon minced fresh ginger

½ cup chopped onion

1 cup peeled and diced sweet potato

1 cup broccoli florets

1 cup snow peas

3 tablespoons soy sauce

1 tablespoon chili-garlic sauce

½ cup cilantro leaves and stems, minced

½ cup light coconut milk

1. Slice the tofu into ½"-thick triangles.

2. Place the tofu into a 4-quart slow cooker. Top with coconut, water, garlic, ginger, onion, sweet potato, broccoli, snow peas, soy sauce, and chili-garlic sauce.

3. Stir to distribute all ingredients evenly. Cook on low for 5 hours.

4. Stir in the cilantro and coconut milk. Cook on low for an additional 20 minutes. Stir prior to serving.

Tofu

Tofu is a white high-protein soybean product that absorbs flavors from the sauce around it. It can be used instead of meat for a vegetarian/pareve dish.

Zucchini Ragout

A ragout is either a main-dish stew or a sauce. This one can be served as either.

INGREDIENTS | SERVES 6

5 ounces fresh spinach

3 zucchini, diced

½ cup diced red onion

2 stalks celery, diced

2 carrots, diced

1 parsnip, diced

3 tablespoons tomato paste

¼ cup water

1 teaspoon freshly ground black pepper

¼ teaspoon kosher salt

1 tablespoon minced fresh basil

1 tablespoon minced fresh Italian parsley

1 tablespoon minced fresh oregano

1. Place all ingredients into a 4-quart slow cooker. Stir. Cook on low for 4 hours. Stir before serving.

Saving on Herbs

The cost of herbs can add up quickly, but you can save a little money by shopping at an international farmers market or buying a blend of spices (an Italian blend would work well in this recipe) instead of buying each individually.

Spicy Red Lentil Dal

Reduce the amount of jalapeño, or omit it completely for a not-so-spicy version.

INGREDIENTS | SERVES 4

1 tablespoon olive oil

1 medium onion, peeled and diced

3 garlic cloves, minced

1 cup dried red lentils, picked over and rinsed

1 teaspoon ground turmeric

1 teaspoon ground cumin

½ teaspoon ground ginger

2 cups Vegetable Broth (see Chapter 4)

1 teaspoon kosher salt, plus more to taste

¼ teaspoon ground black pepper, plus more to taste

2 cups basmati rice, cooked

2 plum tomatoes, seeded and diced

¼ cup chopped fresh cilantro leaves

1 jalapeño pepper, seeded and diced (optional)

1. Heat the oil in a large skillet over medium-high heat. Add the onion. Cook, stirring frequently, until onions are tender, about 5 minutes. Add garlic; stir and cook for another minute. Transfer mixture to a 4-quart slow cooker.

2. Stir in lentils, turmeric, cumin, ginger, and broth. Cover and cook on high for 2 hours or until lentils are tender. If the broth hasn't been completely absorbed, leave cover ajar and cook on high for up to 30 more minutes. Stir in the salt and pepper. Taste and add more salt and/or pepper if needed.

3. Serve dal over the rice, topped with tomatoes, cilantro, and jalapeño pepper, if desired.

Pareve Palak Paneer

Palak paneer is an Indian spinach dish with cubes of paneer cheese. In this pareve version, tofu is used. For a dairy alternative, substitute store-bought paneer or Easy Paneer (see sidebar) for the tofu, and evaporated milk for the almond milk–cream "cheese" mixture.

INGREDIENTS | SERVES 4

Cooking spray

2 tablespoons olive oil

1 small onion, minced

2 garlic cloves, minced

1 tablespoon tomato paste

1 tablespoon curry powder

½ teaspoon ground ginger

1 teaspoon ground cumin

½ teaspoon ground turmeric

2 (10-ounce) packages frozen chopped spinach, defrosted

½ cup almond milk

2 tablespoons pareve cream cheese (such as Better Than Cream Cheese)

1 (12-ounce) package firm or extra-firm tofu, cut into ½" cubes

1 teaspoon kosher salt, plus more if needed

¼ teaspoon cayenne pepper

2 cups cooked basmati rice

1. Spray the inside of a 4-quart slow cooker with the cooking spray.

2. Heat the oil in a large skillet over medium heat. Add the onion and sauté for 5 minutes, stirring frequently, until the onion is softened. Add the garlic and stir for another 30 seconds.

3. Add the tomato paste, curry, ginger, cumin, and turmeric and stir for an additional 30 seconds. Scrape the mixture into the prepared slow cooker. Stir in the spinach. Cover and cook on low for 4 hours.

4. Using an immersion blender, purée the spinach mixture.

5. In a medium bowl, whisk together the almond milk and cream cheese until smooth. Stir the mixture into the slow cooker along with the tofu, salt, and cayenne pepper. Cover and cook for an additional 15 minutes. Taste and add more salt if needed. Serve over the basmati rice.

Easy Paneer

Grease an 8" × 8" cake pan with 1 tablespoon butter. Press the contents of a 15-ounce container of ricotta cheese evenly into the pan. Bake at 350°F for 30–40 minutes or until the cheese dries out and just starts to brown. Remove from oven and let cool enough to handle. Cut into ½" cubes. Cover and refrigerate up to 3 days if not using right away.

Ratatouille

Serve this flavorful entrée with crusty bread to soak up the delicious juices.

INGREDIENTS | SERVES 12

3 tablespoons olive oil, divided

1 large eggplant, peeled and cut into ½" cubes

3 cups yellow squash, cut into ½" cubes

½ pound green beans, cut into 1" pieces

1 (10-ounce) package mushrooms, cleaned and quartered

½ cup celery, chopped

1 cup red onion, chopped

4 cloves garlic, chopped

1 (28-ounce) can diced tomatoes, undrained

¼ teaspoon salt

1 teaspoon fresh rosemary, minced (or ½ teaspoon dried)

1 teaspoon fresh thyme leaves, minced (or ½ teaspoon dried)

¼ cup white wine (optional)

¼ cup flat-leafed parsley, chopped

2 tablespoons balsamic vinegar

1. Grease a 3- or 4-quart slow cooker with ½ tablespoon of olive oil. Add remaining oil and remaining ingredients except parsley and balsamic vinegar.

2. Cook on low for 4–6 hours. Uncover; add parsley and balsamic vinegar. Re-cover and increase heat to high for 15–30 minutes. Serve hot or warm.

Flat-Leaf Parsley

Flat-leaf parsley, also known as Italian parsley, is more flavorful than curly-leaf.

Eggplant and Spinach with Red Curry Paste

Despite the long list of ingredients, this is an easy dish to whip up. Serve with brown or white rice.

INGREDIENTS | SERVES 6

1 tablespoon olive oil

1 small onion, peeled, cut in half and thinly sliced

2 garlic cloves, minced

2 teaspoons ground ginger

2 teaspoons garam masala

2 teaspoons ground cumin

½ teaspoon ground coriander

2 tablespoons Thai red curry paste

4 Japanese eggplants cut into 1" chunks

2 (10-ounce) packages frozen chopped spinach, defrosted and squeezed dry

1 (15-ounce) can fire-roasted diced tomatoes, undrained

¼ cup light coconut milk

2 teaspoons kosher salt, plus more if needed

⅛ teaspoon cayenne pepper, plus more if needed

1. Heat oil in a large skillet over medium-high heat. Add onion and cook, stirring frequently, for 5 minutes or until softened. Add the garlic and stir for 30 more seconds.

2. Add the ginger, garam masala, cumin, coriander, and red curry paste; stir for another 30 seconds.

3. Add eggplant and spinach. Stir to coat with the spices. Stir in the diced tomatoes. Transfer to a 4-quart slow cooker. Cover and cook on low for 4–6 hours.

4. Stir in the coconut milk, salt, and cayenne pepper. Cook for an additional 15 minutes. Taste and add more salt and pepper, if needed.

Thai Red Curry Paste

Kosher red curry paste is a combination of chili peppers, garlic, lemongrass, and other herbs and spices. Despite its name, there is no curry powder in it. It is available at large supermarkets, Asian grocery stores, and by mail order. Or you could use a mixture of 1 teaspoon of lime juice and 1½ tablespoons of chili-garlic sauce (such as Huy Fong), which is not exactly the same thing but will be delicious nonetheless.

CHAPTER 10

Side Dishes

Rice-Stuffed Peppers

Try a mixture of green, red, orange, and yellow peppers for this dish.

INGREDIENTS | SERVES 4

4 large bell peppers of uniform size

½ teaspoon ground chipotle pepper

¼ teaspoon hot Mexican chili powder

¼ teaspoon black pepper

½ teaspoon kosher salt

1 (15-ounce) can fire-roasted diced tomatoes with garlic

1 cup cooked long-grain rice

1½ cups broccoli florets

¼ cup finely diced onion

½ cup water

Cooked Rice Shortcut

Next time you cook up a batch of rice, double the amount needed. Spoon cooled leftover rice into a freezer bag. Flatten bag, label the quantity and freeze. Next time a recipe calls for cooked rice simply defrost in the microwave and continue with the recipe.

1. Cut the tops off of each pepper to form a cap. Remove the seeds from the cap. Remove the seeds and most of the ribs from inside the pepper.

2. Place the peppers, open side up, in a 4- or 6-quart slow cooker.

3. In a medium bowl, mix the spices, tomatoes, rice, broccoli, and onion. Spoon the mixture into each pepper until it is filled to the top. Replace the cap.

4. Pour the water into the bottom of the slow cooker insert. Cook on low for 6 hours.

Spiced "Baked" Eggplant

Make this a main dish by serving over rice.

INGREDIENTS | SERVES 4

1 pound eggplant, cubed

⅓ cup onion, sliced

½ teaspoon red pepper flakes

½ teaspoon crushed rosemary

¼ cup lemon juice

1. Place all ingredients in a 1½- to 2-quart slow cooker. Cook on low for 3 hours, or until the eggplant is tender.

Cold Snap

Take care not to put a cold ceramic slow cooker insert directly into the slow cooker. The sudden shift in temperature can cause it to crack. If you want to prepare your ingredients the night before use, refrigerate them in reusable containers, not in the insert.

Savory "Creamed" Spinach

Fresh spinach reduces greatly when cooked, so to get a bigger bang for your buck, use frozen spinach when possible.

INGREDIENTS | SERVES 6

1 tablespoon margarine

1 clove garlic, minced

1 tablespoon flour

1 cup unsweetened rice milk or soymilk

½ teaspoon salt

½ teaspoon crushed red pepper

½ teaspoon dried sage

2 (12-ounce) packages frozen spinach, thawed and drained well

1. Melt the margarine in a 2-quart slow cooker over low heat. Add the garlic and sauté for 2 minutes before stirring in the flour.

2. Slowly pour in the rice milk or soymilk and whisk until all lumps are removed.

3. Add all remaining ingredients. Stir and cook over low heat for 1–2 hours. If desired, purée with an immersion blender before serving.

Variations

Make this savory dish even richer by adding a sprinkling of pareve cheese such as Daiya Mozzarella Style Shreds.

"Creamed" Spinach

*Finally! A great-tasting pareve version of a side dish traditionally
served alongside roast beef or with Thanksgiving dinner.*

INGREDIENTS | SERVES 6

2 pounds baby spinach, rinsed, drained,
and coarsely chopped

1 cup soy or rice milk

1 small onion, finely diced

1 clove garlic, minced

1 tablespoon olive oil

½ teaspoon nutmeg

½ teaspoon kosher salt, plus more to
taste

¼ teaspoon pepper, plus more to taste

½ cup pareve sour cream or cream
cheese

Slurry of 1 tablespoon flour mixed with 1
tablespoon water

1. Combine everything except the sour cream or cream
   cheese and flour slurry in a 4-quart slow cooker. Cover
   and cook on low for 4 hours.

2. Uncover and stir in pareve sour cream or cream
   cheese and flour slurry. Re-cover and continue to cook
   on low for another 15–30 minutes or until heated
   through.

3. Taste and add additional salt and/or pepper if
   necessary. If too watery, continue to cook, uncovered,
   for up to an additional 30 minutes. If desired, purée the
   mixture using an immersion blender before serving.

Sweet Potatoes with Coconut Milk

This is an alternative to that marshmallow-studded side dish.
The peanuts can be omitted if there are allergy issues.

INGREDIENTS | SERVES 4

Nonstick cooking spray
3 pounds sweet potatoes
⅓ packed cup brown sugar
1 cup coconut milk
¼ cup shredded coconut
½ cup chopped peanuts

Yams versus Sweet Potatoes

Yams and sweet potatoes are so close that they can be used interchangeably in cooking. Sweet potatoes are a rich orange inside and have a deeper brown skin. They're also by far the sweeter of the two. Both tubers are very high in soluble fiber. To add extra fiber, sprinkle them with nuts, cook them with apples, or mix them with sweet green peas.

1. Spray the inside of a 4-quart slow cooker with nonstick spray.

2. Peel sweet potatoes and slice them into ½"-thick rounds.

3. Overlap the sweet potato slices in prepared cooker. Sprinkle evenly with the brown sugar.

4. Pour the coconut milk over the sweet potatoes, then sprinkle them with shredded coconut.

5. Cover and cook on low for 6–8 hours. Serve hot, topped with chopped peanuts.

Scalloped Winter Vegetables

White and sweet potatoes add a pleasing visual contrast to this recipe. Replace the butter with olive oil and the evaporated milk with soy or rice milk for a pareve alternative.

INGREDIENTS | SERVES 6

3 tablespoons olive oil, divided

2 russet potatoes, peeled and thinly sliced

2 sweet potatoes, peeled and thinly sliced

1 medium parsnip, peeled and sliced

1 medium turnip, peeled and sliced

3 tablespoons all-purpose flour

½ teaspoon salt

¼ teaspoon pepper

1 cup evaporated milk (low-fat or fat-free)

1 medium onion, chopped

Storing Potatoes

Don't store potatoes or sweet potatoes in the refrigerator or their starches will convert to sugar, which will make the potatoes taste too sweet. Instead, keep them in a cool, dark, well-ventilated place, such as a root cellar or cabinet.

1. Grease a 3- to 4-quart slow cooker with ½ tablespoon of the olive oil.

2. Add russet potatoes, sweet potatoes, parsnip, and turnip; stir to combine.

3. In a small saucepan, heat remaining olive oil over medium heat; whisk in flour, salt, and pepper to make a roux. Continue to whisk constantly for 1 minute. Gradually whisk in evaporated milk, cooking over low heat.

4. Bring milk to a boil, stirring constantly, until milk has thickened into a sauce, about 6–8 minutes. Remove from heat.

5. Arrange half of the sliced vegetables in casserole dish; top with half of the chopped onion and half of the white sauce; repeat to make second layer. Cover and cook on low for 3–4 hours. Serve hot.

Broccoli Amandine

A simple yet delicious way to serve broccoli.

INGREDIENTS | SERVES 4

1 (16-ounce) bag frozen broccoli florets

2 teaspoons olive oil

1 teaspoon kosher salt

¼ teaspoon black pepper

1 tablespoon lemon juice

¼ cup sliced or slivered toasted almonds

1. Place the broccoli florets in a 2-quart heat-safe covered casserole dish. Microwave on full power for 3 minutes to defrost completely.

2. Transfer broccoli to a 4-quart slow cooker. Add the olive oil, salt, pepper, and lemon juice. Cover and cook on high for 45 minutes or until broccoli is tender. Serve sprinkled evenly with the toasted almonds.

Corn Bread

Corn bread is the perfect accompaniment to chili or soup.

INGREDIENTS | SERVES 8

Cooking spray

1½ cups stone-ground cornmeal

¾ cup all-purpose flour

1 cup soymilk or rice milk

1 tablespoon sugar

¼ teaspoon salt

1 cup corn kernels (if frozen, defrost before using)

3½ tablespoons vegetable oil

2 eggs

1. Spray a 4-quart round slow cooker with cooking spray.

2. In a medium bowl, whisk together remaining ingredients.

3. Pour the batter into the slow cooker and cook on high for 2 hours. Slice the corn bread and lift out the slices.

A Bit about Corn Bread

Corn bread is a generic name for quick breads made with cornmeal. In the northern states, corn bread is generally sweet and made with yellow cornmeal. In the South, corn bread is traditionally unsweetened and made with white cornmeal.

Spiced Cauliflower, Potatoes, and Peas

This Indian-inspired vegetable dish has spicy flavor, not spicy heat.

INGREDIENTS | SERVES 4

Cooking spray

1 head cauliflower, rinsed and cut into 1" chunks

1 large potato, peeled and diced

1 medium onion, peeled and diced

½ cup frozen peas, completely defrosted

1 teaspoon ground ginger

3 cloves garlic, minced

1 teaspoon ground cumin

2 teaspoons chili powder

1 tablespoon garam masala

2 teaspoons kosher salt

½ teaspoon turmeric powder

1 tablespoon vegetable oil

¼ cup packed fresh cilantro leaves

1. Spray the inside of a 4- to 6-quart slow cooker with cooking spray.

2. Add all the ingredients except cilantro to the slow cooker; stir until well combined.

3. Cover and cook on low for 3 hours. Transfer to serving dish and top with the cilantro leaves.

Garam Masala

Garam Masala (pronounced GAH-ram Ma-SAH-lah) is an aromatic mixture of many different spices. If none is available, substitute with ½ teaspoon each of cumin, coriander, cardamom, black pepper, and cinnamon, ¼ teaspoon nutmeg, and ⅛ teaspoon cloves.

Citrusy Beets

Beets can be served as a warm side dish or a chilled salad over a bed of greens.

INGREDIENTS | SERVES 4

12 baby beets, halved, ends trimmed
1 cup orange juice
Juice of ½ lime
¼ red onion, sliced
½ teaspoon pepper

1. Add all ingredients to a 2- or 4-quart slow cooker and cook on low for 4 hours.

Cauliflower Curry

Serve as a side dish, or over rice for a filling pareve meal.

INGREDIENTS | SERVES 4

Cooking spray
Florets from 1 head of cauliflower (about 2 cups), rinsed and drained
1 (15-ounce) can diced tomatoes, drained
1 medium onion, peeled and diced
1 large baking potato, peeled and cut into 1" cubes
1 cup low-fat coconut milk
1½ teaspoons curry powder
½ teaspoon ground coriander
½ teaspoon ground cinnamon
¼ teaspoon black pepper
⅛ teaspoon crushed red pepper
1 teaspoon kosher salt
1 cup frozen peas, defrosted

1. Spray the inside of a 4-quart slow cooker with cooking spray.

2. Add cauliflower, tomatoes, onion, and potato to prepared cooker.

3. In a medium bowl, mix the remaining ingredients except the peas together and pour over vegetables in slow cooker.

4. Cover and cook on low for 4–6 hours or until the cauliflower is tender.

5. Uncover and stir in peas. Re-cover and cook on low heat setting for 10–15 minutes or until peas are heated through.

Rosemary Fingerling Potatoes

Fingerling potatoes are small, long potatoes that look a little like fingers.
Use new potatoes if fingerlings are unavailable.

INGREDIENTS | SERVES 6

2 tablespoons olive oil
1½ pounds fingerling potatoes
1 teaspoon salt
¼ teaspoon black pepper
2 tablespoons fresh rosemary, chopped
1 tablespoon fresh lemon juice

1. Add the olive oil, potatoes, salt, and pepper to a 4-quart slow cooker. Cover and cook on low heat for 3–4 hours or on high for 1½–2 hours. Potatoes are done when they can be easily pierced with a fork.

2. Remove the cover and mix in the rosemary and lemon juice.

Time Saver

To save on time when cooking potatoes, cut them into the smallest pieces the recipe will allow and cook at the highest temperature. For this recipe, you can quarter the potatoes and cook on high heat.

Rosemary-Garlic Mashed Potatoes

Slow-cooked mashed potatoes are the perfect side for busy holiday cooks. Not only does this dish leave a burner free for other cooking, there is no need to boil the potatoes before mashing them.

INGREDIENTS | SERVES 10

3 pounds red skin potatoes, quartered
4 cloves garlic, minced
¾ cup Vegetable Broth (see Chapter 4)
1 tablespoon minced fresh rosemary
2 teaspoons salt
¼ cup unsweetened rice milk or soymilk
1 tablespoon pareve margarine
⅓ cup pareve sour cream

1. Place the potatoes in a 4-quart slow cooker. Add garlic, broth, rosemary, and salt. Stir.

2. Cover and cook on high until potatoes are tender, about 3–4 hours.

3. Add the rice milk or soymilk, margarine, and pareve sour cream. Mash with a potato masher.

Dill Red Potatoes

Fresh dill is the perfect herb to season a summer dish.

INGREDIENTS | SERVES 6

2 tablespoons extra-virgin olive oil

1½ pounds red potatoes

1 teaspoon salt

¼ teaspoon black pepper

2 tablespoons fresh dill, chopped

1 tablespoon fresh lemon juice

1. Add the olive oil, potatoes, salt, and pepper to a 4-quart slow cooker. Cover, and cook on low heat for 3–4 hours or high heat for 1½–2 hours. Potatoes are done when they can easily be pierced with a fork.

2. Remove the cover and mix in the dill and lemon juice.

Sweet Potato Salad

This salad, like many others, can be served warm and straight out of the slow cooker or chilled before serving.

INGREDIENTS | SERVES 6

3 tablespoons olive oil

1 onion, chopped

3 cloves garlic, minced

1 pound sweet potatoes, peeled and cubed

½ teaspoon dried ginger

½ teaspoon paprika

1 teaspoon cumin

1 teaspoon salt

¼ teaspoon black pepper

1 tablespoon fresh lemon juice

¼ cup fresh parsley, chopped

1. Add the olive oil to a 4-quart slow cooker and sauté the onion and garlic on high heat until they are golden brown, about 2–3 minutes.

2. Add the rest of the ingredients except for the lemon juice and parsley. Cover and cook on low heat for 4 hours.

3. Mix the lemon juice and parsley into the sweet potato salad.

Potato Peels

For most recipes, it's the cook's personal preference whether or not to leave the skins on or peel them. Although in this recipe either way works fine, consider leaving them on—the 2 grams of fiber per serving contained in the skin equals or exceeds the amount in many whole-grain foods.

Maple-Glazed Sweet Potatoes

You can reduce the amount of sugar in this very easy recipe by using a no-sugar-added syrup.

INGREDIENTS | SERVES 4

4 cups sweet potatoes, cubed

2 tablespoons butter or margarine

¼ cup maple syrup

⅓ cup chopped pecans

Recipe Substitutions

It's okay to use inexpensive pancake syrup instead of pure maple syrup in this recipe. It won't be as flavorful as pure maple syrup, but it will do the job.

1. Add all ingredients to a 4-quart slow cooker. Cover and cook on low heat for 4–5 hours.

Garlic-Parsley Potatoes

The ingredients are similar to mashed potatoes in this dish, but you enjoy a stronger potato flavor by leaving them in bigger pieces.

INGREDIENTS | SERVES 8

½ cup margarine

6 cloves garlic, minced

1 onion, diced

1½ pounds red potatoes, quartered

½ cup unsweetened soymilk or rice milk

1 teaspoon salt

¼ teaspoon black pepper

¼ cup packed parsley leaves, chopped

1 tablespoon fresh lemon juice

1. Add the margarine to a 4-quart slow cooker and sauté the garlic and onion on high heat until they are golden brown, about 2–3 minutes.

2. Add the rest of the ingredients except for the parsley and lemon juice. Cover and cook on low heat for 4–5 hours.

3. Mix in the parsley and lemon and serve.

Mediterranean Chickpeas

*Chickpeas, also known as garbanzo beans, are the main ingredient
in this delicious dish that can be served hot or cold.*

INGREDIENTS | SERVES 8

2 (15-ounce) cans chickpeas, drained

1 cup water

2 teaspoons kosher salt

¼ cup extra-virgin olive oil

1 teaspoon black pepper

1 cup fresh basil, chopped

5 cloves garlic, minced

2 tomatoes, diced

½ cup kalamata olives, sliced

1. Add all ingredients to a 4-quart slow cooker. Cover and cook on low heat for 4 hours.

Caramelized Onions

*Caramelized onions are a great addition to roasts, dips, soups, and sandwiches.
Make in advance to speed up recipes that call for long sautéing time.
Substitute margarine for the butter or use all vegetable oil for a pareve version.*

INGREDIENTS | YIELDS 4 CUPS

4 pounds Vidalia or other sweet onions

3 tablespoons butter, thinly sliced

3 tablespoons vegetable oil

Storing Caramelized Onions

Store caramelized onions in an airtight container. They will keep up to 2 weeks refrigerated or up to 6 months frozen. If frozen, defrost overnight in the refrigerator before using.

1. Peel and slice the onions in ¼" slices. Separate slices into rings.

2. Place the onions into a 4-quart slow cooker. Scatter butter or margarine slices over top of the onions and drizzle with vegetable oil. Cover and cook on low for 10 hours.

3. If after 10 hours the onions are wet, turn the slow cooker up to high and cook uncovered for an additional 30 minutes, or until the liquid evaporates.

Orange-Glazed Carrots

Serve as an appetizer or accompaniment to a roasted meat entrée.

INGREDIENTS | SERVES 10

2 tablespoons olive oil, divided

2 pounds fresh baby carrots

¼ packed cup dark brown sugar

1 teaspoon grated fresh ginger (or ½ teaspoon ground)

½ cup raisins (or dried cranberries)

Juice and zest of 3 large oranges

1. Grease a 4- or 6-quart slow cooker with ½ tablespoon of the olive oil.

2. Arrange baby carrots on bottom of prepared cooker. Stir in brown sugar, ginger, raisins, orange juice and zest and remaining olive oil.

3. Cover and cook on high for 2–4 hours. If sauce is too liquidy, remove cover and cook for another half hour on high. Serve hot.

Spicy Eggplant

No need for Chinese takeout! Serve this dish with the Hot and Sour Soup (Chapter 4) and Teriyaki Chicken (Chapter 5). Reduce the heat by halving the amount of chili paste.

INGREDIENTS | SERVES 6–8

Cooking spray

6 Japanese eggplants, rinsed and cubed

2 tablespoons balsamic vinegar

1 tablespoon hoisin sauce

1 tablespoon vegetable oil

1 teaspoon chili paste, such as Sambal Oelek

2 cloves garlic, minced

1 tablespoon sesame seeds

2 scallions, green parts only, chopped

1. Lightly spray the inside of a 4-quart slow cooker with the cooking spray. Add the cubed eggplant.

2. In a medium bowl, mix the remaining ingredients except the sesame seeds and scallions and pour over the eggplant cubes. Cover and cook on low for 4–6 hours or until eggplant is very tender.

3. Transfer eggplant to a serving dish. Sprinkle on the sesame seeds and chopped scallion before serving.

Japanese Eggplants

Japanese eggplants, also known as baby eggplants, have thinner and more tender skins than the larger variety. There is no need to peel them, which saves prep time.

Acorn Squash with Walnuts

This recipe can also be made with pecans instead of walnuts.

INGREDIENTS | SERVES 4

2 acorn squash, halved and seeded

¼ packed cup dark brown sugar

½ teaspoon ground cinnamon

½ teaspoon kosher salt

4 tablespoons butter or margarine, softened

2 tablespoons toasted chopped walnuts

1. Place acorn squash halves cut side up in a 6-quart slow cooker.

2. In a medium bowl, combine remaining ingredients. Spoon resulting mixture evenly into center of each squash half.

3. Cook on high for 3–4 hours or on low for 5–6 hours, or until squash is tender.

Marsala Glazed Mushrooms

You can use any red wine, but the nutty taste of marsala wine goes perfectly with mushrooms.

INGREDIENTS | SERVES 4

2 pounds white button mushrooms, cleaned and sliced

2 garlic cloves, minced

2 tablespoons olive oil

½ teaspoon kosher salt, plus more to taste

¼ teaspoon black pepper, plus more to taste

1 teaspoon finely chopped fresh rosemary

1 teaspoon finely chopped fresh sage

2 tablespoons marsala wine

¼ cup chopped fresh parsley leaves

1. Mix all ingredients except the wine and parsley in a 4-quart slow cooker.

2. Cover and cook on low for 2–4 hours. Uncover and cook on low for another 30 minutes to allow excess moisture to evaporate. Add the wine and continue to cook uncovered for another 15 minutes.

3. Transfer to serving bowl and sprinkle evenly with chopped parsley.

CHAPTER 11

Great Grains and Beans

Cassoulet

Besides chicken, sausage is a traditional ingredient in this dish.
If kosher sausage is not available in your area, simply omit it.

INGREDIENTS | SERVES 10

Nonstick spray

2 tablespoons olive oil

1 large onion, diced

1 carrot, finely chopped

1 stalk celery, finely chopped

3 garlic cloves, minced

1 (12- to 16-ounce package) spicy or sweet kosher sausage, cut into 1" lengths

2 tablespoons tomato paste

1 teaspoon dried thyme (or 1 tablespoon fresh thyme, minced)

2 (12-ounce) cans chicken broth, low-sodium preferred

1 cup dry white wine

1 whole chicken, cut into quarters or eighths, most of skin removed

3 (15-ounce) cans great northern beans, drained and rinsed

1. Spray the inside of a 6-quart slow cooker with nonstick spray.

2. Heat the olive oil over medium heat in a large skillet. When hot, add the onion, carrot, celery, and garlic. Cook until the vegetables are just beginning to soften, stirring often, about 5 minutes.

3. Add sausage and continue to cook, stirring often, for another 3–5 minutes or until sausage just starts to brown. Stir in the tomato paste, thyme, chicken broth, and wine. Remove from heat.

4. Carefully pour about a third of the sauce into prepared slow cooker. Arrange the chicken in the sauce, overlapping pieces to fit. Pour beans over chicken, then pour remaining sauce over everything else. Cover and cook for 4–6 hours on low until the beans and meats are both tender.

Cassoulet

Named for its cooking vessel, the cassole, cassoulet is a rich, slow-cooked white bean casserole that originated in the south of France.

Parmesan Mushroom Risotto

The white wine adds a gourmet touch to this dairy dish, but if you prefer, the wine can be replaced with an equal amount of water.

INGREDIENTS | SERVES 6

1 teaspoon olive oil

½ cup finely diced onion

2 cloves garlic, minced

8 ounces sliced mushrooms, any variety

2 cups Vegetable Broth (see Chapter 4)

2 cups Arborio rice

2 cups water

½ cup dry white wine

½ teaspoon salt

¼ cup grated Parmesan cheese

1 tablespoon butter, softened

2 tablespoons minced parsley leaves (for garnish)

Additional ¼ cup Parmesan cheese (for garnish)

1. Heat the oil in a nonstick pan. Sauté the onion, garlic, and mushrooms until soft, about 4–5 minutes.

2. Add ½ cup broth and the rice and cook until the liquid is fully absorbed, about 5 minutes.

3. Transfer the rice mixture into a 4-quart slow cooker. Sir in the water, wine, salt, and remaining broth.

4. Cover and cook on high for 1½–2 hours or until all the liquid has been absorbed. Stir in Parmesan cheese and butter. Sprinkle with parsley and/or additional Parmesan cheese, if desired, before serving.

Wild Mushroom Risotto

This makes a great side dish, but you can also try it as a main course, paired with a green salad.

INGREDIENTS | SERVES 6

1 teaspoon olive oil

¼ cup finely diced shallot

2 cloves garlic, minced

8 ounces sliced assorted wild mushrooms

2 cups Vegetable Broth (see Chapter 4)

2 cups Arborio rice

3 cups water

½ teaspoon salt

1. Heat the oil in a small skillet. Sauté the shallot, garlic, and mushrooms until soft, about 4–5 minutes.

2. Add ½ cup broth and the rice and cook until the liquid is fully absorbed, about 5 minutes.

3. Scrape the rice mixture into a 4-quart slow cooker. Add the water, salt, and remaining broth.

4. Cover and cook on low for 1 hour. Stir before serving.

Arborio Rice

Arborio rice is an Italian short-grained rice traditionally used in making risotto. If Arborio rice is not available, use any medium or short-grained rice. Do not substitute long-grained because it will become mushy.

Boston Baked Beans

Serve these at your next cookout or over the pareve version of
Boston Brown Bread (see recipe in this chapter).

INGREDIENTS | SERVES 8

1 large sweet onion, peeled and diced

3 (15-ounce) cans cannellini, great northern, or navy beans, drained and rinsed

1 cup barbecue sauce

½ cup molasses

1 teaspoon dry mustard powder

1 (1.5- to 2-ounce) package kosher beef jerky, finely chopped

Salt, to taste

1. Add all ingredients to a 4-quart slow cooker. Stir until combined.

2. Cover and cook on low heat for 6 hours. Taste for seasoning and add additional salt, if needed.

Kosher Beef Jerky

Kosher beef jerky is available in the kosher aisle of larger supermarkets, many butchers, and via mail order. It comes in several varieties: use original, hickory, or the flavor you prefer. Bacos can be substituted—use ¼ cup of the chips style.

Boston Brown Bread

Replace the buttermilk with soymilk mixed with 1 tablespoon lemon juice for a pareve version.

INGREDIENTS | SERVES 20

3 empty 16-ounce cans
Nonstick cooking spray, as needed
Bamboo skewers, to fit slow cooker
½ cup rye flour
½ cup all-purpose flour
½ cup cornmeal
1 tablespoon sugar
½ teaspoon baking powder
½ teaspoon baking soda
½ teaspoon cinnamon
½ cup sweetened dried cranberries
½ teaspoon ground ginger
1 cup buttermilk
⅓ cup molasses
Water, as needed

Boston Brown Bread

Boston brown bread is traditionally steamed in cans, making it perfect for the slow cooker.

1. Spray the insides of the 3 empty cans with cooking spray. Place a layer of bamboo skewers on the bottom of a 6-quart slow cooker.

2. In a medium bowl, whisk together the flours, cornmeal, sugar, baking powder, baking soda, cinnamon, cranberries, and ginger. Set the mixture aside.

3. In another bowl, stir together the buttermilk and molasses. Pour into the dry mixture and stir until combined.

4. Evenly divide the dough among the 3 cans. Cover each can with foil; stand the cans inside the slow cooker. Add water until it is halfway up the sides of the cans. Cook on low for 4–5 hours or until a toothpick inserted into the bread comes out clean.

5. Carefully remove the cans and allow them to cool for 5 minutes. Then gently tap the cans and remove the bread. Allow the bread to cool on a wire rack. Slice them into 20 slices.

Barley and Mushrooms

Barley is a great food to eat when you want to feel full because it absorbs more liquid during cooking than other grains. That's why it's such a favorite in soups. It's also a highly digestible fiber.

INGREDIENTS | SERVES 4

4 tablespoons olive oil, divided

1 cup uncooked barley

1½ cups diced onion

1 (10-ounce) package mushrooms, cleaned and sliced

1 teaspoon kosher salt

¼ teaspoon pepper

2 (12-ounce) cans beef broth, low-sodium preferred

½ cup chopped Italian flat-leafed parsley (for garnish)

1. Coat the inside of a 3- or 4-quart slow cooker with ½ tablespoon of the olive oil.

2. Heat 1 tablespoon olive oil over medium heat in a large skillet. When hot, add the barley and cook, stirring often, until it begins to smell toasty, about 2 minutes. Transfer the barley to the slow cooker.

3. Heat remaining oil in the same skillet over medium-high heat. Add the onion and mushrooms. Sauté until the onions soften and begin to brown. Add both vegetables to the cooker along with the salt, pepper, and beef broth.

4. Cover and cook on low for 4–6 hours.

5. If there is too much liquid in the slow cooker, uncover and cook on high for an additional 30 minutes. Serve garnished with parsley.

Baked Barley Porridge with Cheddar Cheese, Chives, and Apples

Soy sauce is an unexpected ingredient in this recipe, but it adds a welcome savory flavor and nutty color to the porridge.

INGREDIENTS | SERVES 4

Cooking spray
1 cup pearl barley
2 cups water
2 cups low-fat or fat-free milk
½ cup chopped dried apples
1 tablespoon reduced-sodium soy sauce
½ cup shredded reduced-fat Cheddar cheese
2 tablespoons chopped chives

1. Spray the inside of a 3- or 4-quart slow cooker with cooking spray.

2. Heat a medium-sized frying pan over medium heat, then add the barley. Stir constantly for a minute or two until barley just begins to toast and smell nutty.

3. Immediately remove from heat and place mixture in prepared slow cooker. Carefully pour in the water and milk.

4. Stir in the apples and soy sauce.

5. Cover and cook on low for 8–9 hours. Sprinkle the cheese over the top, then cover and cook an additional 15 minutes or until the cheese melts.

6. Sprinkle with chives. Serve hot.

Mushroom-Barley Amandine

The nutty flavor of barley is accented by two kinds of almonds in this recipe. Replace the butter with an additional 2½ tablespoons olive oil for a pareve version.

INGREDIENTS | SERVES 8

2½ tablespoons butter, divided
1 tablespoon olive oil
½ cup slivered almonds
1 onion, chopped
3 cloves garlic, minced
1 (8-ounce) package sliced mushrooms
1½ cups medium pearl barley
3 cups vegetable broth
½ cup sliced almonds

1. Grease a 3- or 4-quart slow cooker with ½ tablespoon butter.

2. In a large skillet, melt the remaining butter with the olive oil over medium heat. Add the slivered almonds and cook just until starting to brown, about 2 minutes; remove with a slotted spoon and set aside.

3. Add the onion, garlic, and mushrooms to the skillet; sauté until onions just start to brown and mushrooms reduce, about 6–8 minutes. Add the barley and stir until coated.

4. Add the broth and toasted almonds to the pan; bring to a simmer. Transfer the mixture to the prepared slow cooker and top with sliced almonds. Cook on low for 4–6 hours or until the barley is tender and the broth is absorbed.

Portobello Barley with Parmesan Cheese

This method of cooking barley makes this dairy dish as creamy as risotto but with the bonus of being high in fiber.

INGREDIENTS | SERVES 8

1 teaspoon olive oil

2 shallots, minced

2 cloves garlic, minced

3 Portobello mushroom caps, sliced

1 cup pearl barley

3¼ cups water

¼ teaspoon salt

½ teaspoon freshly ground black pepper

1 teaspoon crushed rosemary

1 teaspoon dried chervil

½ cup grated Parmesan cheese, divided

1. Heat the oil in a nonstick skillet. Sauté the shallots, garlic, and mushrooms until softened, about 4–5 minutes.

2. Place the mushroom mixture into a 4-quart slow cooker. Add the barley, water, salt, pepper, rosemary, and chervil. Stir. Cook on low for 8–9 hours or on high for 4 hours.

3. Turn off the slow cooker and stir in half the Parmesan cheese. Serve immediately, topped with the remaining Parmesan cheese.

Open-Faced Black Bean Burrito

Salsas come in many different flavors depending on which ingredients are used, but any type of salsa (except fruit-based salsa) will work in this recipe.

INGREDIENTS | SERVES 8

1 (16-ounce) bag dried black beans
Water, enough to cover beans by 1"
4 teaspoons salt, divided
1 tablespoon chili powder
2 teaspoons cumin
2 teaspoons garlic powder
1 teaspoon black pepper
1 (15-ounce) can corn, drained
2 fresh tomatoes, diced
8 large flour tortillas
4 cups cooked brown rice
2 cups shredded Cheddar cheese
2 cups salsa
¼ cup cilantro, chopped

Alternate Suggestions

Burrito fillings can easily be used in other dishes. Try the beans, rice, and toppings over a bed of lettuce for a taco salad, in soft corn tortillas for delicious tacos, or as a hearty meal on their own.

1. Rinse the black beans, then soak overnight. Drain the water, rinse again, then add to a large pot and cover with water. Boil on high heat for 10 minutes, then drain.

2. Add black beans, fresh water to cover by about 1 inch, and 2 teaspoons of salt to a 4-quart slow cooker. Cover and cook on medium heat for about 5–6 hours. Check the beans at about 5 hours to see if they are fork-tender and continue cooking if necessary.

3. Once the beans are done, drain in a colander and allow to cool to room temperature.

4. In a large bowl, mix the remaining salt, chili powder, cumin, garlic powder, black pepper, corn, and tomatoes.

5. Place a tortilla on a plate, add a scoop of the brown rice and then a scoop of the black bean mixture. Top with the cheese, salsa, and cilantro, if desired.

Middle Eastern Chicken

The small amount of crushed red pepper flakes in this recipe provides flavor, not heat.

INGREDIENTS | SERVES 6–8

Cooking spray

8 chicken thighs

2 cups boiling water, divided

1 (15-ounce) can diced tomatoes, drained

½ cup dried apricots, cut up

1 (15-ounce) can chickpeas, drained and rinsed

2 garlic cloves, minced

2 teaspoons ground cumin

1 teaspoon ground turmeric

½ teaspoon ground coriander

⅛ teaspoon crushed red pepper flakes

2 tablespoons lemon juice

1 cup uncooked Israeli couscous

1. Spray the inside of a 4- or 6-quart slow cooker with cooking spray.

2. Place chicken in the bottom of the slow cooker. Add 1 cup of the boiling water and the remaining ingredients except the lemon juice and the Israeli couscous.

3. Cover and cook on low for 5–6 hours. Stir in the lemon juice, the couscous, and the remaining boiling water. Re-cover and cook for an additional 10 minutes or until the couscous is tender. Serve hot.

Chana Masala

The main ingredient in this popular Indian dish is chickpeas. Serve with jasmine or basmati rice.

INGREDIENTS | SERVES 8

2 (15-ounce) cans chickpeas, drained and rinsed

1 cup water

4 teaspoons salt

¼ cup margarine

1 onion, diced

5 cloves garlic, minced

1 tablespoon cumin

½ teaspoon cayenne pepper

1 teaspoon ground turmeric

2 teaspoons sweet paprika

1 teaspoon garam masala

1 cup tomatoes, diced

1 lemon, juiced

2 teaspoons grated ginger

1. Add all ingredients to a 4-quart slow cooker. Cover and cook on low heat for 6 hours.

Indian Cuisine

Due to the size of India and its abundance of spices, Indian cuisine varies by region, community, and religion, but they are all similar. Herbs and spices such as coriander, curry powder, and garam masala are commonly used as well as rice and a variety of lentils.

Summer Vegetable Bean Salad

Serve this salad warm, straight out of the slow cooker, or chilled over a bed of lettuce.

INGREDIENTS | SERVES 8

1 (15-ounce) can black beans

1 (15-ounce) can red kidney beans

1 (15-ounce) can white beans

1 cup water

4 teaspoons salt

1 red onion, diced

1 green bell pepper, diced

1 red bell pepper, diced

¼ cup cilantro, chopped

½ cup red wine vinegar

½ cup extra-virgin olive oil

1 teaspoon black pepper

1. Add all ingredients to a 4-quart slow cooker. Cover and cook on low heat for 4 hours.

White Beans

Great northern beans, navy beans, and cannellini beans are all referred to as white beans. Each has its own unique qualities; cannellini beans work best if you want the bean to hold its shape and texture after a long cooking time.

Vegetarian Refried Beans

Besides served as a side dish, leftover refried beans can become a quick lunch!
Spoon into a flour tortilla, cover with shredded Cheddar cheese, and microwave
for 1 minute or until the cheese melts. Sprinkle with taco sauce, roll up, then serve.

INGREDIENTS | YIELDS ABOUT 2 CUPS

1 (16-ounce) bag dried pink or pinto beans

Water, as needed

2 teaspoons table salt

2 teaspoons garlic powder

1 teaspoon ground cumin

1 teaspoon chili powder

½ teaspoon kosher salt (or to taste)

Few drops hot sauce (or to taste)

1. Rinse the beans, then soak overnight. Drain the water, rinse again, then add to a large pot and cover with water. Boil on high heat for 10 minutes, then drain.

2. Add beans, fresh water to cover, and 2 teaspoons of table salt to a 4-quart slow cooker. Cover and cook on medium heat for about 5–6 hours. Check the beans at about 5 hours to see if they are very tender, and continue cooking if necessary.

3. Once the beans are done, drain in a colander and transfer to a large saucepan. Stir in the garlic powder, the cumin, the chili powder, the kosher salt, and the hot sauce.

4. Purée mixture with an immersion blender.

5. Place saucepan over medium heat and cook until mixture starts to boil. Immediately reduce heat to low and simmer, uncovered, for 10–15 minutes or until thickened slightly.

6. Remove from heat. The refried beans will continue to thicken more upon standing. Taste and add more salt, spices, and hot sauce, if needed. Serve warm.

Spinach with Chickpeas and Israeli Couscous

This pareve side dish can also be a light lunch for 4 people.

Toasted Almond Slivers or Slices

Toasting almonds, or nuts of any kind for that matter, really intensifies their flavor! Heat a small skillet over medium heat. Add almonds and sauté for 2 minutes or just until they start to lightly brown and become fragrant. Immediately transfer almonds to a heat-safe bowl to stop the browning process.

1. In a 4-quart slow cooker, add the chickpeas and cover with water by several inches. Soak overnight. The next day, drain and replace water. Cover and cook on low for 8 hours. Drain.

2. Heat olive oil in a small sauté pan over medium heat. Add garlic; stir for 30 seconds, then add couscous. Continue to stir for 2–3 minutes or just until couscous starts to brown.

3. Add the couscous mixture, the baby spinach, and the almonds to the slow cooker; stir to combine. Pour the boiling water over the mixture.

4. Cover and cook for 10 minutes or until couscous is tender. Stir in salt and pepper. Taste and add more salt and/or pepper if needed. Serve immediately.

Quinoa Pilaf

A tasty alternative to the more familiar rice pilaf.
Use vegetable broth instead of chicken broth for a pareve version.

INGREDIENTS | SERVES 8

4½ tablespoons olive oil, divided
1 medium onion, diced
1 carrot (or 4 baby carrots), chopped
1 celery rib, chopped
2 cups quinoa, rinsed well
2 (10-ounce) cans low-sodium chicken broth
½ teaspoon white pepper
1 bay leaf

1. Grease the inside of a 4-quart slow cooker with ½ tablespoon olive oil.

2. Heat remaining oil in a medium skillet over medium-high heat. When hot, add the onion, carrots, and celery; cook until the onions soften, about 5–6 minutes.

3. Add the quinoa to the skillet and cook until it just begins to become translucent, 3–4 minutes. Stir in broth and heat until it just starts to simmer, about 2–4 minutes.

4. Pour the quinoa mixture into prepared cooker. Stir in pepper and bay leaf.

5. Cover and cook on low heat for 3–4 hours or until quinoa is tender and broth is totally absorbed. Remove the bay leaf before serving.

Chicken and Rice

Brown rice, white rice, wild rice, or any combination will all work in this recipe.

INGREDIENTS | SERVES 8

2 tablespoons olive oil

1 cup mushrooms, sliced

½ cup onions, sliced

2 cups white rice, uncooked

2 tablespoons margarine

2 cups water

2 cups chicken broth

1 pound boneless, skinless chicken breast, cut into ½"-thick slices

½ teaspoon kosher salt

⅛ teaspoon black pepper

1. Add the olive oil to a 4-quart slow cooker and sauté the mushrooms and onions on high heat until browned, about 3–5 minutes.

2. Add the rest of the ingredients to the slow cooker. Cover and cook on low heat for 6 hours.

Beanie Weenies

If serving this dish to young children, slice the hot dog rounds into smiles (halves) to avoid a choking hazard.

INGREDIENTS | SERVES 8

1 tablespoon olive oil

1 large yellow onion, peeled and diced

1 (12-ounce) package frankfurters, sliced into ½" rounds

3 (15-ounce) cans navy or cannellini beans, drained and rinsed

½ cup barbecue sauce

¼ cup molasses

2 teaspoons yellow mustard

2 teaspoons Worcestershire sauce

1 bay leaf

1. Heat the oil in a large skillet over medium heat. Add the onion and cook, stirring frequently, for 5 minutes or until the onion softens. Push onions to the sides and add the sliced franks. Sauté until the franks brown, about 3–4 minutes.

2. Transfer frank mixture to the slow cooker; stir in remaining ingredients.

3. Cover and cook on low heat for 4 hours. Remove the bay leaf before serving.

Sloppy Beanie Weenies

For a fun way to serve the Beanie Weenies, ladle into hot dog buns. And keep a supply of paper towels handy!

Farro Salad with Feta

The farro in this salad is best at room temperature or lightly chilled. If made in advance, cover and chill; remove from refrigerator about a half hour before combining with remaining ingredients.

INGREDIENTS | SERVES 8

1 cup whole grain farro, rinsed and picked over

2 cups Vegetable Broth (see Chapter 4)

½ teaspoon kosher salt, or to taste

¼ teaspoon ground black pepper, or to taste

4 cups baby greens

1 cup grape or cherry tomatoes

8 ounces feta cheese, crumbled

¼ cup olive oil

2 tablespoons balsamic vinegar

2 teaspoons dried oregano or dill, for garnish

1. Add farro and broth to a 4-quart slow cooker. Cover and cook on high for 1½–2 hours, or until farro is tender and all of the broth is absorbed.

2. Fluff with a fork while mixing in the salt and pepper. Taste and add more salt and/or pepper if needed. Remove farro from cooker and allow to cool to room temperature.

3. Just before serving, divide greens among 8 salad bowls. Top each with farro, cherry tomatoes, and feta cheese. Whisk together the oil and the balsamic vinegar; drizzle over salads. Sprinkle with oregano or dill, if desired.

Farro

Farro is an ancient grain that is making a modern comeback. It has a look and nutty taste similar to brown rice. Be sure to buy whole grain and not the pearled variety, which will become mushy during the long cooking process. Farro is available in larger supermarkets and health food stores.

Cuban-Style Chicken with Black Beans

*Take the heat down a notch by halving the quantity of the chilies
in adobo sauce, or omitting them completely.*

INGREDIENTS | SERVES 4–6

2 (15-ounce) cans black beans, rinsed and drained

2 large sweet potatoes, peeled cut into 2" chunks

1 small red pepper, seeded and cut into ½" strips

4 garlic cloves, minced

2 tablespoons olive oil

1 whole chicken cut into eighths, most of the skin removed

2 teaspoons chopped chipotle chilies in adobo sauce

½ cup salsa

1 tablespoon paprika

1 cup Chicken Stock (see Chapter 4)

¼ cup fresh cilantro leaves, chopped

1. Combine black beans, sweet potatoes, red pepper, garlic, and olive oil in a 6-quart slow cooker. Place chicken on top of potato mixture.

2. Mix together the chipotle chilies, salsa, and paprika; spread over the chicken. Pour chicken stock on top. Cover and cook on low for 8 hours or on high for 4 hours.

3. Sprinkle with cilantro just before serving.

Greek-Style Kasha and Lentils

The feta cheese can be omitted for a pareve side dish.

INGREDIENTS | SERVES 4

Cooking spray

2 eggs, lightly beaten

2 cups medium or coarse uncooked kasha

1 cup dried brown lentils, rinsed and picked over

½ teaspoon dried oregano

3 garlic cloves, minced

5 cups Vegetable Broth (see Chapter 4)

½ teaspoon kosher salt

⅛ teaspoon ground black pepper

½ cup sliced black olives

3 Roma tomatoes, seeded and diced

1 cup feta cheese, crumbled

¼ cup Italian parsley leaves, finely chopped (for garnish)

1. Spray the inside of a 4-quart slow cooker with the cooking spray.

2. In a medium bowl, combine the eggs and kasha, stirring to make sure that the kasha is completely coated with egg.

3. Heat a large skillet over medium-high heat. Pour in the kasha mixture. Stir continuously with a wooden spoon or spatula, breaking up the mixture until the egg dries and the kasha has toasted and separated. Add the kasha mixture to the prepared slow cooker.

4. Add the lentils, oregano, garlic, and vegetable broth to the slow cooker and stir to mix. Cover and cook on low for 3–4 hours or until the broth has completely been absorbed and the lentils are tender.

5. Stir in the salt, pepper, olives, and tomatoes. Cover and cook for an additional 15 minutes. Sprinkle on the feta cheese and garnish with the chopped parsley, if desired, before serving.

Vegetarian Cholent with Kishke

Kishke, also known as stuffed derma, is made of matzoh meal, oil, vegetables, and spices stuffed into a large sausage-like casing.

1 medium onion, diced

1 carrot, peeled and cut into 1" pieces

1 cup lima beans, rinsed and picked over

1 cup navy beans, rinsed and picked over

1 cup pearl barley, rinsed and picked over

2 Yukon gold potatoes, peeled and cut into large chunks

2 medium sweet potatoes, peeled and cut into large chunks

1 teaspoon paprika

4 garlic cloves, minced

8 ounces white mushrooms, cleaned and quartered

1 pound whole kishke, defrosted if frozen

4 cups water, plus more if needed

2 teaspoons kosher salt, plus more if needed

½ teaspoon black pepper, plus more if needed

1. In a 4- or 6-quart slow cooker, place ingredients in the following order: Chopped onion, carrot, beans, barley, Yukon gold potatoes, sweet potatoes, paprika, garlic, mushrooms, kishke, and water.

2. Cover and cook on low for 12–26 hours. Check and add water at any time if cholent looks too dry. If there is too much liquid at the end of the cooking time, uncover and let cook for an additional 30 minutes. Add salt and pepper. Taste and add additional salt and/or pepper if needed. Slice kishke before serving.

Chicken and Sausage Paella

There is no seafood in this version of the classic Spanish rice dish.

INGREDIENTS | SERVES 6

Cooking spray

1 medium onion, diced

3 garlic cloves, minced

1 (12-ounce) package sausage, sliced into ½" rounds

1 (14.5-ounce) can diced tomatoes, undrained

1 small green or red pepper, seeded and cut into ½" strips

1 tablespoon paprika

2 teaspoons kosher salt

¼ teaspoon ground black pepper

⅛ teaspoon saffron, crushed

1½ cups Chicken Stock (see Chapter 4)

4 skinless, boneless chicken breasts, cut into 1" strips

1 cup frozen peas, thawed

3 cups cooked rice

1. Spray the inside of a 6-quart slow cooker with the cooking spray.

2. Combine the onion, garlic, sausage, tomatoes, green or red pepper, paprika, salt, black pepper, saffron, and chicken stock in the prepared slow cooker. Arrange the chicken breasts on top.

3. Cover and cook on low for 4–6 hours. Stir in the peas. Cover and cook on low for an additional 15 minutes. Serve over rice.

CHAPTER 12

Noodles, Pasta, and Sauces

Creamy Vodka Sauce

If you prefer not to use vodka in this recipe, you can skip Step 1 and use ½ cup tomato sauce instead. Serve this Creamy Vodka Sauce over cooked penne pasta or fried eggplant. Top with freshly grated cheese if desired.

INGREDIENTS | YIELDS ABOUT 3½ CUPS

1 cup vodka

2 tablespoons olive oil

2 medium shallots, peeled and minced

3 cloves of garlic, peeled and minced

2 (28-ounce) cans crushed tomatoes in purée

1 teaspoon dried oregano

1 teaspoon sugar

Salt and freshly ground pepper, to taste

2 cups evaporated milk

1. Add the vodka to a 3- or 4-quart slow cooker. Cook uncovered on high for 1 hour or until reduced by half.

2. Add the olive oil and minced shallots to a microwave-safe bowl. Cover and microwave on high for 1 minute. Uncover and stir in the garlic. Cover and microwave on high for 30 seconds. Add to the slow cooker along with the tomatoes, oregano, sugar, salt, and pepper. Stir to combine. Cover and cook on low for 10–12 hours.

3. Shortly before serving, stir the evaporated milk into the sauce. Cook uncovered on low until heated through. Taste for seasoning and, if necessary, add additional oregano, sugar, salt, and pepper if needed.

4. Any leftover sauce can be refrigerated in a covered container for up to 3 days or frozen for up to 3 months.

Marinara Sauce

This classic sauce is delicious over spaghetti or in Spinach Lasagna (see recipe this chapter).

INGREDIENTS | SERVES 8

1 tablespoon olive oil

1 large onion, diced

2 cloves garlic, minced

1 tablespoon minced fresh basil

1 tablespoon minced fresh Italian parsley

1 stalk celery, diced

1 (28-ounce) can whole tomatoes in purée

1 (28-ounce) can crushed tomatoes

1 (15-ounce) can diced tomatoes in juice

1. Heat the olive oil in a medium nonstick skillet. Sauté the onion and garlic until the onion is soft, about 3 minutes.

2. Add the onions and garlic to a 6-quart slow cooker. Add the herbs, celery, and tomatoes. Stir to distribute the spices. Cook on low for 10–12 hours.

Tomato and Sausage Sauce

Sausage is a delicious alternative to meatballs in this rich tomato sauce. There are chicken, veal, and beef kosher sausages, each with many different flavors from which to choose. Try making this recipe with a different type each time and select your favorite. Or favorites!

INGREDIENTS | SERVES 6

1 (12-ounce) package sweet Italian sausages, sliced

2 tablespoons tomato paste

1 (28-ounce) can crushed tomatoes

3 cloves garlic, minced

1 onion, minced

3 tablespoons minced basil

1 tablespoon minced Italian parsley

¼ teaspoon crushed rosemary

¼ teaspoon freshly ground black pepper

1. Brown the sausage slices in a nonstick skillet over medium-high heat, about 2–3 minutes each side. Drain any grease. Add the sausages to a 4-quart slow cooker, along with the remaining ingredients. Stir.

2. Cook on low for 8 hours.

Mushroom and Red Wine Sauce

Try this sauce over your favorite pasta.

INGREDIENTS | SERVES 8

2 tablespoons olive oil, divided

1 pound white button mushrooms, sliced

1 cup red wine

1 large onion, diced

2 cloves garlic, minced

1 tablespoon minced fresh basil

1 tablespoon minced fresh Italian parsley

1 (28-ounce) can whole tomatoes in purée, undrained

1 (28-ounce) can crushed tomatoes

1 (15-ounce) can diced tomatoes, undrained

Which Wine?

The best wine to use in any recipe is one that you like to drink. If it's unfit by the glass, it's unfit for your dish!

1. Heat 1 tablespoon of the olive oil in a medium skillet over medium-high heat. Add the mushrooms and cook, stirring frequently, until the mushrooms start to give off their juices, about 5 minutes. Continue to cook until the juices evaporate, about 2 more minutes.

2. Add the wine and let wine come to a simmer. Reduce heat to medium; continue to simmer uncovered for 2 minutes. Transfer the mushrooms and wine to a 4-quart slow cooker.

3. Return the skillet to the burner and increase heat to medium-high. Heat the remaining olive oil, then add the onion and cook, stirring frequently, until the onion is soft, about 5 minutes. Add the garlic and stir continuously for 30 more seconds.

4. Add the onion mixture to the slow cooker. Stir in the remaining ingredients. Cover and cook on low for 10–12 hours.

Eggplant and Tomato Sauce

Serve this sauce over a thick pasta such as rotini.

INGREDIENTS | SERVES 8

2 tablespoons olive oil, divided
1 large onion, diced
2 cloves garlic, minced
4 Japanese eggplants, diced
1 tablespoon minced fresh basil
1 tablespoon minced fresh Italian parsley
1 (28-ounce) can whole tomatoes in purée, undrained
1 (28-ounce) can crushed tomatoes
1 (15-ounce) can diced tomatoes, undrained

1. Heat 1 tablespoon of the olive oil in a medium skillet over medium-high heat. Add the onion and cook, stirring frequently, until the onion is soft, about 5 minutes.

2. Add the garlic and stir continuously for 30 more seconds.

3. Add the eggplant and stir for another 2 minutes.

4. Transfer the eggplant mixture to the slow cooker. Stir in the remaining ingredients. Cover and cook on low for 10–12 hours.

Spinach Lasagna

Baby spinach is more tender than full-sized leaves, so no pre-cooking is necessary.

INGREDIENTS | SERVES 8

Cooking spray

4 cups Marinara Sauce (see recipe in this chapter)

2 (15-ounce) cans diced tomatoes, drained

3 cloves garlic, minced

1 tablespoon dried oregano

1 (16-ounce) carton whole ricotta cheese

½ cup grated Parmesan cheese

½ cup flat-leaf parsley leaves, chopped

2 teaspoons kosher salt

½ teaspoon black pepper

1 (16-ounce) package lasagna noodles, uncooked

1 (8-ounce) bag baby spinach

1 (16-ounce) package whole mozzarella cheese, grated

1. Lightly spray the interior of a 5- or 6-quart slow cooker with the cooking spray.

2. In a medium bowl, combine the marinara sauce, the tomatoes, the garlic, and the oregano.

3. In another medium bowl, combine the ricotta cheese, the Parmesan cheese, the parsley, the salt, and the pepper.

4. Spoon about ⅓ cup of the tomato sauce mixture into the slow cooker to cover the bottom with a thin layer. Top with a single layer of noodles, breaking them as necessary to fit. Layer a third of the baby spinach evenly over the noodles. Spread a third of the ricotta mixture and a third of the remaining sauce. Sprinkle evenly with a third of the mozzarella cheese.

5. Cover with another layer of lasagna noodles, and half each of the remaining spinach, ricotta, sauce, and mozzarella. Finish with a final layer of lasagna noodles and the remaining spinach, ricotta mixture, sauce, and mozzarella (some lasagna noodles might be left over).

6. Cover and cook on to low until the noodles are tender, 2–3 hours (check after 2 hours).

Macaroni and Cheese

This is a very creamy version of everyone's favorite comfort food.

INGREDIENTS | SERVES 6

Cooking spray

2 eggs, lightly beaten

2 (12-ounce) cans evaporated milk

½ pound elbow macaroni, uncooked

3 cups shredded Cheddar cheese

1 cup freshly grated Parmesan cheese

½ teaspoon kosher salt

¼ teaspoon ground black pepper

½ teaspoon dried mustard

¼ teaspoon ground nutmeg

Miss the Crunchy Topping?

Transfer the cooked macaroni and cheese to a broiler-safe casserole dish. Top with ½ cup of soft bread crumbs mixed with 1 tablespoon of melted butter. Place in a preheated broiler for 1½–2 minutes or until the crumbs are golden brown.

1. Coat the inside of a 4-quart slow cooker with cooking spray.

2. In a large bowl, whisk eggs with evaporated milk. Mix in remaining ingredients. Transfer to prepared slow cooker.

3. Cover and cook on low for 2–4 hours, or on high for 1–3 hours, until the macaroni has softened and the sauce has thickened. If center does not look completely cooked, turn off cooker and let sit, covered, for 30 minutes.

Lamb Ragu

Ragu is a slow-cooked Italian meat sauce, usually served over pasta.
For a nonalcoholic version, substitute 2 cups chicken broth for the wine and water.

INGREDIENTS | SERVES 8

2 tablespoons vegetable oil

1 medium onion, peeled and diced

2 garlic cloves, peeled and minced

2 pounds stew lamb, cut into 1" cubes

2 carrots, peeled and cut into 1" chunks

½ teaspoon kosher salt

¼ teaspoon black pepper

1 tablespoon fresh rosemary, minced

1 teaspoon dried oregano

1 teaspoon dried sage

1 cup dry red wine

1 cup water

2 tablespoons tomato paste

2 (15-ounce) cans diced tomatoes, drained

1 pound rigatoni, cooked according to package directions

½ cup Italian flat parsley leaves, chopped (for garnish)

1. Heat oil in a large skillet over medium-high heat. Add onion and cook until onions just start to brown, stirring occasionally, about 5 minutes. Add garlic and sauté for 30 seconds. Transfer onion mixture to a 4- or 6-quart slow cooker.

2. Add the lamb cubes to the skillet and brown for 3 minutes on each side.

3. Place carrots in slow cooker, then top with lamb cubes. Add remaining ingredients except pasta and parsley leaves to the slow cooker. Cook for 8–12 hours on low. Serve ragout over rigatoni, garnished with parsley.

Rigatoni

Rigatoni is a tube-shaped pasta with ridges. It is traditionally served with a chunky meat sauce. Another suitable pasta is penne rigate, a pasta similar to rigatoni but cut on the diagonal.

Chicken Paprikash with Egg Noodles

If you prefer not to cook with wine, replace it with an equal amount of chicken broth.

INGREDIENTS | SERVES 8

1 tablespoon margarine

1 tablespoon extra-virgin olive oil

1 large yellow onion, peeled and diced

2 cloves of garlic, peeled and minced

3 pounds boneless skinless chicken thighs

Salt and freshly ground pepper, to taste

2 tablespoons paprika

½ cup Chicken Stock (see Chapter 4)

¼ cup dry white wine

1 (16-ounce) container pareve sour cream or cream cheese

Cooked wide egg noodles

Additional paprika (optional)

Thickening or Thinning

If the resulting sauce for the chicken paprikash is too thin, uncover and cook for up to an additional 30 minutes. If too thick, add a little more chicken stock.

1. Add the margarine, oil, and onion to a microwave-safe bowl; cover and microwave on high for 1 minute. Stir, re-cover, and microwave on high for another minute or until the onions are transparent. Stir in the garlic; cover and microwave on high for 30 seconds. Add to a 4- or 5-quart slow cooker.

2. Cut the chicken thighs into bite-sized pieces. Add the chicken to the slow cooker, and stir-fry for 5 minutes on high. Stir in the salt, pepper, paprika, broth, and wine; cover and cook on low for 8 hours.

3. Stir in the pareve sour cream; cover and continue to cook long enough to bring the sour cream sauce to temperature, or for about 30 minutes. Serve over cooked noodles. Sprinkle each serving with additional paprika if desired. Serve immediately.

Chicken in Plum Sauce with Japanese Soba Noodles

You can use commercial plum sauce or the one in Chapter 2 for this rich, sweet entrée.

INGREDIENTS | SERVES 4

Nonstick spray

1¼ cups plum sauce

2 tablespoons margarine, melted

2 tablespoons orange juice concentrate, thawed

1 teaspoon Chinese five-spice powder

1 tablespoon soy sauce, plus more if desired

8 chicken thighs, skin removed

1 (9.5-ounce) package Japanese soba noodles, cooked according to package directions

Toasted sesame seeds (optional)

1. Spray the inside of a 4- or 6-quart slow cooker with nonstick spray. Add the plum sauce, margarine, orange juice concentrate, five-spice powder, and soy sauce to the slow cooker; stir to combine.

2. Add the chicken thighs. Cover and cook on low for 6–8 hours. Serve over soba noodles. Top each serving with toasted sesame seeds and additional soy sauce, if desired.

Japanese Soba Noodles

Japanese soba noodles are made from buckwheat flour. If you are gluten-intolerant be sure to check the label since many brands also contain wheat. Soba noodles can be served cold in salads or hot in soups and other dishes. They are available in the Asian section of larger supermarkets. If not available, substitute angel hair pasta.

Kasha Varnishkes

Kasha is a whole grain product usually made from buckwheat. This eastern European dish combines kasha with onions and bow-tie noodles. Use vegetable broth for a pareve version.

INGREDIENTS | SERVES 4 AS AN ENTRÉE, 8 AS A SIDE DISH

Cooking spray

2 eggs, lightly beaten

2 cups medium or coarse uncooked kasha

1 tablespoon olive oil

1 large yellow onion, halved and thinly sliced

1 small carrot, peeled and finely chopped (optional)

8 ounces white button mushrooms, sliced

3½ cups Chicken Broth (see Chapter 4)

½ teaspoon kosher salt, plus more to taste

⅛ teaspoon ground black pepper, plus more to taste

1 (12-ounce) box of bow-tie noodles, cooked according to package directions

¼ cup Italian parsley leaves, finely chopped (for garnish)

Why Is the Egg in Kasha Varnishkes Necessary?

Besides the additional protein, the egg coats the kasha grains, helping to keep them separate and fluffy.

1. Spray the inside of a 4-quart slow cooker with the cooking spray.

2. In a medium bowl, combine the egg and kasha, stirring to make sure that the kasha is completely coated with egg. Set aside.

3. Heat the oil in a large skillet over medium-high heat. Add the sliced onion and carrot (if using). Cook, stirring frequently, until the onions soften, about 5 minutes.

4. Add the mushrooms and continue to sauté for another 5–8 minutes or until the mushrooms give off their liquid and the liquid evaporates. Transfer the mushroom mixture to the slow cooker.

5. Return the skillet to medium-high heat. Pour in the kasha mixture. Stir continuously with a wooden spoon or spatula, breaking up the mixture until the egg dries and the kasha has toasted and separated. Stir kasha into the slow cooker. Pour in the chicken broth and stir to combine. Cover and cook on high for 1½–2 hours or until the broth has completely been absorbed.

6. Use a fork to fluff the kasha and to stir in the salt, pepper, and the cooked bow-tie noodles. Taste and add more salt and/or pepper if needed. Garnish with the chopped parsley, if desired, before serving.

Pierogies and Onions

For a dairy alternative, substitute potato-Cheddar pierogies for the potato-onion variety, and use ½ stick of butter in place of the olive oil.

INGREDIENTS | SERVES 4

3 tablespoons olive oil, divided

1 large yellow onion, peeled and thinly sliced into rings

2 (1-pound) packages potato-onion pierogies (approximately 24 pierogies)

1. Pour 2 tablespoons of the oil into a 4-quart slow cooker. Add the onions and stir to separate the rings. Place the pierogies on top of the onion rings. Drizzle remaining oil over the pierogies.

2. Cover and cook for 2–3 hours on low until the pierogies are tender. Serve immediately.

Cheesy Tortellini

This recipe is also great with spinach tortellini.

INGREDIENTS | SERVES 4

2 cups Marinara Sauce (see recipe in this chapter)

1 (15-ounce) can diced tomatoes, undrained

1 (8-ounce) package mushrooms, sliced

1 (12-ounce) package frozen cheese tortellini

1 (8-ounce) package shredded mozzarella cheese

½ cup grated Parmesan cheese

1. Combine the marinara sauce, diced tomatoes, and mushrooms in a 4-quart slow cooker. Cover and cook on low for 6 hours.

2. Thirty minutes before the sauce is ready, cook frozen tortellini according to package directions. Drain. Stir the tortellini into the sauce. Top with both cheeses.

3. Cover and continue to heat on low for another 15 minutes, or until cheeses have melted.

Pasta with Artichokes and Sun-Dried Tomatoes

Use a thin pasta, such as spaghetti, linguine, or tagliatelle.

INGREDIENTS | SERVES 8

1 (8-ounce) jar sun-dried tomatoes packed in oil, undrained

2 (8-ounce) packages frozen artichoke hearts, defrosted

4 garlic cloves, minced

1 (1-pound) package of pasta

½ cup grated Parmesan cheese

¼ cup loosely packed parsley leaves, coarsely chopped (for garnish)

1. Combine sun-dried tomatoes (with their oil), artichoke hearts, and garlic in a 4-quart slow cooker. Cover and cook on high for 2 hours.

2. Cook pasta according to package directions; drain and divide among 8 plates. Spoon the artichoke mixture over pasta.

3. Top with the Parmesan cheese and sprinkle evenly with the parsley, if desired. Serve immediately.

Spinach and Cheese Stuffed Shells

Serve with a salad and slices of Italian bread.

INGREDIENTS | SERVES 6

4 cups Marinara Sauce (see recipe in this chapter), divided

30 jumbo pasta shells

1 (10-ounce) package frozen chopped spinach, defrosted and squeezed dry

1 (15-ounce) container ricotta cheese

⅔ cup plain dried bread crumbs

½ cup grated Parmesan cheese

1 (8-ounce) package mozzarella cheese

1 egg, lightly beaten

¼ teaspoon ground nutmeg

¼ teaspoon ground black pepper

¼ cup loosely packed fresh Italian parsley leaves, chopped (for garnish)

Always Cook Extra Shells

Cook more pasta shells than required for a recipe since a few may break during boiling or when they are filled.

1. Spread ½ cup of the Marinara Sauce on the bottom of a 4-quart slow cooker. Set aside.

2. Cook shells in boiling salted water for 4 minutes (shells will not be fully cooked). Drain and rinse under cold water to stop the cooking process. Set aside.

3. In a large bowl, combine spinach, ricotta, bread crumbs, Parmesan, mozzarella, egg, nutmeg, and black pepper. Stuff each pasta shell with 2 heaping tablespoons of the spinach-cheese mixture. Place a layer of stuffed shells in the prepared slow cooker. Spoon a little sauce over each shell, then continue to layer in the shells until all are in the cooker. Spoon the remaining sauce evenly over the top layer of shells.

4. Cover and cook on low for 5–6 hours or on high for 3–4 hours. Sprinkle with parsley leaves before serving, if desired.

Ravioli Casserole

With three different cheeses (not counting the filling), this is a very cheesy pasta dish.

INGREDIENTS | SERVES 6–8

3 cups Marinara Sauce (see recipe in this chapter), divided

2 (10- to 12-ounce) packages frozen raviolis

1 (8-ounce) package shredded mozzarella cheese

1 (8-ounce) package shredded Cheddar cheese

½ cup grated Parmesan cheese (for garnish)

¼ cup loosely packed Italian parsley leaves, coarsely chopped (for garnish)

1. Spread 1 cup of the Marinara Sauce in the bottom of a 4-quart slow cooker. Add 1 package of the frozen raviolis. Sprinkle half of the mozzarella and the Cheddar cheeses over the raviolis. Pour another cup of the Marinara Sauce evenly over the cheeses. Add the remaining package of raviolis followed by the remaining mozzarella and Cheddar cheeses. Pour the remaining cup of the Marinara Sauce on top.

2. Cover and cook on low for 4 hours or until sauce is bubbly and the raviolis are completely cooked.

3. Sprinkle with the Parmesan cheese and the parsley just before serving, if desired.

Bolognese Sauce over Pasta

Choose a thick pasta, like rotini or ziti, for this hearty sauce.

INGREDIENTS | SERVES 8

1 tablespoon olive oil

1 large onion, diced

1 carrot, peeled and chopped

2 cloves garlic, minced

1 pound ground beef

1 tablespoon minced fresh basil

1 (28-ounce) can whole tomatoes in purée

1 (28-ounce) can crushed tomatoes

1 (15-ounce) can diced tomatoes in juice

1 pound pasta, cooked

1 tablespoon chopped fresh Italian parsley (for garnish)

1. Heat the oil in a skillet on medium-high. Add the onion and carrots. Cook, stirring frequently, until the onions are softened, about 5 minutes. Add the garlic and continue to stir for 30 seconds.

2. Push the vegetable mixture to the sides and add the ground beef. Stir, breaking up the meat, until no pink remains, about 5 minutes.

3. Scrape the meat mixture into a 6-quart slow cooker. Add the remaining ingredients except the pasta and parsley. Cover and cook on low for 6–8 hours. Serve the sauce over pasta. Sprinkle with parsley, if desired, before serving.

Chicken Tetrazzini

After just a few "tweaks" this normally treif (nonkosher) dish can be served in a kosher home.

INGREDIENTS | SERVES 8

1 medium onion, peeled and diced

2 tablespoons unbleached flour

3 skinless, boneless chicken breasts, cut into 1" cubes

½ pound white button mushrooms, sliced

1½ cups Chicken Stock or Vegetable Broth (see Chapter 4)

½ cup almond or rice milk

¼ cup dry sherry (optional)

1 pound uncooked spaghetti, broken in half

½ cup frozen peas, defrosted

1 teaspoon kosher salt

¼ teaspoon ground black pepper

1. In a 6-quart slow cooker, combine the onion, flour, and the chicken breasts. Top with the mushrooms and pour in the stock or broth. Cover and cook on low for 4–6 hours.

2. Stir in the almond or rice milk, sherry (if using), spaghetti, peas, salt, and pepper. Cover and cook on high for 20–30 minutes or until the spaghetti is done.

CHAPTER 13

Desserts

Sweet Ricotta Strata with Plumped Fruit

Similar to a bread pudding, but not quite as sweet, this breakfast strata tastes great when served alongside a fresh berry salad. Plump dried fruit by soaking it in boiling water for 10 minutes, then drain.

INGREDIENTS | SERVES 6

Cooking spray

4 cups cubed baguette (white or whole wheat)

½ cup plumped dried cherries, chopped

½ cup plumped raisins

6 large egg whites

3 large egg yolks

1 tablespoon sugar

½ cup part-skim ricotta cheese, drained

¼ teaspoon salt

Fresh Berry Salad

Combine ½ pint each of washed fresh blueberries, raspberries, and blackberries. Add 2 teaspoons of chopped fresh mint. Gently mix to combine and serve.

1. Spray the inside of a 4-quart slow cooker with cooking spray. Place half of the baguette cubes in the cooker. Sprinkle on half of the cherries and raisins. Repeat with remaining half of baguette cubes and fruit.

2. In a large bowl, whisk the egg whites, egg yolks, sugar, ricotta, and salt together; pour over bread mixture.

3. Cover and cook on the high heat setting for about 1¾–2 hours, or until set. (Do not cook on the low heat setting for a longer time.) Let stand for 5–10 minutes before serving.

Cinnamon and Sugar Almonds

These nuts make a very addictive treat! They're great for shalach manot baskets.
Use margarine in place of butter for a pareve version.

INGREDIENTS | YIELDS 12 OUNCES

12 ounces unsalted whole roasted almonds
½ cup packed brown sugar
1 teaspoon ground cinnamon
¼ teaspoon kosher salt
1 tablespoon butter, melted

1. Place the almonds into a 4-quart slow cooker.

2. Add remaining ingredients and stir until completely combined.

3. Cook on low, uncovered, for 2–3 hours (or on warm setting, covered), stirring occasionally.

4. Spread the mixture onto a cookie sheet lined with parchment paper and cool completely.

Sabra Compote

For a nonalcoholic version, substitute 1 teaspoon grated orange peel for the orange liqueur.

INGREDIENTS | YIELDS 8 SERVINGS

1 (15-ounce) can sliced peaches, drained
1 (15-ounce) can dark sweet cherries, drained
1 (15-ounce) can pear halves, drained
1 (15-ounce) can apricot halves, drained
½ cup mixture dates and dried plums (prunes)
¼ cup light brown sugar, packed
¼ cup orange juice
2 tablespoons Sabra liqueur
½ teaspoon cinnamon
¼ teaspoon ground ginger

1. Place all ingredients in a 4-quart slow cooker. Cover and cook on low for 3–4 hours. Serve warm or chilled.

Sabra

Sabra is a kosher-for-Passover chocolate-orange liqueur imported from Israel. Sabra is also the term used for a Jewish person born in Israel.

Monkey Bread

This pull-apart bread is a lot of fun. Set on a table and let everyone tear off a section to eat.

INGREDIENTS | SERVES 8

2 (8-ounce) cans refrigerated biscuits
½ cup granulated sugar
2 teaspoons ground cinnamon
¼ cup unsalted butter, melted
¼ cup chopped nuts

Refrigerated Biscuits

Refrigerated kosher biscuits may be difficult to find, but they do exist. One source is Whole Foods.

1. Place a heat-safe trivet or crumbled balls of aluminum foil in the bottom of a 4-quart slow cooker. Set aside.

2. Remove biscuits from their cans according to the directions. Tear each biscuit in half and gently roll between hands to form a ball.

3. In a small bowl, mix sugar and cinnamon together.

4. Dip each biscuit ball in melted butter, then in sugar mixture. Place into a heat-safe pan or casserole dish that fits into the slow cooker. Sprinkle chopped nuts evenly over the biscuits.

5. Cover top of pan with several layers of paper towels. Cover slow cooker and heat on high for 3–4 hours.

Warm Rice Pudding

This version is reminiscent of the warm rice pudding, with its thick layer of custard on top, sold in Jewish dairy restaurants in the Bronx years ago.

INGREDIENTS | SERVES 8

Cooking spray

2 eggs, lightly beaten

⅓ cup granulated sugar

1 teaspoon vanilla extract

¼ teaspoon kosher salt

1 (12-ounce) can evaporated milk (regular, low-fat, or fat-free)

2 tablespoons unsalted butter, melted

2 cups cooked long-grain rice

½ cup raisins

½ teaspoon ground cinnamon

2 cups Cherry Sauce (see recipe in this chapter), warmed

1. Spray the inside of a 4-quart slow cooker with cooking spray.

2. Combine remaining ingredients except cinnamon and cherry sauce in the slow cooker; mix well.

3. Cover and cook on high for 1 hour. Sprinkle cinnamon evenly over surface, then re-cover and cook on low for 2 more hours or on high for 1 more hour (pudding will not be completely set in center). Turn off slow cooker. Let stand, covered, for a half hour to let pudding firm up.

4. To serve, divide rice pudding among 8 serving bowls. Ladle cherry sauce over pudding. Serve warm.

Cherry Sauce

Tapioca starch creates a more translucent gel than when flour or cornstarch is used. And it has no "flour-y" taste, either. Serve over Warm Rice Pudding (see recipe in this chapter) or ice cream.

INGREDIENTS | YIELDS APPROXIMATELY 4 CUPS

2 (15-ounce) cans sweet cherries in heavy syrup, undrained

⅔ cup granulated sugar

4 teaspoons tapioca starch

1. Stir together all the ingredients in a 3- or 4-quart slow cooker. Cover and cook on low for 3–4 hours. Sauce will be thin. Transfer to a covered container and store in the refrigerator (up to 5 days) where it will thicken as it cools.

Double Chocolate Brownies

Substitute margarine in place of the butter for a pareve version.

INGREDIENTS | SERVES 12

Cooking spray
¾ cup unbleached flour
½ cup cocoa powder
½ teaspoon baking powder
½ teaspoon kosher salt
½ cup (1 stick) unsalted butter, cut up
1 cup sugar
2 eggs, lightly beaten
1 teaspoon vanilla extract
¾ cup semisweet chocolate chips
½ cup chopped walnuts (optional)

How to Cut Parchment to Fit

Using the bottom of the slow cooker insert as a template, draw around on the parchment with a felt-tipped pen. Remove insert, then cut around the circle *inside* the line by ¼". Voila! Perfect fit!

1. Lightly spray the insert of a 4-quart slow cooker with cooking spray. Cut a circle of parchment paper and place on the bottom inside the insert. Lightly press down paper (so it stays put), then lightly spray parchment as well.

2. In a small mixing bowl, whisk together flour, cocoa, baking powder, and salt. Set aside.

3. In a medium-sized heat-safe bowl, melt butter in microwave at 100 percent power for 45 seconds. Stir until completely melted. Whisk in sugar, then eggs.

4. Using a rubber spatula, stir the prepared flour mixture into the butter mixture just until incorporated. Fold in vanilla extract, chocolate chips, and chopped walnuts, if using. Spread chocolate mixture on bottom of prepared cooker.

5. Cover and cook on low for 3 hours. The outer edges will be dry with the center still wet. Leave cover off and continue to cook for another 30 minutes. The center should still be underdone, but will firm up as it cools.

6. Let cool completely. Run a table knife around the edges of the brownies. Carefully lift the brownies from the slow cooker and let cool completely before cutting.

Chocolate Cake

This chocolate cake is a classic dessert that needs only a simple vanilla glaze to dress it. Substitute soymilk, almond milk, or rice milk in place of the dairy milk for a pareve version.

INGREDIENTS | SERVES 8

2 cups all-purpose flour
2 cups sugar
¾ cup unsweetened cocoa powder
1¾ teaspoons baking powder
1¾ teaspoons baking soda
1¼ cups regular or low-fat milk
2 eggs
½ cup vegetable oil
1¼ cups water

1. In a medium bowl, mix all the dry ingredients.

2. In another medium bowl, mix all the wet ingredients.

3. Spray a 4-quart slow cooker with cooking spray.

4. Combine the dry and wet ingredients just until moistened and pour into the slow cooker.

5. Cover and cook on high heat for 1–2 hours.

6. Remove cake from slow cooker and let cool.

Simple Vanilla Glaze

Make this very easy vanilla glaze by stirring together 1 cup sifted powdered sugar, 1 tablespoon melted margarine, 1 teaspoon vanilla extract and 1 tablespoon water or milk. Stir in another tablespoon of water or milk at a time if glaze needs thinning (will thicken upon standing). Pour glaze evenly over top of cake, allowing glaze to drip down sides. Let glaze set before serving.

Pareve Carrot Cake

Substitute your favorite cream cheese frosting for a dairy version.

INGREDIENTS | SERVES 8

1½ cups all-purpose flour

½ teaspoon baking soda

1 teaspoon baking powder

¼ teaspoon salt

¾ teaspoon cinnamon

¼ teaspoon ground cloves

⅛ teaspoon freshly grated nutmeg

2 large eggs or 2 mashed bananas

¾ cup sugar

⅓ cup margarine

¼ cup water

1 cup carrots, grated

¼ cup raisins

½ cup chopped walnuts

Carrot Cake Glaze

Repeatedly pierce the top of the cake with a fork. Then in a microwave-safe measuring cup add ½ cup lemon, orange, or unsweetened pineapple juice; 1 teaspoon freshly grated lemon or orange zest; and 1½ cups of sifted powdered sugar and stir to combine. Microwave on high for 30 seconds. Stir and repeat until sugar is dissolved. Pour warm glaze evenly over the cake.

1. In a mixing bowl, add the flour, baking soda, baking powder, salt, cinnamon, cloves, and nutmeg. Stir to combine.

2. In a food processor, add the eggs or bananas, sugar, and margarine. Process to cream together. Scrape into the flour mixture.

3. Pour in the water and add the grated carrots to the mixing bowl. Stir and fold to combine all ingredients. Fold in the raisins and nuts.

4. Spray the inside of a 4-quart slow cooker with nonstick spray. Add the carrot cake batter and use a spatula to spread it evenly in the crock.

5. Cover and cook on low for 2 hours, or until cake is firm in the center.

Pumpkin Challah Pudding with Caramel Sauce

Dried cranberries can substitute for the raisins in this recipe.

INGREDIENTS | SERVES 8–12

Cooking spray

1 challah loaf, cut into 1" cubes (about 10 cups)

2 eggs, lightly beaten

1 (16-ounce) can solid pack pumpkin (not pie filling)

1 cup packed brown sugar

2 teaspoons ground cinnamon

½ teaspoon cardamom

¼ teaspoon ground nutmeg

⅛ teaspoon ground cloves

2 (14-ounce) cans evaporated milk

1½ teaspoons vanilla extract

½ cup raisins

½ cup coarsely chopped pecans

Whipped cream (optional)

Caramel Sauce

¼ cup packed brown sugar

2 sticks (1 cup) unsalted butter

2 cups heavy cream

1 teaspoon vanilla extract

1. Spray the inside of a 4- to 6-quart slow cooker with cooking spray. Add in the challah cubes.

2. In a large bowl, whisk together the eggs, pumpkin, brown sugar, cinnamon, cardamom, nutmeg, cloves, evaporated milk, and vanilla until completely combined.

3. Pour mixture over the challah cubes. With a large spoon, gently mix in the raisins and the pecans. Make sure everything is moistened.

4. Cover and cook on low for 3–3½ hours or on high for 1½–2 hours, until set and a toothpick inserted into the center comes out clean.

5. Meanwhile, in a heavy saucepan, whisk the brown sugar and butter over medium heat until butter is melted. Whisk in cream and cook, stirring, for about 3–5 minutes or until sugar is dissolved and sauce is smooth. Do not let boil. Immediately remove from heat. Stir in vanilla extract. Keep warm.

6. Spoon challah pudding into dessert bowls. Drizzle warm sauce on top. Garnish with whipped cream (if using).

Green Tea Tapioca Pudding

Tapioca pudding is simple in the slow cooker. There's no need to stir!

INGREDIENTS | SERVES 6

2 cups fat-free evaporated milk

1 teabag green tea

¼ cup small pearl tapioca

1 teaspoon matcha or green tea powder

½ cup sugar

1 egg

Tapioca

Tapioca comes in several forms. Large pearl tapioca can be boiled to a chewy texture and served Taiwanese-style in cold drinks. Small pearl tapioca is better used in puddings and desserts. Tapioca starch is also used as a thickener in savory dishes.

1. Heat evaporated milk in a 2-quart saucepan just until it barely simmers (do not allow to boil). Remove from heat and add teabag. Let steep for 2 minutes.

2. Pour the milk mixture, tapioca, matcha or green tea powder and sugar into a 4-quart slow cooker. Whisk until the sugar dissolves. Cook for 1½ hours on high.

3. Stir in the egg. Cook for an additional half hour on low. Serve warm.

Red Lentil Payasam

Payasam is an Indian dessert. It is traditionally made with rice, beans, or lentils. Although it is referred to as a pudding, it has more of a creamy soup consistency. Southern Indian Jews serve it on special occasions, such as at weddings or after shloshim (the ritual 30 days of mourning).

INGREDIENTS | SERVES 4

1 cup red lentils, rinsed well

1½ cups water, heated to boiling

¾ packed cup dark brown sugar

1 (15-ounce) can whole coconut milk

½ teaspoon ground cardamom

4 teaspoons toasted coconut

4 teaspoons pistachio nuts, finely chopped

1. Mix the red lentils, water, and brown sugar together in a 4-quart slow cooker. Cover and cook on low for 2 hours.

2. Uncover and stir in the coconut milk and ground cardamom. Re-cover and cook for an additional hour. Serve topped with toasted coconut and pistachio nuts.

Date Pudding

This is a rich, decadent dessert that, when served with the quick sauce (see sidebar), is in the tradition of an English sticky toffee pudding. In fact, you can double the number of servings if you layer the pudding in parfait glasses with the sauce, chopped toasted pecans, and whipped cream.

INGREDIENTS | SERVES 8

2½ cups dates, pitted and snipped

1½ teaspoons baking soda

1⅔ cups boiling water

2 cups dark brown sugar, packed

½ cup unsalted butter, softened

3 large eggs

2 teaspoons vanilla extract

3½ cups all-purpose or cake flour

4 teaspoons baking powder

¼ teaspoon kosher salt

Cooking spray

Whipped cream (optional)

Quick Sauce

Add 1½ cups packed brown sugar, ½ cup unsalted butter, and 3 cups heavy cream to a saucepan over medium heat. Stirring constantly, bring to a boil and then, while continuing to stir constantly, reduce the heat and maintain a simmer for 6 minutes.

1. Add the dates to a mixing bowl and toss them together with the baking soda. Pour the boiling water over the dates. Set aside.

2. Add the brown sugar and butter to a food processor. Process to cream them together, and then continue to process while you add the eggs and vanilla.

3. Use a spatula to scrape the brown sugar mixture into the bowl with the dates. Stir to mix.

4. Add the flour, baking powder, and salt to a bowl; stir to mix. Fold into the date and brown sugar mixture.

5. Treat a 4-quart slow cooker with cooking spray. Pour the batter into the slow cooker. Cover and cook on low for 4 hours or until the center of the pudding cake is set but still moist. Serve warm with quick sauce and a dollop of whipped cream if desired.

Chocolate Crème Brûlée

This elegant dessert can be cooking while you have dinner.
Replace the evaporated milk with coconut milk for a delicious pareve alternative.

INGREDIENTS | SERVES 4

2 cups evaporated milk, regular or low-fat

2½ tablespoons cocoa powder

½ teaspoon vanilla extract

4 egg yolks

½ cup sugar

2 packed tablespoons brown sugar

1 cup water

Vanilla Extract Is Essential

When a recipe calls for vanilla, use real vanilla extract. Although real vanilla extract is more expensive than imitation, the flavor is far superior. Store vanilla extract in a cool, dark place to preserve the flavor.

1. In a small bowl, whisk the evaporated milk, cocoa, vanilla, egg yolks, and sugar until the sugar dissolves. Pour the mixture into a small pan and bring it to a boil. Remove the pan from the heat and allow the mixture to cool. Divide it among 4 (5- to 6-ounce) broiler-safe ramekins.

2. Pour 1 cup of water into the bottom of an oval 6-quart slow cooker. Place the ramekins in the water. Cook on high for 3 hours or until the custard is set.

3. Sprinkle each Crème Brûlée with ½ tablespoon brown sugar. Place them under the broiler and broil until the sugar caramelizes.

Apple Brown Betty

Apple Brown Betty is an American dessert that dates back to colonial times. Use a baking type of apple that holds its shape, such as jonathan, rome, honeycrisp, gala, or braeburn.

INGREDIENTS | SERVES 6

Cooking spray
3½ cups cubed apples
1 tablespoon lemon juice
1 tablespoon sugar
½ teaspoon cinnamon
½ teaspoon ground ginger
¼ teaspoon nutmeg
¼ teaspoon allspice
1¾ cups ½ inch bread cubes

Lemon Juice

Lemon juice is a cook's best friend. It adds a bright note to most dishes. It is low in calories but high in vitamin C. It can even keep cut apples or pears from turning brown.

1. Spray a 2-quart slow cooker with cooking spray. Add the apples, lemon juice, sugar, and spices. Stir. Cook on high for 2 hours.

2. Preheat oven to 250°F. Spread the bread cubes in a single layer on a baking sheet. Bake until browned, about 8 minutes.

3. Sprinkle the toasted bread cubes over the apples. Cook on high for 10 minutes prior to serving.

Berry Cobbler

Try this with a mix of blackberries, raspberries, golden raspberries, and blueberries.
If the berries are very tart, add an extra tablespoon of sugar.

INGREDIENTS | SERVES 8

4 cups mixed fresh berries
2½ tablespoons brown sugar
3 tablespoons minced fresh mint
1 cup flour
1½ tablespoons sugar
½ teaspoon ground ginger
1 egg
¼ cup evaporated milk (regular or low-fat)
1½ tablespoons vegetable oil
Cooking spray

1. In a large bowl, toss the berries, brown sugar, and mint. Set aside.

2. Whisk the dry ingredients in a medium bowl. Beat in the egg, evaporated milk, and oil until a thick dough forms.

3. Spray a 4-quart slow cooker with cooking spray. Spread the dough along the bottom, taking care to cover the entire bottom with no gaps. Add the berries in an even layer.

4. Cook on low for 2 hours.

Keep Your Berries Well

Berries are very fragile. For the best flavor, leave them out at room temperature rather than in the refrigerator. Avoid bruising berries by washing them directly before use. Buy local berries and eat them as soon as possible to avoid spoilage.

Pineapple Upside-Down Cake

Admittedly, it's a trick to invert this cake onto a serving plate. It's much easier to allow the cake to cool, cut it into 8 slices, and serve it from the crock of the slow cooker. Invert each slice as you place it on the dessert plate.

INGREDIENTS | SERVES 8

1 (18-ounce) box yellow or butter cake mix

Cooking spray

¼ cup butter, melted

2 packed tablespoons brown sugar

1 (15-ounce) can crushed pineapple, undrained

Maraschino cherries (optional)

1. Prepare the cake mix according to the package directions.

2. Treat the bottom and sides of a 4-quart slow cooker with cooking spray.

3. Pour the butter into the slow cooker, lifting and tilting the crock to evenly coat the bottom. Evenly sprinkle the brown sugar over the butter. Carefully spoon the crushed pineapple over the brown sugar, and then pour in any juice remaining in the can. If using, cut the maraschino cherries in half and arrange as many as you want, cut side up, over the pineapple.

4. Carefully pour (or ladle) the prepared cake batter over the mixture on the bottom of the slow cooker. Cover and cook on low for 4 hours or until a toothpick inserted into the cake comes out clean. If the cake is too moist on top, remove the cover and cook for another 15–30 minutes. Allow to cool and then serve.

Strawberry Pandowdy

The pandowdy gets its name from the dowdy appearance that is achieved by breaking up the crust halfway through the cooking time to allow the juices to soak through.

INGREDIENTS | SERVES 4

4 cups whole strawberries, stems removed

½ teaspoon ground ginger

1½ tablespoons sugar

½ teaspoon cornstarch

¾ cup flour

3 tablespoons cold unsalted butter, cubed

3 tablespoons cold water

⅛ teaspoon table salt

What's the Difference Between a Betty, a Cobbler, a Pandowdy, and a Slump?

A betty is a baked dish made by alternating layers of spiced, sugared fruit and buttered bread crumbs. A cobbler is a fruit stew in which biscuit dough is dropped onto the fruit before cooking. A pandowdy is a spoon pie with fruit on the bottom and a rolled pie crust on top that is broken up halfway through the cooking time. A slump is a spoon pie as well that includes cooked fruit topped with biscuit dough.

1. Place the strawberries, ginger, sugar, and cornstarch into a 2-quart slow cooker. Toss to distribute evenly.

2. Place the flour, butter, water, and salt into a food processor. Mix until a solid ball of dough forms. Roll it out on a clean surface until it is about ¼"–½" thick and will completely cover the fruit in the insert.

3. Drape the dough over the strawberries. Cover and cook on high for 40 minutes. Remove the lid. Using the tip of a knife, cut the dough into 2-inch squares while still in the slow cooker. Keep the lid off and continue to cook on high for an additional 40 minutes. Serve hot.

Summer Blueberry Slump

A slump is a fruit dessert served with fresh, steamed dumplings.

INGREDIENTS | SERVES 8

4 cups fresh blueberries

1½ tablespoons sugar

1 teaspoon minced fresh ginger

1 cup flour

½ teaspoon ground ginger

1 egg

¼ cup evaporated milk, regular or low-fat

1½ tablespoons canola oil

Cooking spray

1. In a large bowl, toss the berries, sugar, and fresh ginger together. Set aside.

2. Whisk the flour and ground ginger in a medium bowl. Beat in the egg, evaporated milk, and canola oil until a thick dough forms. Shape into 2 dumplings.

3. Spray the inside of a 4-quart slow cooker with cooking spray. Add the berries in an even layer. Drop in the dumplings.

4. Cook on low for 2 hours.

Chai Tapioca Pudding

In a way, this pudding can be nicknamed Lucky Tapioca. The Hebrew alphabetical representation for the number 18 is "chai" (pronounced "hi"), meaning life, so 18 is considered a lucky number.

INGREDIENTS | SERVES 6

2 chai tea bags

2 cups evaporated milk (low-fat or fat-free)

⅓ packed cup brown sugar

½ teaspoon ground cinnamon

½ teaspoon ground star anise

½ teaspoon mace

½ teaspoon ground cardamom

¼ cup small pearl tapioca

1 egg

1. Steep the tea bags in the evaporated milk for 20 minutes. Discard the bags. Whisk in the sugar, spices, and tapioca.

2. Pour the mixture into a 2- or 4-quart slow cooker and cook on low for 1½ hours. Stir in the egg and continue to cook for 30 minutes.

Ginger Poached Pears

*Fresh ginger best complements pear flavor, but if you only have ground,
start by adding a smaller amount and then increasing after tasting.
Optionally, serve with Creamy Hot Fudge Sauce (see recipe in this chapter).*

INGREDIENTS | SERVES 8

5 pears, peeled, cored, and cut into wedges

3 cups water

1 cup white granulated sugar

2 tablespoons ginger, minced

1 teaspoon cinnamon

1. Add all ingredients to a 4-quart slow cooker. Cover and cook on low heat for 4 hours.

Creamy Hot Fudge Sauce

*Try this over frozen yogurt or ice cream. Replace the evaporated milk and
the butter with coconut milk and margarine for a pareve version.*

INGREDIENTS | YIELDS 2 CUPS

1 (12-ounce) can evaporated milk

10 ounces semisweet or bittersweet chocolate chips

1 teaspoon vanilla extract

½ teaspoon unsalted butter

⅛ teaspoon table salt

1. Place all ingredients in a 1½- to 2-quart slow cooker. Cook on low, stirring occasionally, for 2 hours. The sauce will thicken as it cools.

2. Refrigerate leftovers. Reheat in the slow cooker for 1 hour on high or on the stovetop on low or simmer settings until warmed through, stirring frequently, about 10 minutes.

Banana Bread

For a special breakfast treat, spread slices of banana bread with strawberry jam.

INGREDIENTS | SERVES 8

Cooking spray
2 cups all-purpose flour
1 cup granulated sugar
¼ teaspoon baking soda
2 teaspoons baking powder
½ teaspoon table salt
3 medium ripe bananas, mashed
6 tablespoons unsalted butter, softened
2 large eggs, beaten
¼ cup plain yogurt
1 teaspoon vanilla extract
1¼ cups walnuts

Spiced Banana Bread

For cinnamon-spiced banana bread, in Step 2 add 1 teaspoon of ground cinnamon and ¼ teaspoon each of ground cloves, ginger, allspice, and nutmeg to the flour.

1. Spray the inside of a 4-quart slow cooker with the cooking spray.

2. In a medium-sized mixing bowl, whisk together the flour, sugar, baking soda, baking powder, and salt. Set aside.

3. In a food processor, add the bananas, butter, eggs, yogurt, and vanilla. Pulse to cream together.

4. Add the walnuts and flour mixture to the food processor. Pulse to combine and to chop the walnuts. Scrape down the sides of the container with a spatula; continue to pulse until mixed.

5. Add the batter to the prepared slow cooker, using a spatula to spread it evenly across the bottom of the crock.

6. Cover and cook on high for 2½–3 hours, or until a toothpick inserted in the center of the bread comes out clean.

7. Allow to cool uncovered before removing it from the slow cooker.

Easy Applesauce

Homemade applesauce is easy to make and tastes much better than what you can get in the store.
It freezes well, too, so you can make extra when apples are in season. Use your favorite sweet-type apple.

INGREDIENTS | YIELDS ABOUT 4 CUPS

10 medium apples, peeled, cored, and sliced

2 tablespoons fresh lemon juice

2 tablespoons water

6" cinnamon stick (optional)

Sugar, to taste (optional)

1. In a 4-quart slow cooker, add the apples, lemon juice, water, and cinnamon stick, if using. Stir to mix.

2. Cover and cook on low for 5 hours, or until the apples are soft and tender.

3. For chunky applesauce, mash the apples with a potato masher. For smooth applesauce, purée in a food processor or blender, use an immersion blender, or press through a food mill or large-mesh strainer.

4. While applesauce is still warm, add sugar to taste, if desired. Store covered in the refrigerator for up to 2 weeks, or freeze up to 6–10 months.

Bananas Foster

Bananas Foster is usually made from flambéed bananas served over vanilla ice cream,
but as this recipe proves, the bananas can be made in a slow cooker, too.
For a pareve version, replace the butter with margarine and top with pareve ice cream.

INGREDIENTS | SERVES 8

1 cup dark corn syrup

⅛ cup rum

½ teaspoon vanilla extract

1 teaspoon cinnamon

¾ cup unsalted butter

½ teaspoon kosher salt

10 bananas, peeled and cut into bite-sized pieces

4 cups vanilla ice cream

1. In a medium bowl, stir in the corn syrup, rum, vanilla extract, cinnamon, butter, and salt.

2. Add mixture and bananas to a 4-quart slow cooker. Cover and cook on low heat for 1–2 hours. Serve over a scoop of vanilla ice cream.

Dried Fruit Compote

The dried fruits plump up deliciously in this simple compote.

1 (10- to 12-ounce) package dried apricots

1 (10- to 12-ounce) package dried plums (prunes)

1 (6-ounce) package dried apple slices

¼ cup raisins

1 cup apple cider or unsweetened apple juice

1 teaspoon ground cinnamon

½ teaspoon ground nutmeg

¼ teaspoon ground cloves

½ teaspoon ground ginger

¼ cup apricot marmalade

1 tablespoon lemon juice

1. Place the apricots, plums, apples, raisins, and cider or unsweetened apple juice in a 4-quart slow cooker. Cover and cook on low for 4 hours.

2. Stir in the spices, the marmalade, and the lemon juice. Re-cover and cook on low for an additional hour. Serve warm or chilled.

Chocolate Peanut Clusters

The low temperature of a slow cooker is perfect for melting chocolate without burning it.

INGREDIENTS | YIELDS 60–70 CLUSTERS

2 (24-ounce) packages semisweet chocolate chips

¼ cup solid vegetable shortening

1 (24-ounce) jar dry-roasted salted peanuts

Add Some Raisins!

Try stirring in ½ cup raisins during the last 15 minutes of cooking time.

1. Combine all of the ingredients in a 4-quart slow cooker. Cover and cook on low for 1 hour.

2. Stir, then cook for an additional hour, stirring every 15 minutes.

3. Drop by rounded teaspoons onto wax or parchment paper. Allow 30 minutes to 1 hour to harden, then store in an airtight container, separated by layers of wax paper, at cool room temperature for up to a week, or freeze for up to 1 month.

Rocky Road Candy

Did you know that Rocky Road ice cream is known in Canada as Heavenly Hash? Well, now you do!

INGREDIENTS | YIELDS APPROXIMATELY 60–70 CANDIES

2 (24-ounce) packages semisweet chocolate chips
¼ cup solid vegetable shortening
1 (8-ounce) bag chopped walnuts
½ (10-ounce) bag mini marshmallows

1. Combine the chocolate chips, vegetable shortening, and walnuts in a 4-quart slow cooker. Cover and cook on low for 1 hour.

2. Stir, then cook for an additional hour, stirring every 15 minutes.

3. Stir in the marshmallows.

4. Drop by rounded teaspoons onto wax or parchment paper. Allow 30 minutes to 1 hour to harden, then store in an airtight container, separated by layers of wax paper, at cool room temperature for up to a week, or freeze for up to 1 month.

Mocha Truffles 3 Ways

The white chocolate is necessary to mellow out the taste. To give as gifts, place each truffle in a paper bon-bon cup and package in candy boxes (available in craft stores).

INGREDIENTS | YIELDS ABOUT 75 TRUFFLES

⅔ cup heavy cream, heated to a simmer

1 stick (½ cup) unsalted butter, cut up

3 teaspoons instant coffee granules, divided

1 (24-ounce) package semisweet chocolate chips

1 (6-ounce) package white chocolate chips

25 coffee beans

½ cup unsweetened cocoa powder

½ cup confectioner's sugar, plus more if needed

Warm Hands, Melted Chocolate

Every 5–10 truffles or so, rinse your hands in cold water. It will make the soft chocolate mixture stick less.

1. Combine the cream, butter, and 1 teaspoon of the coffee granules in a 4-quart slow cooker. Stir in the semisweet chocolate and the white chocolate. Cover and cook on low for 1 hour or until chocolate has completely melted and the mixture is glossy and smooth, stirring every 15 minutes.

2. Pour the chocolate mixture into a large shallow dish. Refrigerate for 1–2 hours, or until the gloss is gone and the mixture holds it shape when rolled in a ball. Meanwhile, line 2 large cookie sheets with wax paper; set aside.

3. Scoop out heaping teaspoons of the chocolate and, using your hands, roll into balls about ¾"–1" in diameter. Place truffles on the prepared cookie sheets. Press one coffee bean on top of 25 truffles. Refrigerate for at least 1 hour or until truffles are firmed up.

4. In a small bowl, mix together the cocoa powder with the remaining coffee granules. One at a time, roll 25 truffles (without the coffee beans) in the cocoa mixture, turning to completely coat. Return truffles to one of the cookie sheets. Refrigerate for another hour or until completely firm.

5. Using the confectioner's sugar as a coating, repeat with the remaining 25 truffles.

6. Store each truffle type, in separate airtight containers, in the refrigerator for up to a week, or freeze for up to 1 month.

Pumpkin Pudding

Be sure to use solid packed pumpkin rather than pumpkin pie filling.

INGREDIENTS | SERVES 8

Cooking spray
1 (12-ounce) can evaporated milk
1 (16-ounce) can solid packed pumpkin
¾ cup granulated sugar
½ cup baking mix, such as Bisquick
2 eggs, lightly beaten
2 tablespoons unsalted butter, melted
1 teaspoon ground cinnamon
½ teaspoon ground nutmeg
⅛ teaspoon ground cloves
2 teaspoons vanilla extract
Whipped cream (for garnish)

1. Spray the inside of a 4-quart slow cooker with the cooking spray.

2. In a large bowl whisk together the remaining ingredients until smooth. Scrape into the prepared slow cooker. Cover and cook on high for 3–4 hours or on low for 6–8 hours.

3. Decorate with whipped cream before serving, if desired.

Peach Melba

Peach Melba proves that a French dessert need not be complicated.
Use real ice cream or a pareve version, depending upon the meal with which it is served.

INGREDIENTS | SERVES 8

2 (10-ounce) packages frozen raspberries in syrup, defrosted
½ cup white granulated sugar
½ teaspoon ground cinnamon
2 tablespoons fresh lemon juice
2 (15-ounce) cans peach slices, drained
1 quart vanilla ice cream
8 teaspoons sliced almonds (for garnish)
Mint leaves (for garnish)

1. Add the raspberries and their syrup to a 4-quart slow cooker. Stir in the sugar, cinnamon, and lemon juice. Cover and cook on low heat for 4 hours.

2. Transfer the raspberry sauce to a covered container. Allow to cool for 30 minutes, then place in the refrigerator for several hours to cool completely.

3. Divide the peach slices among 8 dessert bowls. Place a ½-cup scoop of ice cream on top of each serving. Drizzle with the chilled raspberry syrup. Garnish with a teaspoon of the almonds and a few mint leaves over each, if desired. Serve immediately.

Mexican-Style Flan

The usual water bath is not needed due to the low gentle heat of the slow cooker.
For a lower-fat version, substitute low-fat or fat-free evaporated milk.

INGREDIENTS | SERVES 8

1½ cups granulated sugar, divided
4 eggs
2 (13-ounce) cans evaporated milk
2 teaspoons vanilla extract
½ teaspoon kosher salt
Whipped cream (for garnish)

1. In a small saucepan over medium heat, constantly stir 1 cup of the sugar until it melts and becomes golden brown, about 5 minutes. As soon as it is golden brown, immediately remove from heat and pour into the insert of a 4-quart slow cooker, tilting to coat bottom and sides. Set aside.

2. In a 2-quart or larger bowl, whisk the eggs, then stir in evaporated milk, remaining ½ cup sugar, vanilla, and salt. Pour mixture into prepared slow cooker. Cover and cook on low for 3–4 hours, or until a knife inserted halfway between center and edge of mold comes out clean.

3. Carefully remove insert and place on cooling rack for 15 minutes, then refrigerate for at least 2 hours, or until completely chilled.

4. Hold a large plate over the top of the insert, then quickly invert. Flan should release onto the plate, covered in the liquefied caramelized sugar. Spoon or cut into 8 servings and serve with whipped cream, if desired.

CHAPTER 14

Passover

Spiced Apple Cider Turkey

This recipe makes candied sweet potatoes while it cooks the turkey in the sweetened cider sauce.

INGREDIENTS | SERVES 8

Cooking spray

1 (3-pound) boneless turkey breast

Salt and freshly ground black pepper, to taste

2 apples

4 large sweet potatoes

½ cup apple cider or apple juice

½ teaspoon ground cinnamon

¼ teaspoon ground cloves

¼ teaspoon ground allspice

2 tablespoons brown sugar

1. Spray the inside of a 6- or 7-quart slow cooker with cooking spray. Add turkey breast and season it with salt and pepper.

2. Peel, core, and slice the apples; arrange the slices over and around the turkey.

3. Peel the sweet potatoes and cut each in half; add to the slow cooker.

4. In medium bowl, add the cider or juice, cinnamon, cloves, allspice, and brown sugar; stir to combine and pour over the ingredients in the slow cooker.

5. Cover and cook on low for 8 hours or until the internal temperature of the turkey is 170°F.

Simple Brisket

After a few minutes of browning, the brisket can be left to cook by itself while you pay more attention to all those other Passover preparations.

INGREDIENTS | SERVES 6–8

Cooking spray

2 tablespoons vegetable oil

1 large onion, diced

2 garlic cloves, minced

1 (3-pound) brisket, trimmed of excess fat

1 teaspoon powdered pareve beef bouillon

1 cup water

2 tablespoons balsamic vinegar

1 teaspoon ground ginger

½ teaspoon pepper

1. Lightly spray the inside of a 6-quart slow cooker with cooking spray.

2. Heat vegetable oil in a large skillet over medium heat. Add onion and garlic; stir frequently for 3–4 minutes or until onions just start to brown. Push to the sides of the pan and add brisket. Let sear undisturbed for 4 minutes, then carefully use tongs to turn brisket over. Let sear for another 4 minutes.

3. Transfer brisket and onions to prepared slow cooker.

4. In a medium bowl, stir together the bouillon, water, balsamic vinegar, ginger, and pepper. Pour mixture over brisket. Cover and cook on low for 7–8 hours or until brisket is very tender.

5. Turn off the slow cooker. When safe to handle, remove insert and allow contents to cool for 30 minutes. Transfer to a heat/refrigerator-safe covered dish and refrigerate overnight.

6. The next day, place brisket on cutting board. Slice as thinly as possible across the grain. Return to covered dish. Heat in preheated 350°F oven for 30 minutes or until hot.

Stuffed Breast of Veal

Veal is a spectacular alternative to the usual brisket or turkey.
Have the butcher cut a pocket into the veal breast.

INGREDIENTS | SERVES 6–8

Cooking spray

2 tablespoons olive oil

2 tablespoons margarine

1 small onion, finely diced

1 celery stalk, finely chopped

8 ounces white button mushrooms, sliced

½ cup loosely packed parsley leaves, chopped

4 cups matzoh farfel

1 teaspoon kosher salt

½ teaspoon ground black pepper

1 teaspoon fresh sage leaves, minced

1 tablespoon fresh thyme leaves

½ cup Chicken Stock or Vegetable Broth (see Chapter 4)

1 (4- to 5-pound) breast of veal

If There Is Any Leftover Stuffing . . .

Place leftover stuffing mixture in a casserole dish sprayed with the cooking spray. Bake covered at 350°F for 30 minutes. If a crust is desired, uncover and bake for an additional 10 minutes or until top is browned.

1. Spray the inside of a 6-quart slow cooker with cooking spray.

2. Heat the oil and the margarine in a large skillet over medium-high heat. Add the onion and celery. Cook, stirring frequently, for 5–8 minutes, or until onions soften.

3. Stir in mushrooms and cook for another 5 minutes or until mushrooms start to reduce and give up their liquid. Stir in remaining ingredients except the veal. Remove from heat.

4. Stuff the matzoh mixture loosely into the veal pocket (not all may be needed; see sidebar on what to do with any leftover stuffing). Secure pocket closed with toothpicks. Place veal into prepared slow cooker. Cover and cook on low for 6–8 hours or on high for 4–6 hours. Remove toothpicks before slicing and serving.

Lemon Chicken with Potatoes, Onions, and Olives

Because of the saltiness of the olives, no extra salt is needed.

INGREDIENTS | SERVES 4

2 large onions, cut in half then thinly sliced

1 tablespoon olive oil

2 large potatoes, peeled and cut into large chunks

1 whole chicken, cut up and partially skinned

½ teaspoon black pepper

½ cup whole black olives

1 lemon, thinly sliced

1. Place onion slices in a 6-quart slow cooker. Drizzle oil over onions, and mix to coat onions in the oil.

2. Evenly arrange potato chunks over onions. Place the chicken, skin side up, on top of the potatoes. Sprinkle pepper and scatter olives over chicken. Place lemon slices over chicken, overlapping if necessary.

3. Cover and cook on low for 8 hours or until the chicken juices run clear when pierced with a knife. Discard lemon before serving.

Chicken with 40 Cloves of Garlic

This dish has become a Passover favorite simply because of its name. According to the book of Exodus, after escaping from Egyptian slavery, Moses and the Israelites wandered the desert for forty years.

INGREDIENTS | SERVES 4

2 tablespoons olive oil

1 whole chicken, cut into eighths and most of skin removed

½ cup dry white wine

¼ teaspoon black pepper

½ tablespoon fresh rosemary, chopped

½ teaspoon dried thyme

40 garlic cloves (about 4 garlic bulbs), peeled

1. Heat the oil in a large skillet over medium-high heat. Brown the chicken for about 4–5 minutes each side.

2. Transfer the chicken to a 6-quart slow cooker. Pour the wine over the chicken. Sprinkle with the black pepper, rosemary, and thyme. Scatter the garlic cloves around the chicken.

3. Cover and cook for 3–4 hours on low or until the juices run clear when the chicken is pierced with a knife.

Don't Be Afraid of All That Garlic!
The long cooking process mellows the taste of the garlic. Mash the cooked garlic to use as a spread or to mix into mashed potatoes.

Lamb Shanks with Lemon

This is a simple yet delicious alternative to the usual chicken or brisket for the Seder table.

INGREDIENTS | SERVES 4

1 tablespoon olive oil

1 large onion, peeled and chopped

3 garlic cloves, minced

4 lamb shanks

¼ teaspoon minced fresh rosemary

½ teaspoon kosher salt

¼ teaspoon ground black pepper

1 lemon, thinly sliced

½ cup dry white wine

¼ cup water

1. Heat the oil in a large skillet over medium-high heat. Add onion. Cook, stirring frequently, for about 5 minutes, or until onions soften. Add garlic and stir for 1 minute. Transfer the mixture to a 6-quart slow cooker and set aside.

2. Return skillet to heat and add lamb shanks. Let shanks sear for 3 minutes undisturbed. Carefully turn shanks over and repeat browning for another 3 minutes. Place shanks over onion mixture in slow cooker. Sprinkle with rosemary, salt, and pepper. Arrange lemon slices over shanks. Pour in white wine and water. Cover and cook on low for 6–8 hours or until shanks are tender. Discard lemon slices before serving.

Matzoh Ball Soup

Although it is not strictly traditional, adding dill or parsley to the matzoh balls adds a fresh note to this slow-cooked soup.

INGREDIENTS | SERVES 6

2 quarts Chicken Stock (see Chapter 4)
1 stalk celery, diced
2 carrots, cut into coin-sized pieces
1 parsnip, diced
1 onion, diced
1½ cups diced cooked chicken
2 tablespoons vegetable oil
2 large eggs, slightly beaten
½ cup matzoh meal
2 tablespoons seltzer
1 teaspoon kosher salt
1½ tablespoons minced fresh dill or parsley

1. Put the stock, celery, carrots, parsnip, and onion into a 4-quart slow cooker. Cook on low for 6–8 hours. Add the chicken 1 hour before serving.

2. About 45 minutes before serving, mix the oil, eggs, matzoh meal, seltzer, salt, and dill (or parsley) in a large bowl until matzoh meal is completely moistened. Refrigerate mixture for 15 minutes.

3. Rinse hands in cold water (repeat as necessary), then form mixture into 1" balls. Drop them into the soup, cover, and cook for 20 minutes.

Matzoh Meal Year-Round

Leftover matzoh meal can be used year-round. Use in place of crushed crackers or bread crumbs to bread fish or chicken before frying, for Chanukah potato latkes, or in meatballs.

Tzimmes

This traditional long-cooking sweet vegetable stew is served at Passover as well as other Jewish holidays.

INGREDIENTS | **SERVES 12–16**

Cooking spray

4 large carrots, peeled and cut into 1" chunks

1 medium onion, peeled and diced

5 large sweet potatoes, peeled and cut into large chunks

1 (8-ounce) package pitted prunes, halved

1 cup (4 ounces) dried apricots, halved

¼ cup raisins

2 tablespoons honey

½ teaspoon ground cinnamon

½ teaspoon ground ginger

1 teaspoon kosher salt

⅛ teaspoon ground pepper

½ cup orange juice

¾ cup apple juice

1. Lightly spray the inside of a 6-quart slow cooker with the cooking spray. Add the carrots, onion, sweet potatoes, prunes, dried apricots, raisins, and honey to the slow cooker. Stir to combine.

2. Sprinkle in the cinnamon, ginger, salt, and pepper.

3. Pour in the orange and apple juices. Cover and cook on high for 10–12 hours.

Passover Potatoes Au Gratin

Serve this dairy dish with a simple salad for lunch.

INGREDIENTS | SERVES 4

Cooking spray

2 tablespoons margarine, divided

1 medium onion, peeled and diced

1 (5-ounce) box scalloped potatoes (any variety)

2 cups hot water

4 ounces Cheddar or Swiss cheese (or a combination of both), shredded

1. Spray the inside of a 4-quart slow cooker with cooking spray.

2. Melt margarine in a sauté pan over medium-high heat. Add diced onion. Cook, stirring occasionally, until onions soften and start to brown, about 5–8 minutes. Transfer to prepared slow cooker.

3. Add the potatoes and sprinkle the seasoning mix over the top of them. Dot with the remaining margarine. Pour in the water. Cover and cook on low for 5 hours.

4. Uncover and sprinkle on the cheese. Re-cover and continue to cook for another 15 minutes or until cheese has melted.

Passover Scalloped Chicken

Here's an easy meal that's delicious enough to serve year-round.

INGREDIENTS | SERVES 4

Cooking spray

2 tablespoons margarine, divided

1 medium onion, peeled and diced

1 (5-ounce) box scalloped potatoes (any variety)

1 cup cooked diced chicken

2 cups hot water

1. Spray the inside of a 4-quart slow cooker with cooking spray.

2. Melt margarine in a sauté pan over medium-high heat. Add diced onion. Cook, stirring occasionally, until onions soften and start to brown, about 5–8 minutes. Transfer to prepared slow cooker.

3. Add the potatoes and sprinkle the seasoning mix over the top of them. Spread the chicken on top of the potatoes. Dot with remaining margarine. Pour in the water. Cover and cook on low for 5 hours.

Potato Kugel

Kugel means pudding, sweet or savory, with or without noodles. This version is a noodle-free savory version.

INGREDIENTS | SERVES 8

Cooking spray

6 Yukon gold potatoes, peeled and grated

1 medium onion, diced

½ cup boiling water

3 eggs

1 teaspoon kosher salt

¼ teaspoon black pepper

1 teaspoon pareve chicken bouillon powder

2 tablespoons vegetable oil

1. Spray the inside of a 4-quart slow cooker with cooking spray.

2. In a large mixing bowl, combine the grated potatoes, diced onion, and boiling water. Transfer to prepared slow cooker.

3. In the same mixing bowl, whisk together the eggs, salt, pepper, bouillon powder, and oil. Stir egg mixture into potato mixture.

4. Cover slow cooker and cook on high for 1 hour, then on low for 6–8 more hours.

Balsamic Asparagus with Lemon

This spring vegetable is perfect for the Seder table!

INGREDIENTS | SERVES 6–8

2 pounds asparagus, rinsed and tough ends trimmed

1 tablespoon balsamic vinegar

¼ cup boiling water

¼ cup dry white wine

2 teaspoons olive oil

½ teaspoon kosher salt

¼ teaspoon black pepper

1 lemon, thinly sliced

1. Place the trimmed asparagus in a 4-quart slow cooker.

2. In a medium bowl, whisk together the balsamic vinegar, water, wine, olive oil, salt, and pepper; pour over the asparagus. Top evenly with the lemon slices.

3. Cook on high for 2–3 hours or until the asparagus is tender. Discard lemon slices before serving.

Trimming Asparagus

An easy way to trim asparagus is to simply bend each stalk until it snaps. It will break at the correct spot every time!

Aunt Carol's Matzoh Cheese Kugel

Aunt Carol is one of my husband's aunts. She makes this recipe every Passover, and says even cheese-haters love it. Don't substitute matzoh farfel for the crumbled matzoh, because the small pieces will "melt" into the cheese.

INGREDIENTS | SERVES 4–6

Cooking spray

6 matzohs

5 eggs

¾ cup milk, regular or low-fat

¼ cup half-and-half

1 pound small-curd cottage cheese

1 teaspoon kosher salt

¼ cup granulated sugar, plus another ¼ cup for garnish

1 teaspoon ground cinnamon

3 tablespoons butter, melted

1. Spray the inside of a 4-quart slow cooker with cooking spray.

2. Coarsely crumble matzohs into small pieces, ½" or less; place in the slow cooker and set aside.

3. In a large mixing bowl, whisk together the eggs, the milk, and the half-and-half.

4. Then add in the cottage cheese, salt, ¼ cup of the sugar, cinnamon, and melted butter and use a spatula to combine. Pour mixture evenly over matzoh pieces. Do not stir. Use a spatula if necessary to make sure the matzoh pieces are moistened.

5. Cover and cook on low for 3 hours. Turn off cooker, set cover slightly ajar, and let center firm up for 15–30 minutes. Serve warm, sprinkled with additional sugar.

Breakfast Quinoa with Fruit

Quinoa, pronounced "KEEN-wah," is actually a seed, not a grain, closely related to spinach. It is gluten-free and (where available) kosher for Passover.

INGREDIENTS | SERVES 4

Cooking spray
1 cup quinoa, rinsed
2 cups water, heated to a simmer
1 pear, thinly sliced
1 packed tablespoon dark brown sugar
½ teaspoon ground ginger
¼ teaspoon cinnamon
⅛ teaspoon cloves
⅛ teaspoon nutmeg
½ cup dried apricots, quartered

1. Spray the inside of a 4-quart slow cooker with cooking spray.

2. Add all the ingredients except the dried apricots and stir. Cover and cook on low for 2–3 hours, or until the quinoa is fully cooked. Stir in the dried apricots and serve.

Kichel Cake

Be sure the cherries are patted dry so that their juice doesn't stain the batter. Margarine is used so that this cake can be served as part of a meat-based meal. Feel free to use butter in place of the margarine, and evaporated milk (any variety) in place of the almond milk, for a dairy alternative.

INGREDIENTS | SERVES 8–12

¾ cup (1½ sticks) margarine, softened, divided

12 ounces Passover egg kichel or ladyfinger cookies, crushed into crumbs, divided

½ cup granulated sugar

4 eggs

⅓ cup almond milk

½ teaspoon vanilla extract

1 cup loosely packed sweetened coconut

¾ cup chopped pecans, lightly toasted

6 maraschino or canned sweet cherries, drained and patted dry with a paper towel

1. Use 1 tablespoon of the margarine and 2 tablespoons of the egg kichel crumbs to grease and flour a heat-safe pan or casserole dish that fits inside a 4-quart slow cooker.

2. In a large bowl, cream remaining margarine and sugar together.

3. Add eggs, one at a time, beating well after each addition. Stir in remaining ingredients except the cherries. Scrape batter into prepared pan.

4. Cut the cherries in half; arrange, cut side down, evenly on top of the batter.

5. Place a heat-safe trivet or crushed aluminum foil in bottom of slow cooker. Carefully place pan on top. Cover pan with 4 layers of paper towels. Set cover slightly ajar and cook on low for 3–4 hours.

Gefilte Fish

It's a little bit of work, but homemade gefilte fish is so much better than the rubbery version sold in jars.

INGREDIENTS | SERVES 10

2 pounds carp

2 pounds pike

1 pound whitefish

3 medium onions, divided

3 carrots, divided

8 cups of water, heated to a simmer

2 celery stalks, cut into 1" chunks

3 teaspoons kosher salt, divided

1 teaspoon ground black pepper, divided

3 tablespoons granulated sugar, divided

3 large eggs

½ cup matzoh meal

1 (6-ounce) bottle horseradish, red or white

What Kind of Fish Is a Gefilte?

Gefilte is not a type of fish, but a ball of chopped and seasoned fish cooked in broth, usually served cold. The fish used is generally carp, pike, whitefish, or some combination of the three, depending upon personal taste. Bubbe (grandma) may have finely chopped all the fish by hand in an ancient wooden chopping bowl (and might even have had a live fish in the bathtub to assure freshness), but nowadays it's much easier to have the fish store grind it for you.

1. Have the fish store grind together the fish, reserving the heads and bones for the stock.

2. Peel and quarter 2 of the onions. Peel and thinly slice 1 of the carrots. Peel and finely chop remaining onion and carrots together; set aside.

3. In a 6- or 7-quart slow cooker, pour in the water and add the reserved fish heads and bones along with the 2 quartered onions, the sliced carrot, celery, 2 teaspoons of the salt, ½ teaspoon of the black pepper, and 2 tablespoons of the sugar. Cover and cook on low for 2 hours. Occasionally skim off any scum that may form on top.

4. Meanwhile, in a large bowl, combine ground fish with the finely chopped onion and carrots, along with remaining sugar, salt, and pepper.

5. In a small bowl, lightly whisk the eggs and then mix into the fish mixture along with matzoh meal. Cover and refrigerate for at least a half hour.

6. Strain the broth. Cover and refrigerate the sliced carrots. Discard remaining solids. Return broth to slow cooker and set on high until broth starts to simmer.

7. With wet hands, take fish mixture and form 10 ovals. Carefully add to hot broth. Cover and reduce heat to low. Cook for 2 hours.

8. Remove gefilte fish with a slotted spoon. Discard broth. Cover and refrigerate gefilte fish until ready to serve. Serve cold, topping each piece with a carrot slice and a teaspoon of horseradish on the side.

Gedilla's Meatballs in Borscht

Gedilla *means "joy" in Yiddish and was the nickname of the Ukrainian-born bubbe who made this dish every Passover. Her original recipe called for, among other ingredients, "less half a lemon." Serve the meatballs with matzoh farfel to soak up the broth.*

INGREDIENTS | SERVES 8–10

1 large onion, peeled and finely chopped (about 1 cup), divided

2 carrots, peeled and chopped

2 large raw beets, peeled and shredded

2 cups shredded cabbage

1 tablespoon olive oil

2 tablespoons sugar

1 teaspoon kosher salt

2 tablespoons fresh lemon juice

1 bay leaf

1 pound ground beef

1 egg, lightly beaten

½ cup matzoh meal

¼ teaspoon black pepper

½ cup tomato juice

4 cups Beef Broth or water, heated to a simmer (see Chapter 4)

2 cups matzoh farfel (for garnish)

1. Add ¾ cup of the chopped onion, the carrots, the beets, and the cabbage to a 4-quart slow cooker. Drizzle in the olive oil; stir to combine. Sprinkle on the sugar, salt, and lemon juice; add the bay leaf. Set aside.

2. In a large bowl combine the ground beef, egg, remaining onion, matzoh meal, and pepper. Using your hands, roll the mixture into balls about 1" in diameter. Place meatballs on top of the vegetables in the slow cooker.

3. Pour the tomato juice and the broth or water over the meatballs. Cover and cook on low for 6–8 hours or on high for 3–4 hours, or until the meatballs are fully cooked and the vegetables are tender.

4. Serve meatballs with some of the broth and vegetables. Optionally, sprinkle on the matzoh farfel just before serving.

Almond Cake with Honey Lemon Syrup

The long cooking time softens up the matzoh meal.

INGREDIENTS | SERVES 12

Honey Lemon Syrup
¼ cup honey
2 tablespoons granulated sugar
¼ cup water
2 tablespoons fresh lemon juice

Almond Cake
Cooking spray
1 (6-ounce) package ground almonds
½ cup matzoh cake meal
1 cup sugar, divided
1 teaspoon ground cinnamon
¼ teaspoon kosher salt
4 large eggs, room temperature
2 tablespoons fresh lemon juice
1 teaspoon grated lemon peel
¼ cup vegetable oil
¼ cup sliced almonds

1. Make the Honey Lemon Syrup: Heat honey, sugar, water, and lemon juice in a 1-quart saucepan over medium-high heat, stirring constantly until sugar is dissolved. Bring to a boil, then remove from heat and let cool. Set aside.

2. Line a 4-quart slow cooker with aluminum foil, allowing the foil to come at least 4" up the sides. Spray with cooking spray. Set aside.

3. In a medium bowl, whisk together the ground almonds, matzoh cake meal, ½ cup sugar, cinnamon, and salt. Set aside.

4. In a large bowl, using an electric mixer on medium speed, beat the eggs, remaining ½ cup sugar, lemon juice, and grated lemon peel for 2 minutes, then increase to high speed (for handheld mixer) or medium-high speed (for a stand mixer such as KitchenAid) for 6–8 more minutes until batter turns pale in color and thickens. Reduce speed back to medium and beat in vegetable oil for another minute. Use a spatula to fold in dry mixture until completely moistened.

5. Scrape batter into prepared slow cooker. Cook on high for 2–2½ hours or until cake starts to pull away from sides of pan and a toothpick inserted into center comes out clean.

6. Holding foil by edges, lift and remove cake from slow cooker; place on cooling rack. Let cool for 10 minutes; cake will sink slightly. Carefully peel foil from cake and place on serving dish. Slice cake into 12 squares. Sprinkle evenly with sliced almonds. Spoon cooled syrup over cake. Let cake absorb syrup for 30 minutes before serving.

Matzoh Lasagna

If kosher-for-Passover Parmesan cheese is not available in your area, simply omit it.

INGREDIENTS | SERVES 8

Cooking spray

4 matzohs

2 cups hot water

4 cups Marinara Sauce (see Chapter 12)

1 (16-ounce) carton small-curd cottage cheese

4 ounces grated Parmesan cheese

1 (16-ounce) package shredded mozzarella cheese

For a Delicious Option . . .

Instead of Marinara Sauce, try this recipe with Eggplant and Tomato Sauce (see Chapter 12).

1. Lightly spray the interior of a 5- or 6-quart slow cooker with cooking spray.

2. Place matzohs in a colander set in the sink. Pour hot water over matzohs. Drain matzohs well.

3. Spoon about ⅓ cup of Marinara Sauce into the slow cooker to cover the bottom with a thin layer. Top with 1 matzoh. Spread a third of the cottage cheese on top of the matzoh. Sprinkle a third each of the Parmesan cheese and the mozzarella cheese over cottage cheese. Spoon a third of the remaining sauce over the cheese.

4. Repeat with remaining matzohs, cheeses and sauce, ending with matzoh and sauce.

5. Cover and cook on high for 2 hours until the cheese has melted and sauce has been absorbed into the matzoh.

Balsamic Sweet Potatoes

Something different for your Seder table.

INGREDIENTS | SERVES 6–8

6 large sweet potatoes, peeled and cut into 2" chunks

¼ cup olive oil

¼ cup balsamic vinegar

3 tablespoons brown sugar

1 teaspoon kosher salt, plus more to taste

¼ teaspoon ground black pepper, plus more to taste

¼ cup toasted pecans, chopped (for garnish)

1. Place the sweet potatoes in a 4-quart slow cooker.

2. In a medium bowl, whisk together the olive oil, vinegar, and brown sugar; stir into the sweet potatoes until they are completely coated. Cover and cook on low for 4–6 hours, or until the sweet potatoes are easily pierced with a fork. Stir in salt and pepper. Taste and add additional salt and/or pepper if needed.

3. Sprinkle with chopped pecans before serving, if desired.

Spinach Soufflé

This is not a true soufflé since the eggs are not separated, but the dish does rise a bit, so it makes for a lovely and delicious presentation.

INGREDIENTS | SERVES 6–8

Cooking spray

1 (8-ounce) package cream cheese, room temperature

2 eggs

½ cup mayonnaise

1 small onion, finely diced

¼ teaspoon ground nutmeg

1 teaspoon kosher salt

¼ teaspoon black pepper

½ cup shredded Cheddar cheese

¼ cup Parmesan cheese

2 (10-ounce) packages frozen chopped spinach, defrosted and squeezed dry

1. Line a 4-quart slow cooker with aluminum foil, covering the bottom and at least 6" up the sides. Spray foil with the cooking spray and set aside.

2. Using an electric mixer, beat the cream cheese on medium speed until softened. Add the eggs and continue to beat until incorporated. Mix in the remaining ingredients in order given at medium-low speed. Scrape the mixture into the prepared slow cooker. Cover and cook on high for 2–3 hours.

3. Remove the soufflé by pulling up on the aluminum foil.

Quinoa with Onions and Toasted Almonds

Look for kosher-for-Passover quinoa in the kosher section of larger supermarkets.

INGREDIENTS | SERVES 4

Cooking spray

2 tablespoons olive oil

1 medium onion, cut in half, then thinly sliced

1 cup quinoa, rinsed and drained

1 teaspoon kosher salt

¼ teaspoon black pepper

1½ cups water, heated to a simmer

¼ cup toasted almonds

2 tablespoons chopped parsley leaves (for garnish)

Quinoa

Quinoa is naturally coated with a bitter substance to protect against predators, making it important to rinse it well before cooking.

1. Spray the inside of a 4-quart slow cooker.

2. Heat oil in a skillet over medium-high heat. Add the onion. Sauté frequently until the onion begins to turn golden brown, about 10–15 minutes.

3. Add the quinoa, salt, and pepper to the skillet and stir for 1 minute to combine.

4. Scrape the quinoa mixture into the prepared cooker. Stir in water.

5. Cover and cook on high heat for 2 hours or until quinoa is tender and water is totally absorbed. Stir in toasted almonds. Transfer quinoa mixture to a serving dish. Garnish with parsley, if desired, before serving.

Spinach Pie

Sheets of matzoh are used to create a pie "crust."

INGREDIENTS | SERVES 4–6

Cooking spray

4 matzohs

2 cups hot water

1½ pounds fresh spinach, washed, drained well, and chopped

3 eggs, lightly beaten

1 teaspoon kosher salt

¼ teaspoon black pepper

¼ teaspoon nutmeg

¼ cup matzoh meal

1 tablespoon olive oil

1 tablespoon ground walnuts or almonds

1. Lightly spray the inside of a 4-quart slow cooker with the cooking spray.

2. Place matzohs in a colander set in the sink. Pour hot water over the matzohs; drain well and set aside.

3. In a large bowl, combine the spinach, eggs, salt, pepper, nutmeg, and matzoh meal. Set aside.

4. Line the prepared cooker with half of the softened matzoh, letting them come up the sides. Spread the spinach mixture on top of the matzoh layer. Cover with the remaining matzohs. Brush the matzohs with the oil and sprinkle walnuts evenly over the top. Cover and cook on high for 2–4 hours.

Plums in Orange Sauce

Any firm ripe purple plum can substitute for the prune plums called for in this recipe.

INGREDIENTS | SERVES 8

8 prune plums, cut in half and pitted

½ cup granulated sugar

⅓ cup orange juice

1 teaspoon finely grated orange zest

1 cinnamon stick

1. Combine all of the ingredients in a 4-quart slow cooker. Cover and cook on low for 3–5 hours or on high for 2–3 hours, or until the plums are tender.

2. Leave cover ajar and cook on high for another 30 minutes to let the syrup reduce slightly (syrup will thicken up more as it cools).

3. Remove and discard the cinnamon stick. Transfer the plums and their syrup to a covered container; refrigerate for several hours until chilled, or overnight. Serve the plums cold with their syrup spooned over them.

CHAPTER 15

Other Holidays

Honey-Mustard Turkey

You can substitute maple syrup for the honey. Another alternative is to substitute Dijon mustard instead of stone-ground and white wine vinegar for the cider.

INGREDIENTS | SERVES 4

Cooking spray
2 turkey thighs, skin removed
4 red potatoes, peeled and quartered
¼ cup stone-ground mustard
⅓ cup honey
1 tablespoon apple cider vinegar
Extra-virgin olive oil (optional)

1. Spray the inside of a 5- or 6-quart slow cooker with cooking spray.

2. Place the thighs in the slow cooker, meaty side down. Layer the potatoes over the thighs.

3. In a small bowl, whisk together the mustard, honey, and vinegar, then pour into the slow cooker. Cover and cook on low for 8 hours.

4. Before serving, drizzle extra-virgin olive oil over the potatoes if desired.

Rosh Hashanah Brisket

Lemon and honey go together very nicely in this simple brisket recipe. Serve with rice or potatoes.

INGREDIENTS | SERVES 6–8

Cooking spray

2 tablespoons olive oil

2 large onions, peeled and diced

2 large carrots, peeled and coarsely chopped

1 (3-pound) brisket, trimmed of excess fat

1 teaspoon ground ginger

¼ teaspoon black pepper

¼ cup honey

2 tablespoons fresh lemon juice

1 (12-ounce) can beef broth or 1½ cups No-Beef Broth (see Chapter 4)

1. Lightly spray inside of a 6-quart oval slow cooker with cooking spray.

2. Heat oil in a large skillet over medium-high heat. Add onions and carrots. Cook, stirring frequently, for 5 minutes or until onions soften. Scrape vegetables into slow cooker and set aside.

3. Return skillet to the burner and add brisket. Let brisket brown, undisturbed, for 3 minutes. Carefully turn brisket over and repeat for 3 more minutes.

4. Place browned roast on top of vegetables in the slow cooker. Sprinkle with ginger and black pepper. Drizzle on honey and lemon juice. Pour beef broth around brisket. Cover and cook on low for 8–10 hours.

5. Let cool for a half hour, then carefully transfer meat, vegetables, and accumulated juices to a covered casserole dish. Refrigerate overnight. The next day, use a spoon to remove and discard the thick layer of chilled fat.

6. Transfer the brisket to a carving board. Slice and return sliced meat to the casserole dish. Cover and rewarm in a 350°F oven for 25–30 minutes. Spoon the juices over meat before serving.

Rosh Hashanah Chuck Roast

This roast tastes better after an overnight chill in the refrigerator.
The excess fat is easier to remove then as well.

INGREDIENTS | SERVES 6–8

Cooking spray

1 tablespoon vegetable oil

1 medium onion, peeled and sliced into thin rings

2 cloves of garlic, minced

3–4 carrots, peeled and cut into 1" pieces

2½- to 3-pound boneless chuck roast

1 teaspoon ground ginger

¼ teaspoon black pepper

2 tablespoons honey

1 tablespoon soy sauce

½ cup of red wine

1 bay leaf

3 cups cooked rice or mashed potatoes

Honey

Honey is traditionally used in Rosh Hashanah foods to represent the wish for a sweet new year.

1. Lightly spray inside of a 6-quart oval slow cooker with cooking spray.

2. Heat oil in a large skillet over medium-high heat. Sauté onion and garlic for 2 minutes, or until the rings easily separate. Scrape onions into slow cooker and top with carrots.

3. Return skillet to burner. Place chuck roast in pan. Let roast brown, undisturbed, for 3 minutes. Carefully turn roast over and repeat for 3 more minutes. Optionally, turn the roast on each end and repeat the browning.

4. Place browned roast on top of vegetables in the slow cooker. Sprinkle with ginger and black pepper. Drizzle on honey. Pour soy sauce and wine over and around roast. Place bay leaf in wine mixture. Cover and cook on low for 5–8 hours. Then discard the bay leaf.

5. Let cool for a half hour then carefully transfer meat, vegetables, and juices to a covered casserole dish. Refrigerate overnight. The next day, use a spoon to remove and discard the thick layer of chilled fat.

6. Transfer roast to a carving board and slice roast. Return sliced meat to the casserole dish. Cover and rewarm in a 350°F oven for 25–30 minutes. Serve meat and vegetables with rice or potatoes, spooning the juices over everything.

Beef Tzimmes

Tzimmes (pronounced TZIH-mess) is served at many Jewish holidays.

INGREDIENTS | SERVES 8

2 tablespoons vegetable oil

1 medium onion, peeled and diced

2 pounds beef stew meat, cut into 1" cubes

2 cups Beef Broth (see Chapter 4)

2 tablespoons tomato paste

1 tablespoon minced fresh rosemary

2 carrots, peeled and cut into 1" chunks

2 sweet potatoes, peeled and cut into 1" chunks

1 cup prunes, cut into halves

1 (8-ounce) can pineapple chunks or tidbits, drained

1 teaspoon kosher salt

¼ teaspoon black pepper

1. Heat oil in a large skillet. Sauté onion for 5 minutes or until it softens and starts to brown. Transfer to a 4- or 6-quart slow cooker and set aside.

2. Add meat cubes to skillet and brown for 3 minutes per side. Transfer to slow cooker and add all remaining ingredients except salt and pepper.

3. Cover and cook on low for 8–10 hours. Add salt and pepper. Taste and add more if needed.

Barley and Mushroom Casserole

Tu B'Shevat, the New Year for trees, is the holiday marking the beginning of spring in Israel when the trees break out of their dormancy. It is traditional during this holiday to eat from the Seven Species (barley, wheat, grapes, figs, pomegranates, olives, and dates), the fruits and grains mentioned in the Bible.

INGREDIENTS | SERVES 4

Nonstick spray
1 tablespoon olive oil
2 medium onions, diced
2 cloves garlic, minced
8 ounces button mushrooms, chopped
2 cups Vegetable Broth (see Chapter 4)
1 cup uncooked pearl barley
1 teaspoon dried thyme leaves
1 bay leaf
1 teaspoon dried basil
1 teaspoon kosher salt
½ teaspoon black pepper

1. Spray the inside of a 4-quart slow cooker with the nonstick spray.

2. Heat the olive oil in a large skillet over medium-high heat. Add the onions and cook, stirring frequently, until they soften and start to brown, about 7–9 minutes.

3. Add garlic and mushrooms. Continue to sauté frequently for another 3–5 minutes or until mushrooms reduce and start to give up their liquid.

4. Scrape vegetables into the prepared slow cooker. Stir in the remaining ingredients except the salt and pepper.

5. Cover and cook on high for 4–6 hours or on low for 10–12 hours. Remove bay leaf. Taste and add salt and pepper. Serve hot.

Mock Chopped "Liver"

Here's a vegetarian substitute that tastes just like the real thing! This spread keeps for 3–4 days covered tightly in the refrigerator, allowing you plenty of time for those last-minutes chores before yom tov guests arrive. Serve with crackers or cocktail bread.

INGREDIENTS | SERVES 10–12

1 cup brown lentils, rinsed and picked over

Water to cover lentils by at least 2"

1 tablespoon olive oil

2 large onions, thinly sliced

3 hard-boiled eggs, peeled

1 cup walnut pieces

½ teaspoon kosher salt, plus more to taste

½ teaspoon black pepper, plus more to taste

½ teaspoon paprika, for garnish (optional)

Lentils and Queen Esther

Queen Esther, heroine of the Purim story, supposedly ate a vegetarian diet to avoid nonkosher foods while in the King's court. In her honor, lentils are traditionally served during this holiday.

1. Add lentils to a 4-quart slow cooker. Pour in water to cover lentils by at least 2". Cover and cook on high for 3 hours. Drain lentils in a colander and rinse with cold water to stop the cooking process.

2. Meanwhile, heat oil in a large skillet over medium heat. Add thinly sliced onions. Sauté frequently until the onions are browned, about 10–15 minutes.

3. Add the drained lentils, cooked onions, eggs, walnuts, salt, and black pepper into a food processor. Process in short pulses until the mixture becomes a smooth, thick paste. Taste and add more salt and pepper, if necessary. Transfer mixture to a serving bowl. Dust with paprika, if desired.

Classic Hummus

Serve this Middle Eastern spread with toasted pita chips.

INGREDIENTS | SERVES 20

8 ounces dried chickpeas, rinsed and drained

Water, as needed

¼ cup tahini

2 tablespoons lemon juice

2 cloves garlic, minced

1 teaspoon ground coriander

½ teaspoon cumin

½ teaspoon kosher salt, or to taste

¼ teaspoon cayenne or black pepper, or to taste

¼ teaspoon paprika, for garnish

1. In a 4-quart slow cooker, add the chickpeas and cover with water by several inches. Soak overnight. The next day, drain and replace water. Cover and cook on low for 8 hours. Drain, reserving the liquid.

2. Transfer the chickpeas to a food processor and add remaining ingredients except paprika. Pulse until smooth, adding the reserved liquid as needed to achieve the desired texture. Taste and add more salt and pepper if needed.

3. Transfer to a serving bowl. Garnish with paprika. Serve with pita chips.

Toasted Pita Chips

No need to buy expensive bags of pita chips! Lightly brush 4 pita rounds with olive oil, then cut each into eighths, pizza style. Place triangles on ungreased baking pan in a single layer. Sprinkle on a couple pinches of kosher salt and bake at 400°F for 10 minutes, or until triangles just start to brown.

Lag B'Omer Sweet and Sour Red Cabbage

This cabbage dish is great alongside barbecued foods.

INGREDIENTS | SERVES 6

½ head red cabbage, shredded

1 medium onion, shredded

1½ tablespoons dark brown sugar

1 teaspoon margarine

¼ cup water

½ cup apple cider vinegar

1 tablespoon white wine vinegar

½ teaspoon freshly ground black pepper

¼ teaspoon salt

⅛ teaspoon ground cloves

½ teaspoon thyme

1. Place all ingredients into a 4-quart slow cooker. Stir to distribute all ingredients evenly.

2. Cook on low for 4–6 hours or until the cabbage is very soft. Stir before serving.

Lag B'Omer

Lag B'Omer is the 33rd day of the Omer (the counting of the 49 days from the second night of Passover to the day before Shavuot). Thousands of students of Rabbi Akiva, a great rabbi from the Torah, died from a great plague that occurred during one such counting of the Omer. Lag B'Omer commemorates the one day when no one died. It is celebrated with outdoor activities such as picnics, barbecues, and bonfires.

New York–Style Cheesecake

Making cheesecake in the slow cooker might sound odd, but it is actually the perfect appliance for the job. The constant low heat and moist environment keep it from drying out or cracking, even when using low-fat ingredients.

INGREDIENTS | SERVES 8

¾ cup low-fat chocolate or cinnamon graham cracker crumbs

1½ tablespoons butter, melted

8 ounces sour cream, at room temperature

8 ounces cream cheese, at room temperature

⅔ cup sugar

1 egg, at room temperature

2 teaspoons vanilla extract

1½ tablespoons flour

1 tablespoon lemon juice

1 tablespoon lemon zest

1 cup hot water

Shavuot and Dairy Products

Shavuot celebrates the giving of the Torah to the Jewish people. Dairy foods, a symbol of modesty, were considered appropriate for such a celebration.

1. In a small bowl, mix together the graham cracker crumbs and butter. Press into the bottom and sides of a 6" springform pan.

2. In a large bowl, mix the sour cream, cream cheese, sugar, egg, vanilla, flour, lemon juice, and zest until completely smooth. Pour into the springform pan.

3. Pour the water into the bottom of a 6-quart slow cooker. Place a trivet in the bottom of the slow cooker. Place the springform pan onto the trivet.

4. Cook on low for 2 hours. Turn off the slow cooker and let the cheesecake steam for 1 hour and 15 minutes with the lid on. Remove the cheesecake from the slow cooker. Refrigerate for 6 hours or overnight before serving.

Italian-Style Cheesecake

Which is better cheesecake, New York–style or Italian-style? Why choose? Make both!

INGREDIENTS | SERVES 8

1 (15-ounce) container of ricotta cheese, at room temperature

¾ cup ground almonds

1½ tablespoons butter, melted

⅓ cup sugar

2 tablespoons honey

2 eggs, at room temperature

2 teaspoons vanilla extract

1 tablespoon cornstarch

¼ teaspoon ground cinnamon

2 teaspoons lemon zest

⅛ teaspoon salt

1. Place ricotta in a colander lined with several layers of paper towels over a bowl. Drain for 30 minutes.

2. Meanwhile, in a small bowl, mix together the ground almonds and butter. Press into the bottom and sides of a 6" springform pan. Set aside.

3. In a large bowl, mix the drained ricotta, sugar, honey, eggs, vanilla, cornstarch, cinnamon, zest, and salt until completely smooth. Pour into the prepared springform pan.

4. Pour 1 cup of water into the bottom of a 6-quart slow cooker. Place a trivet in the bottom of the slow cooker. Place the springform pan onto the trivet.

5. Cook on low for 2 hours. Turn off the slow cooker and let the cheesecake steam for 1¼–1½ hours with the lid on or until the center is firm. Remove the cheesecake from the slow cooker. Refrigerate for 6 hours or overnight before serving.

Sukkot Apple and Pear Spread

Make the most of in-season apples and pears in this easy alternative to apple or pear butter.

INGREDIENTS | YIELDS 3 QUARTS

4 Winesap apples, cored and sliced

4 Bartlett pears, cored and sliced

1 cup water or pear cider

¼ packed cup brown sugar

¼ cup sugar

¼ teaspoon ginger

¼ teaspoon cinnamon

¼ teaspoon nutmeg

¼ teaspoon allspice

1. Place all ingredients into a 4-quart slow cooker. Cook on low for 10–12 hours.

2. Uncover and cook on low for an additional 10–12 hours or until thick and most of the liquid has evaporated.

3. Allow to cool completely, then pour into the food processor and purée. Pour into clean glass jars. Refrigerate for up to 6 weeks.

Sukkot

Sukkot is a fall harvest festival. Jewish people celebrate by eating most, if not all, their meals in small outdoor huts (called sukkahs or sukkot), symbolizing the tents workers lived in while harvesting foods.

Honey-Baked Apples with Raisins and Walnuts

A mixture of apples and honey is traditional for Rosh Hashanah.
It is great for Sukkot, too! You can also try this recipe with slivered almonds or chopped pecans.

INGREDIENTS | SERVES 4

¼ cup chopped walnuts
¼ cup raisins
½ teaspoon cinnamon
¼ teaspoon cardamom
2 teaspoons honey
4 Rome or other large baking apples
¼ cup water
½ cup apple juice or cider

1. In a small mixing bowl combine the walnuts, raisins, cinnamon, cardamom, and honey.

2. Cut off and reserve a ½" slice off the top of each apple, then core almost to the bottom. Fill each apple with the walnut mixture and replace top.

3. Place apples in a 4-quart slow cooker. Pour water and juice over apples.

4. Cover and cook on high for 3–4 hours or on low for 6–8 hours.

Chanukah Carrot "Coins"

These "coins" are a play on the chocolate gelt (money) children receive for Chanukah.

INGREDIENTS | SERVES 4

Cooking spray
1 pound carrots, peeled and sliced into ¼"-thick coins
½ cup orange marmalade
2 tablespoons orange juice
2 tablespoons honey
2 tablespoons unsalted butter or margarine, melted
¼ teaspoon ground ginger
½ teaspoon ground cinnamon
½ teaspoon kosher salt

1. Lightly spray the inside of a 4-quart slow cooker with cooking spray. Add carrots and set aside.

2. In a small bowl whisk together the remaining ingredients. Pour over carrots. Cover and cook on high for 4 hours.

APPENDIX A

Kosher or Pareve Substitutes

Ingredient	Substitute
Milk	soy, rice, coconut, or almond milk
Butter	margarine or olive oil
Chicken or beef broth	vegetable or no-beef broth
Wine	wine vinegar, vegetable broth, or water
Tapioca starch	corn or potato starch
1 tablespoon cornstarch	2 tablespoons flour or 1 tablespoon potato starch
Whole milk	cream, evaporated milk
Yogurt	sour cream, buttermilk, or whipped cream cheese
Buttermilk	yogurt or 1 cup milk mixed with 1 tablespoon of lemon juice
Buttermilk	1 cup soymilk mixed with 1 tablespoon of lemon juice
Ricotta or cottage cheese	tofu
Ricotta cheese	cottage cheese
Ice cream	Tofutti
Cream cheese	Tofutti Better Than Cream Cheese or Follow Your Heart Cream Cheese
Sour cream	Tofutti Better Than Sour Cream or Follow Your Heart Sour Cream
Cheese	sliced and grated pareve "cheese" substitutes such as Tofutti, Daiya, and Sheese
Walnuts	almonds or pecans

Ingredient	Substitute
1 tablespoon fresh herb or spice	1 teaspoon dried
Saffron	turmeric
Dried bread crumbs	stale bread, pulsed in food processor, or matzoh meal
Graham cracker crumbs	Passover egg kichel or ladyfingers, ground together with ¼ teaspoon cinnamon
Raisins	currants, dried cranberries, or chopped dates
Maple syrup	pancake syrup
Ground beef	ground chicken, turkey, lamb, bison, or veal
Ground meat	TVP or TSP (textured vegetable protein or textured soy protein), sold as unflavored dehydrated crumbles such as Bob's Red Mill or hydrated pre-seasoned such as Gimme Lean
Ground pork	ground veal, TVP, or TSP
Pork chop	veal chop
Pulled pork	shredded brisket, pastrami, short ribs, or veal
Pork ribs	beef or veal ribs
Ham	soy analog such as faux ham
Pork sausage	kosher veal or chicken sausage
Pork pepperoni	kosher beef or faux pepperoni
Bacon	turkey bacon, soy analog (such as Bacos) or kosher beef jerky
Shrimp, scallops, or crab	surimi

Additional Resources

All in Kosher Online Supermarket
A great source for kosher products
www.allinkosher.com

Aviglatt.com
Online kosher meats, including Of Tov products
www.aviglatt.com

Bisra Glatt Kosher Meats
Online source for kosher meats and meat products
www.bisrakosher.com

Bob's Red Mill
Online source for grains, beans, and cereals
www.bobsredmill.com

Boca Burger
Online source for kosher vegetarian and vegan analog meat products
www.bocaburger.com

Crock-Pot Corporation
Official site of the first slow cooker available to the public
www.crock-pot.com

The Food Timeline
One of the first, and still the best, website with information and history about almost any food or recipe
www.foodtimeline.org

French's Corporation
Source for French Fried Onions and other products
www.frenchs.com

Follow Your Heart
Source for pareve "cheese" products. Note: Follow Your Heart also sells dairy-based products.
www.followyourheart.com

Huy Fong Foods
Online source of Sriracha, other products, and recipes
www.huyfong.com

Imo Foods
Fantastic source for kosher Asian food products
www.imofood.com

Kof-K
Kosher-certifying agency
www.kof-k.org

The Kosher Express
Online source for kosher meats and other products
thekosherexpress.com

Kosher Supervision of America (KSA)
Kosher-certifying agency
www.ksakosher.com

Light Life
Vegan and vegetarian food products such as Gimme Lean
www.lightlife.com

Mrs. T's Pierogies
Online source for potato pierogies
www.pierogies.com

My Jewish Learning
A great introduction to Jewish religion, customs, and holidays
www.myjewishlearning.com

OK Kosher Certification (The OK)
Nationwide kosher-certifying agency
www.ok.org

OU (Orthodox Union) Kosher
Best known kosher-certifying agency
www.oukosher.org

Pangea Vegan Store
Online source for many pareve "cheeses" such as Daiya and Sheese
www.veganstore.com

Quinoa Corporation
Information, recipes, and source for Passover as well as year-round quinoa products
www.quinoa.net

Sahar Saffron
Good online source of kosher saffron
saharsaffron.com

The Scroll K/ Vaad Hakashrus of Denver
Kosher-certifying agency
www.scrollk.org

Star-K
Kosher-certifying agency
www.star-k.org

Tofutti
Kosher and pareve food products including Better than Cream Cheese and Better than Sour Cream
www.tofutti.com

United Synagogue of Conservative Judaism
Great information about Conservative Judaism
www.uscj.org

Whole Foods Market
Great natural foods supermarket
www.wholefoodsmarket.com

Wolff's Kasha
Online source for all kinds of buckwheat, groats, and recipes
www.wolffskasha.com

Glossary

Bubbe (BUH-bee or BUH-beh)
Yiddish term for grandmother

Challah (HAH-lah)
Braided bread made with egg and honey. It can be served at any meal, but is the traditional bread served during Shabbat, holidays, and special occasions.

Chametz (HAH-metz)
Breads or any products containing grains prohibited during Passover

Cholent (CHUH-lent)
The quintessential Jewish slow food. A stew made of beans, barley, potatoes, and (optionally) meat, slowly cooked overnight or for up to twenty-six hours in order to have a hot meal for lunch or dinner on Shabbat or soon after Shabbat is over.

Hechsher (HECK-sher)
The logo of a rabbinic agency placed on a food product certifying that the product is kosher

Kashering
The soaking and salting of meat or poultry in order to draw out the blood

Kashrut
The kosher dietary laws

Kitniyot (kit-nee-OAT)
Certain seeds and grains (such as corn and rice) whose consumption during Passover by Ashkenazi Jews is prohibited. The Passover recipes in this book follow Ashkenazi traditions and do not contain kitniyot.

Kosher
Fit for consumption, according to Jewish dietary laws

Kosher salt
So named because it is the salt used to kosher (kasher) meats, but can also be used in everyday foods. Because kosher salt has a larger crystal grain than regular table salt, double the amount of kosher salt must be used to have the same saltiness as table salt.

Margarine
A butter substitute. Although some brands of margarine may contain dairy products, the margarine called for in the recipes in this book should always be pareve.

Mashgiach (mahsh-GHEE-ahk)
A person specially trained to supervise and inspect a restaurant or food service to ensure that the food is kosher

Matzoh (MAHT-zah)
The unleavened bread eaten during Passover. It is a large, flat, crisp cracker. Passover matzoh is made from flour and water. Matzoh farfel is matzoh baked then broken up into tiny pieces about ¼"–½" each. Matzoh meal is ground-up matzoh, similar in texture to corn meal. Matzoh cake meal is very finely ground matzoh, almost like flour.

Pareve (PAH-rehv)
Food that contains neither milk nor meat products

Shabbat (shah-BAHT) or Shabbos (SHAH-bos)
The biblical seventh day of rest. Shabbat is observed from just before sundown on Friday night until just after sundown on Saturday night.

Shalach manot (shah-LAHK man-NOHT)
Basket of treats given to friends and neighbors as part of celebrating Purim

Shiva (SHIH-vah)
Seven days of mourning starting the day of the funeral of a direct relative. Neighbors and friends traditionally provide one or more meals for those sitting shiva as well as refreshments for visitors during this week.

Shochet (SHAH-ket)
A person specially trained in Jewish ritual animal slaughter

Shomer Shabbos (SHO-mer SHAB-boss) or **Shomer Shabbat** (SHO-mer sha-BAHT)
Sabbath observer; someone who does not do any activities prohibited on the Sabbath

Treif (TRAYF)
Foods that are prohibited by kashrut; not kosher

Yom Tov
Hebrew for "holiday"

Standard U.S./Metric Measurement Conversions

VOLUME CONVERSIONS

U.S. Volume Measure	Metric Equivalent
⅛ teaspoon	0.5 milliliters
¼ teaspoon	1 milliliters
½ teaspoon	2 milliliters
1 teaspoon	5 milliliters
½ tablespoon	7 milliliters
1 tablespoon (3 teaspoons)	15 milliliters
2 tablespoons (1 fluid ounce)	30 milliliters
¼ cup (4 tablespoons)	60 milliliters
⅓ cup	90 milliliters
½ cup (4 fluid ounces)	125 milliliters
⅔ cup	160 milliliters
¾ cup (6 fluid ounces)	180 milliliters
1 cup (16 tablespoons)	250 milliliters
1 pint (2 cups)	500 milliliters
1 quart (4 cups)	1 liter (about)

WEIGHT CONVERSIONS

U.S. Weight Measure	Metric Equivalent
½ ounce	15 grams
1 ounce	30 grams
2 ounces	60 grams
3 ounces	85 grams
¼ pound (4 ounces)	115 grams
½ pound (8 ounces)	225 grams
¾ pound (12 ounces)	340 grams
1 pound (16 ounces)	454 grams

OVEN TEMPERATURE CONVERSIONS

Degrees Fahrenheit	Degrees Celsius
200 degrees F	95 degrees C
250 degrees F	120 degrees C
275 degrees F	135 degrees C
300 degrees F	150 degrees C
325 degrees F	160 degrees C
350 degrees F	180 degrees C
375 degrees F	190 degrees C
400 degrees F	205 degrees C
425 degrees F	220 degrees C
450 degrees F	230 degrees C

BAKING PAN SIZES

American	Metric
8 × 1½ inch round baking pan	20 × 4 cm cake tin
9 × 1½ inch round baking pan	23 × 3.5 cm cake tin
1 × 7 × 1½ inch baking pan	28 × 18 × 4 cm baking tin
13 × 9 × 2 inch baking pan	30 × 20 × 5 cm baking tin
2 quart rectangular baking dish	30 × 20 × 3 cm baking tin
15 × 10 × 2 inch baking pan	30 × 25 × 2 cm baking tin (Swiss roll tin)
9 inch pie plate	22 × 4 or 23 × 4 cm pie plate
7 or 8 inch springform pan	18 or 20 cm springform or loose bottom cake tin
9 × 5 × 3 inch loaf pan	23 × 13 × 7 cm or 2 lb narrow loaf or pate tin
1½ quart casserole	1.5 litre casserole
2 quart casserole	2 litre casserole

We Have
EVERYTHING®
on Anything!

The Everything® list spans a wide range of subjects, with more than 500 titles covering 25 different categories:

Business	History	Reference
Careers	Home Improvement	Religion
Children's Storybooks	Everything Kids	Self-Help
Computers	Languages	Sports & Fitness
Cooking	Music	Travel
Crafts and Hobbies	New Age	Wedding
Education/Schools	Parenting	Writing
Games and Puzzles	Personal Finance	
Health	Pets	